PERSPECTIVES & IDENTITIES

PERSPECTIVES & IDENTITIES

The Elizabethan Writer's Search To Know His World

Peter Lloyd

The Rubicon Press

The Rubicon Press Limited
57 Cornwall Gardens
London SW7 4BE

© Peter Lloyd, 1989

British Library Cataloguing in Publication Data

Lloyd, Peter, 1920-
Perspectives and identities : the Elizabethan writer's
search to know his world.
1. English literature, 1475-1600-critical studies
I. Title
820.9

ISBN 0-948695-11-0

Designed and typeset by The Rubicon Press
Printed and bound in Great Britain by Biddles Limited of Guildford and
King's Lynn

Contents

List of Illustrations

Anima Mundi from Robert Fludd's *Utriusque Cosmi Historia*.

Elizabeth I (1533-1603) by an unknown artist c. 1575. *By courtesy of the National Portrait Gallery*.

William Shakespeare. The Droeshout portrait. *By courtesy Mansell Collection*.

Wilton House, Wiltshire, c. 1829. Drawn by J.P. Neale. Engraved by J. Redaway. *By courtesy of the Hulton Picture Library*.

Sir Philip Sidney (1544-86). Oil on panel by an unknown artist. *By courtesy of National Portrait Gallery*.

St. George and the Dragon. Woodcut from Spenser's *The Faerie Queene*. Engraving from 1590 edition. *By courtesy of the British Library*.

Dee and his Enemies. Title-page of Dee's Letter addressed to the Archbishop of Canterbury, 1604 (written earlier). *By courtesy of the British Library*.

Sir Walter Ralegh (1552-1618). Engraving by C.H. Jeens after the portrait by Zucchero at Longleat. *By courtesy of the British Library*.

Jacket - Visscher's Map of London, Pl. II. *By courtesy of the Mansell Collection*.

vi

Introduction

Concepts of identity, which are of contemporary concern, were also being considered at the turn of the sixteenth century. In the age of Shakespeare there was concern about Man's place in the macrocosm which surrounded him, for ideas on the nature and structure of the universe were varied. There was a new interest in individual relationships and in the psychology of the individual. Although Renaissance influences from Europe penetrated England slowly and fitfully, arriving late, the effects were considerable. Society was both troubled and liberated when established beliefs were shaken, and in such a situation it is not surprising that writers were led to ponder who and what people were, and to emphasize the place of character as well as incident in drama.

The world of Shakespeare's maturity was one in which many intellectual traditions were being modified. Medieval and early Renaissance notions continued to linger, some of them for a surprisingly long time, but there was uncertainty about Aristotle's outline of the universe and about correlations between the microcosm and the macrocosm. Individual relationships with authority, as well as with society, were seen from different angles, and as belief in an ordered geocentric universe waned, and with it the notion of a world in which people and things had well defined identities, there emerged the idea of an ego-centric man; a person with a new, if uncertain, identity. This person could be inwardly, as well as outwardly, motivated; someone whose mind and emotions were not always subject to external influences and to accidental movements of chemical 'humours' within the body; someone whose Will was more free than in the past. Such a person could be liberated, vigorous, ambitious and full of confidence. Equally he could be worried, uncertain, withdrawn, inactive and a prey to melancholy. There were several faces to be observed in society.

It is interesting that flawed characters like Cassius in *Julius Caesar* and Edmund in *King Lear* express disenchantment with old notions of the influence of the planets, while vigorous characters, albeit a little staid, like Ulysses in *Troilus and Cressida* and Kent in *King Lear*, accept the older idea of a well ordered universe in which Man had his place in a hierarchy and was often subject to external influences. In a well-ordered universe, problems of human identity, and of the identities of material things did not produce complicated psychological uncertainties. Shakespeare may not have altogether approved of the new, self-centred man, but he was aware of him; and flawed characters can always express unacceptable truths. If, in our own age, non-conforming individuals attract attention as well as disapproval, so did they also in Shakespeare's time. The playgoing public became fascinated by outrageous characters bent on self-gratification. There was also a growing interest in everyday misfits - the solitary person, the miser, the hypochondriac, the misanthrope, the hermaphrodite, and so on. These were types inherited from the past, but they were portrayed more subtly and expressed an individual identity which was not limited to the stereotype.

Setting out on voyages of intellectual discovery can produce an elation which is sometimes counterbalanced by a sense of uneasiness. What did the future hold for society when individuals began to question their relationship to Church and to State? What was the intellectual, the person who possessed what Sir Philip Sidney called the "erected wit", to think about his attitude to a corrupt authority? Debates took place in books and in academic coteries, about the exercise and the abuse of power. In some ways the court of Queen Elizabeth was tolerant of unorthodox thinking, provided it was not open and there was no political danger. Once there was the threat of danger, dissidence was dealt with ruthlessly, so that if liberties were extended, intervention by central authority was correspondingly increased. We have seen similar trends in our own times. There were therefore contradictions in attitudes and in policies.

There was a problem about national identity too. England had a new role to play in European affairs and was becoming more aware of its cultural identity. The patriotism expressed in some of Shakespeare's plays indicates an awareness of a national spirit. Yet foreign policy was often dictated by expediency and foreign adventurism was opportunist as well as patriotic. There were some policy vacil-

2

lations and doubts. There were good arguments in favour of a foreign Catholic marriage for Elizabeth, and there were good arguments against it. Emotionally such a prospect could suggest a contamination of national identity. Perspectives were changing not only in the context of politics and religion, but also in that of philosophy and literature. There were still appeals to classical authority and to foreign example. There was still an inclination to borrow from, and to imitate foreign sources, but there were also attempts to express individual views, views which were English in character. The enthusiasm and the doubt expressed in politics was reflected in different ways in literature. All ages manifest contradictory elements, but that of Elizabeth, and of her successor James, was notable for the paradoxes and contradictions expressed by writers, and frequently left unresolved. The age was uncertain of its political and cultural identity. Sometimes it exhibited an adolescent quality, an almost ebullient immaturity. It produced enthusiasm, assurance, vigour and imagination, but equally uncertainty, equivocation, depression, and inactive introspection.

The first chapter of this book outlines some of the inherited notions which had a strong emotional appeal, even when questioned intellectually. Long before Galileo, there had been doubts about the authority of Aristotle and about the Ptolemaic concept of the universe. Nevertheless, the views of previously accepted classical authorities were so strong that intelligent people found themselves puzzled, divided, and prone to think along contradictory lines. New perspectives opened up, but the way did not always seem clear and might even have been illusionary. In painting, a growing knowledge of perspective seemed to bring reality to the eye, but it was a technique of illusion too. What was reality when there were different ways of looking at the same thing? Could identity be established? Was it changeable? Was allegory a way of expressing general truths or of promoting obscuranticism? Symbolism in Elizabethan poetry could heighten awareness of the need to penetrate beneath surfaces.

Bacon tried to bring order into thinking and was aware of the 'idols' which confused the mind, but he, too, held contradictory views and could be muddled in thought. Occasionally there was a tendency to try to have things all ways. If respected authorities contradicted each other, or were questioned in the light of new discoveries, it did not necessarily mean that they could be discounted. They could be re-interpreted, and they might be correct if viewed from other angles. The growing interest in problems of perspective meant that people began to accept that a change in position caused a change in view; in thought as well as in art. Writers of drama knew, of course, that individual viewpoints could be remarkably different, and the growing importance of the individual underlined these differences together with the need to resort to authority to bring people to order. Some held that established values should be re-asserted.

The Elizabethans inherited a muddled legacy of thought from the past. There were confusions not only about the nature of the universe and about Man's place within it but also about links between the mind and the body, about the function and the scope of free will, and about the significance of 'personality'. The chapter on 'New Perspectives' indicates that the questioning of traditional ways of thought encouraged the desire to look beneath surfaces, to turn things over, and to examine them from different angles. People were not always what they seemed to be and outward appearances could be misleading. It was the notion of human identity that created problems. The quality of material things sometimes depended on their inter-relationships, and these too were being questioned. The identity, or definition of words, became uncertain. Shakespeare was concerned about the meaning of words and his doubts are referred to in the chapter on mistaken identity.

It was understandable if writers, as well as those concerned with policies of State, occasionally changed ground. In changing posture they create inconsistencies and contradictions which they did not always reconcile. Classical authority could provide a court of appeal, but could be questioned if it seemed contrary to newly enlightened experience. The chapter on 'Shifting Viewpoints' discusses the Elizabethan tendency to change intellectual stance and to absorb contradictions which were not resolved. There was ambivalence towards old and new influences, and plagiarism, or re-translation even stimulated original thought. Long works were sometimes unfinished and changed direction in the course of being written.

4

Influences from Europe could be confusing. The Hermetic thinkers spread darkness as well as light upon the question of the individual's relation to God and to the community. Some tried to create harmony in a world of religious strife, but their unorthodox ideas promoted dissidence. The work and life-style of John Dee and Giordano Bruno, which might have influenced Sidney, emphasized the importance of the individual - the *uomo nuovo*; but not in the Machiavellian sense, for the individual was seen by them to become god-inspired after initiation and training. The human being could in some cases achieve a super-ego and a super-human dignity.

Philip Sidney and Walter Raleigh are examples of writers who were at times uncertain of identity in the new world of Renaissance thought. The chapter entitled 'The Lance and the Quill' deals with Sidney's need to play a role in life, and to develop new lines of thought; but his ideals were somewhat old-fashioned and the new concepts he pondered in the *Arcadia* were often contradictory and not reconciled within a basic pattern of thought. His work was unfinished and he felt compelled to revise it drastically, eventually requesting it to be burnt. He showed a concern for human identity - for the integrity of the individual, for his 'persona' - and he touched upon the question of sexual ambiguity. Raleigh, an altogether different person, played several roles in life and is another example of changing viewpoints and incomplete endeavours.

It is not surprising that as perspectives altered, the old dramatic device of disguise should take on a new significance. What had once been an ancient stage convention in classical Greece and Rome, and a common ritual in primitive performances the world over, became a sophisticated device for entertainment and even a way of reinforcing the serious thought that surfaces did not represent reality. It was important to know what lay behind the mask. Appearances could be deceitful and veil true identity. The chapter on Shakespeare's use of disguise attempts to show how the old convention was used to express deep concerns about people and the way they communicate with each other. It was not always necessary to use costume as a disguise. Attitudes and expressions could be assumed in order to mislead. Dramatists attempted to uncover the real self and some, like Shakespeare, realized perhaps that definitions would always be elusive. 'Humours' did not explain everything, and theories on 'humours' were complicated and uncertain as the first chapter indicates. "Know thyself" was a popular aphorism in the Elizabethan age, and there were several attempts to anatomize the human temperament. Lear wished to anatomize Regan, Sidney told himself to "look into thy heart", and in 1599 Sir John Davies wrote a poem called *Nosce Teipsum*. There was a general curiosity to discover the inner self, the person behind the mask, the reality behind the myth or symbol and the truth behind the fiction. Disguise in real life was as common as in drama, but it became more a matter of widespread concern. Counterfeiting and role playing were seen to be doubtful activities and Sidney illustrates in the *Arcadia* the repercussions, both within and without the self, of playing false roles.

In pursuing themes of mistaken identity, Shakespeare went beyond conventional tricks of disguise and became interested in the wider implications of masking personality. Problems of identity created ravelled plots but also revealed that individuals could be complicated. Stage characters, who were at first simply motivated and static in presentation, became multi-faceted and difficult to 'know'. It was natural for Shakespeare and for some other dramatists, to show interest in personality and in human relationships rather than in well constructed plots. It is important not to err by over-correcting the nineteenth century stress on Shakespearean characters. Individualism in drama is dealt with in another chapter.

The underlying themes considered in this book show that doubts about the validity of inherited concepts caused changes in perspective which in turn caused shifting viewpoints. Contradictions and paradoxes occurred; equivocators existed in literature as well as in politics. The search for identity outgrew entertainment. The old belief that identity was conferred by naming (Adam had given names in the Garden of Eden), was only partially held - "What's in a name?" Juliet says. Categories were not necessarily fixed, values might in certain circumstances be relative - Sidney's *Arcadia* seemed to point in that direction. Ideas like 'beauty' and 'ugliness' were not easy to define, for "lilies that fester smell far worse than weeds".

Much depended on individual perspective and this affected concepts of identity.

I   New Perspectives

In 1543 the first printed copy of *De Revolutionibus* by the astronomer Copernicus was issued. It was the same year as his death. He had refuted the generally accepted idea that the earth was the centre of the universe and was encircled by the sun and the stars. He had been working on his thesis several years before his death and his view that the earth moved was known to students of astronomy. His discovery had little noticeable effect. His book was not forbidden, and only in the early seventeenth century when Galileo confirmed his views, and was faced with the Inquisition for his pains, did the intellectual world of Europe wake up to the implications of a new astronomy. Belief in traditional ideas of the universe based on the works of Aristotle, Plato and Ptolemy,[1] and modified by the commentaries of medieval scholars, was strong. Even after Galileo, old ideas persisted side by side with opposing concepts. Milton made use of the Ptolemaic system of astronomy in *Paradise Lost*, though aware that it had been invalidated. It was not just that old ideas died hard. They were much more than a preserve of scholars, theologians and misguided mathematicians. They had reference to a way of life that affected people generally. Traditional ideas about the structure of the universe were related to attitudes to Church and to State, to political authority and to personal relationships. Details might be for scholars, but broad concepts distilled from respected authorities were readily grasped and became elements of faith. A faith in an ordered universe, with the earth as the central point round which the stars revolved, and in which everything had its appointed place, could not be entirely shaken by the theories of Copernicus and later astronomers. If it were true that the earth moved, this would not necessarily explode the whole medieval and renaissance system.

Nicolaus of Cusa in the fifteenth century had taught that the earth went round the sun, and there was classical authority to support those who denied the predominance of the earth in the planetary system. Copernicus himself still thought in terms of a harmonious and neatly structured universe as did his contemporaries. He accepted much of the Ptolemaic theories.. It was possible to pursue a new line of investigation and to reveal a new truth without calling in question all the teachings of authority. Disputes on major matters were not uncommon in the Middle Ages and it was acceptable in the Elizabethan age to hold contradictory notions in matters of faith and practical thinking. There was no question of heresy until later, when the Church became more concerned. Some Elizabethan notions were based on observed fact, but occasionally facts were distorted to make a moral point; a habit which Bacon criticized.

Observed facts were beginning to count more and more, and some old established doctrines were being challenged. Robert Recorde in his *Castle of Knowledge* (1551) did not confirm the ideas of Copernicus, but he warned against condemning matters not fully understood. Giordano Bruno, the subject of another chapter, owed some of his speculations to Copernicus as well as to Hermetic thinking, and he stayed for a while in London where he had several eminent acquaintances. He lectured at Oxford and he was known to Sir Philip Sidney. He undoubtedly argued his views in English intellectual circles. Tycho Brahe, the astronomer, was a man of two worlds. He could not believe that the earth moved, but he saw the need to modify the Ptolemaic system. In 1572 an unknown star shone in the heavens and faded after about seventeen months. Brahe's calculations indicated that the star was remote. It lay beyond the moon and was therefore in the space thought to contain the fixed stars. This gave cause for concern. It was generally held that while the region below the moon was subject to change and decay, the region above the moon was perfect and unchangeable. The arrival of the new star cast doubt on these ideas. The appearance of a comet in 1577 confirmed Brahe's calculations. As an astronomer of a new school he believed in the importance of observed fact, accurate calculation and recording. On the other hand, he held onto the belief that the sun went round the earth even though this led him into difficulties. He finally produced the theory that the comet looped round the sun. Johann Kepler, who had corresponded with Brahe, later came to the conclusion that the earth must move. He defended new approaches to astronomy at Tübingen in 1593 and emphasized the importance of the sun, rather than the earth, in the planetary system. Kepler's work came to fruition in the early seventeenth century, but it was based on previous study and illustrates the exploratory and questioning attitude of the end of the sixteenth century.[2]

In 1576 Thomas Digges outlined Copernicus' theory. He also claimed that the universe was infinite and that the stars, far from being fixed within their proper spheres, were scattered in space.[3] Francis Bacon mentions Copernicus in the *Dignity and Advancement of Learning* and is critical of Aristotelian thinking at several points. He placed great emphasis on scientific observation as against acceptance of doctrine. As scientific instruments became more accurate new observations called in question many traditional views. New convex lenses revealed stars not previously seen or catalogued by ancient authority. Together with the scientific thinkers, unorthodox theologians like Nicolaus of Cusa, and speculative thinkers like Bruno and Campanella (1568-1639), who grew to maturity in the sixteenth century, were not able fully to accept the inherited Ptolemaic system.

Thus it was that although old ideas on the nature and structure of the universe and of humanity's place within the overall scheme of things continued to be held, they had become somewhat shredded towards the end of the sixteenth century. If the impact of Copernicus had not been great, the intellectual atmosphere had changed by the time of Galileo, who faced hostile authority when he vindicated his predecessor's thesis. The implications were better understood by leaders of the Catholic church; the threat was greater. In 1600 Bruno was burned to death for, among other matters, his views on astronomy.

Investigation by astronomers and criticism of ancient Greek concepts of the spacial system were no doubt encouraged by a general growth of a spirit of enquiry among philosophical and political thinkers. Montaigne's *Apologie* had questioned Aristotelian thinking in 1569 and his work was translated into English by Florio. On the political front Machiavelli had questioned the political and moral order. *The Prince* was not translated into print until after 1636, but Machiavelli's ideas were known and he could have been read in the original as far back as 1584. His impact was strong enough for his views to be distorted by shocked opponents of his school of thought. Gabriel Harvey, the Cambridge don, knew about Machiavelli and was likely to have discussed his opinions among his friends and followers. Bacon gave him credit for writing about what men actually do. Although Bacon did not dispute the value of religious faith, he did not favour blind irrationality based on an uncritical acceptance of ancient authorities. Theological systems were often, he thought, a mountain which was "fruitful of controversies and barren of works".[4] They sometimes represented false idols which·were formed out of dogmas and received systems. In pleading for careful observation and verification of fact in pursuit of truth Bacon was expressing an intellectual trend of his time. Earlier scholars, of course, like Erasmus and Sir Thomas More had also helped to move thinking along more rational lines.

The Protestant movement spawned several dissident movements, but also created its own establishment and its own orthodoxy. There were attacks and defences on matters of accepted belief. Familists, Anabaptists and other sects helped to create a climate which stimulated debate and enquiry. Some of the Martin Marprelate tracts were a challenge to authority. Some members of the Catholic faith withheld allegiance to the Crown. These were some of the factors which contributed to ideological debate and promoted the notion of liberty of conscience, and this in turn placed a responsibility on the individual. It was an interesting development for writers of drama, but it raised problems of individual identity.

The influence of Hermetism, mentioned in a later chapter, encouraged free-thinking and experimentation, and it was perhaps for this reason that Bacon was attracted to magical movements. It is difficult for us today to understand how any development of scientific thought could be connected to beliefs in magic, but the latter reinforced the need for experiment and for investigation beneath surfaces. Some Hermetists were backward looking, and their ideas were based on ancient occult philosophies, but they also had a tendency to aim for a new world in which contraries would be resolved and individualism would not be out of place.

Not all intelligent people were on the side of investigation and revaluation. Critical though Bacon was of dogma, he supported religious faith and was no revolutionary. Richard Hooker's *Of the Laws of Ecclesiastical Polity* was published in 1594 and counterbalanced Puritan exaggerations. Other writers put forward conservative views. Debate took place over a wide set of issues and intelligent ventures in one field encouraged ventures in others. Whatever view was taken it would appear that people and things were not what they seemed to be. It was necessary to probe beneath surfaces; face values could mask strange underlying truths. There was a rich field of exploration for the writer of drama to tap here.

It is useful to remind oneself of the ideological package handed down from the Middle Ages and further wrapped around by Renaissance commentators. It had been loosely assembled from Greek writers like Aristotle and Plato. Ptolemy, who lived in Alexandria from 139 to 161 A.D., improved on the work of predecessors such as Hipparchus, and became the main medieval authority for ancient astronomy. His system, based on that of Aristotle and Plato, placed the earth at the centre of the universe with the heavenly bodies revolving around it. His concept of the universe was known as the Ptolemaic system, and it formed the core of the package. He produced sets of complicated calculations, a theory of epicycles to account for the irregularity of planetary motions, and various geographical maps. Plotinus, who was born in Egypt in 205 A.D., contributed a neo-Platonist mysticism to the contents of the package together with an oriental theory of Emanation (which later contributed to Hermetic thinking). In 533, mention was made of the writings attributed to Dionysius the Areopagite. They came to have a strong influence on the development of theology, and described the heavenly hierarchies in the Ptolemaic universe. Astronomy and theology became interrelated and supported each other.

There were additional contributions from theologians, from St. Thomas Aquinas, and from later writers concerned with political and social order. Ficino and Pico della Mirandola held unorthodox views in the fifteenth century, but nevertheless supported the traditional concept of an ordered universe with the earth at its centre. Sir Thomas Elyot, whose work had a strong moral and political influence in the following century translated Pico's *Rules of a Christian Life* in 1534. Earlier he had written the *Book of the Governor*, a conservative treatise on moral philosophy. This package of concepts had grown into a comprehensive collection of reference by the sixteenth century. It provided descriptions of the universe, together with explanations of Man's place and function within the system. The individual knew his place in the great scheme of things and there was little need to question identities.

Despite a minority of contrary views the universe was conceived as finite. At its centre was the unmoving earth which was ruled by Man, to whom all other creatures were totally subordinate. The sun, moon and stars circled the earth in spheres. There was disagreement about the number of spheres, but there were probably eight, and some thought that as the spheres of planets turned they produced a celestial harmony, a harmony which was heard by Adam before he fell from Grace. Above the moon was perfection and order; below was change and decay as on earth. In addition to the sun, moon and earth were five planets under the supervision of divine spirits, and surrounding the entire system was the realm of fixed stars and the 'Primum Mobile' which God had set in motion. There was some dispute about the direction of movement, and the speed of turning, for such matters had to account for the observed planetary movements in the skies. Beyond the 'Primum Mobile' was the mysterious Empyreum of God and the heavenly hosts.

According to Dionysius there were divine orders and within these orders there were categories. Seraphs, Cherubs and Thrones were at the peak of the hierarchy and were contemplative spirits. Cherubs were thought to preside over the remote planet of Saturn. Below Saturn were the spheres of Jupiter, Mars and the Sun, and nearer to earth were Venus, Mercury and the Moon. The second order of heavenly spirits consisted of Dominations, Virtues and Powers, and the third order of Principalities, Archangels and Angels. Angels acted as God's messengers and formed a link with mankind. The categories were largely ignored and the term Angel came to mean any divine spirit. Spenser and Milton[5] accorded Archangels a higher place in the celestial chain, but if details were often confused it was generally accepted that there were degrees among the heavenly hosts.

12

Dionysius implied that distinctions did not produce conflict (except in the case of Satan and his followers) as each order and category consisted of spirits contented with their station and divine duties. Conflict did, however, exist in the regions below the Moon where the elements were in a state of flux and uncertainty. In these regions, matter was subject to decay and evil spirits had their abodes. This view of the universe could be related to Plato's concept of ideas, for he made a distinction between the permanent and the changing; between the real and the copy. It could also be related to the astronomers' views of the universe. Thus astronomy, classical philosophy and theology came together to present a picture, a picture which had its lessons for politics and general behaviour on earth. Man's place and his duties could be defined.

In the sublunary regions there were four elements, and they, too, had an order of importance. Fire was the most refined element and was to be found in remote areas of the skies. In descending order were to be found air, water and earth. Unfortunately, the elements intermingled and, like people on the earth, did not always keep in place. When they came into conflict on a large scale perturbations would shake the skies. Elements had qualities and could be identified. Fire was hot and dry, air was hot and moist in quality, while water, a heavier and less refined element had cold and moist properties. Earth was the heaviest element and was cold and dry. These qualities corresponded to the 'humours' in the human body, and there was therefore a link between human beings and the surrounding universe. Living creatures of all kinds, and even the material things which surrounded them, fitted into the scheme. All things, all creatures great and small, were interconnected to some measure.

As there were hierarchies in the heavens, so were there hierarchies among mankind. There were rulers, and under them were nobles and other leaders. The Church had its dignitaries and its lower orders. Ordinary people also were grouped into categories - gentlemen, citizens and labourers. The feudal system had broken up by the sixteenth century, but it left as its legacy a sense of order, place and duty. The individual was still aware of his place and function. Society was not altogether static, for in the sublunary world change was to be expected and in the late sixteenth century there were thrusts of initiative at different levels. It was possible to rise and to fall. Nevertheless, many thought along lines laid down by Sir John Fortescue in the previous century - "man was set over man and beast over beast". Each had a proper place in a universal scheme.

If Man's identity was clear, so were the identities of inanimate objects. Material things had greater or lesser properties depending on their worth to the human race. If their properties were understood they could be used for good or evil. On a higher level, but below that of the animal kingdom, there was a vegetable existence medicine, interconnected with the human race. It provided food, medecine, poison, shelter and materials as well as the benefit of scenic beauty. On a lower level were inanimate objects such as minerals, stones and liquids. The higher forms of life in the animal kingdom were graded. Noble beasts like the lion were in a superior grade and far above inferior forms of life such as shell fish or insects. Often categories of life were debated. Montaigne somewhat downgraded the stature of Man, stressing the brutish side to his nature, while elevating the qualities of certain animals. He considered that higher forms of animals could reason, but this was doubted by others. Detailed matters could be argued over, but in general there was no doubt that there were hierarchies on earth as in the heavens. People, animals and things had defined identities.

It might be asked whether rebellion could ever be justified in this kind of world and there was indeed argument over this. If more and more detail was being questioned, if the structure of the universe was uncertain, and if the egocentricity of the individual was gaining in importance, could not political authority be a subject for debate? Was there a law superior to that of monarchical government - a divine or natural law? Some believed there was and Sidney hints at this in the *Arcadia*. In a perfect world there would be no sin and all creatures would accept their role and their stamped identity in the world order. The Fall of Man changed all that. Leaders became corrupt and lacking in a sense of duty and responsibility. Could one not rebel against unjust or unlawful authority? It was a possible viewpoint, but it was a dangerous one. Sidney's attitude towards rebellion is ambivalent, as a later chapter shows. God might punish wicked rulers, the Wheel of Fortune might cast down the mighty, but this did not mean that long-suffering subjects had the right to rise against lawful authority. The French writer, Jean Bodin,[6] who was often forward-thinking, held the view that subjects were never justified in rebelling against their rulers. Opinions were diverse, and there was at one time a feeling that a League of Protestant Princes might take things over in Europe against the authority of the Catholic, Philip of Spain. The conservative attitude of Ulysses in Shakespeare's *Troilus and Cressida* was common and linked political ideas with ideas on God's arrangements in the universe. Ulysses' comments[7] are well known, but it is worth quoting them at length:

> The heavens themselves, the planets, and this centre,
> Observe degree, priority and place,
> Insisture, course, proportion, season, form,
> Office, and custom, in all line of order:

When this order was disturbed the skies were shaken with convulsions. Tempests raged in the air, pestilence ravaged the land, and discord broke out on earth.

> . . . . . O, when degree is shaked,
> Which is the ladder to all high designs,
> The enterprise is sick!

> Take but degree away, untune that string,
> And, hark, what discord follows! each thing meets
> In mere oppugnancy:

Ulysses goes on to describe a picture of chaos and violence, adding:

> . . . . . The general's disdained
> By him one step below; he by the next;
> That next, by him beneath: so every step,
> Exampled by the first pace that is sick
> Of his superior, grows to an envious fever
> Of pale and bloodless emulation:

According to this view the ordered structure of the universe should be a model for political and social order upon the earth.

In *Coriolanus* there is a further inter-relation: the functions of the political State are likened to the functions of the body. The senate and the belly are alike in distributing sustenance to inferior organs and thus promoting health. The belly would not submit to rebellious demands of the body's members any more than the senate would be dictated to by a riotous mob. In this play the hungry rabble demand corn and Menenius points out that the dearth of food is due to the will of the gods, not to the fault of the senate. When, nevertheless, the people press for more corn and succeed in their demands, discord follows. Coriolanus is then banished and the state is threatened.

Pride and the abuse of power are themes in Shakespeare's play, but the upsurge of the rabble is not treated with much sympathy. Moral issues are not simple and are complicated by individual psychology. It is noticeable, however, that once the old order is broken up Coriolanus loses his role and identity. He struggles to retain them in another way. He tries to suppress emotion and "Like a dull actor now I have forgot my part". Having gone over to the enemy, but eventually deciding to yield to his mother and forgive Rome, Aufidius is glad that Coriolanus has set "thy mercy and thy honour at difference in thee".[8] Coriolanus is torn and so too, are political issues and events.

Shakespeare was following the example of many in inter-relating the anatomies of the human body, the body politic and the material qualities of the universe. In the human body, wrote Sir Walter Raleigh, "there is a representation of the universal world and (by allusion) a kind of participation of all the parts thereof, therefore was Man called microcosmos, or the little world".[9] The microcosmos resembled the macrocosmos with which it was linked. The poet Phineas Fletcher in the *Purple Island*, which attempted to portray the nature of Man, compares the body to the earth. Organs, veins, sinews and other parts, are described and charted as if they were fields, trees, rivers, roads and islands. Chapman in *Eugenia I* also sees arrangements in the universe reflected in the human body:

In all chief parts that in the great world move
Proportion and similitude have place
With this our little world. The great world's face
Inserted stars hath, as lucifluent eyes;
The sun doth with the heart analogise,
And through the world heat and light disperse,
As doth the heart through man's small universe.

Such correspondences were meant to be reassuring. Not only
were there inter-relationships on a vertical plane; there were also
inter-relationships on a horizontal plane. There were overall patterns could one but see them, and it sometimes helped to describe,
and to define, one thing in terms of another. It was the task of
scholars to explain away difficulties and anomalies by reference to
underlying or hidden meanings. The use of allegory was not merely
an attempt to add colour or to heighten effect through symbolism,
it was a genuine way of looking at things since meaningful correspondences lay beneath surfaces. Allegory obscured and concealed
as far as the ignorant were concerned, but it could reveal to the
initiated. It deepened mystery when the awareness of mystery was
essential to a knowledge of the truth. There might be layers of
meaning. Thus Vergil's *Aeneid* was more than an epic of Rome; it
was an allegory of the human soul. Life was an intricate tapestry
of correspondences; a tissue of occult links, resemblances and significant numbers. These were noticeable when astrologers sought to
link the individual's fate to the movements of the stars. Hermetism
sought out occult significances.

Comparative models were frequently found to provide examples to emulate, and comparisons helped to define identity. The
lion might be likened to the sun or to Mars to underline its qualities.
Important people had their importance emphasized by describing
them in terms of stars or gods. The Queen was often likened to
Diana or the Moon. In an ordered, inter-linking world comparisons
could be made, lessons learned and models imitated. It is in some
ways ironic that when the mould began to break and traditional
concepts became dubious, comparisons were then used to shock
and to help the subversive process. Comparisons could either help
to define identity or to undermine it; much depended on how and
why they were used.

17

The microcosm and the macrocosm were not only interlinked materially. The human mind and its operations was bound up in the general scheme of things. The stars influenced the fate and the thinking of individuals. The elements of fire, air, water and earth comprised the atmosphere around Man, and the body was composed of similar elements which were hot, cold, moist and dry. They were sometimes in conflict in the body as they could be in the heavens. Their activities affected the brain and the whole psychology of the individual, contributing to the moulding of character and the motivation for action. Elements were absorbed through food and drink and through the process of breathing. Marlowe's Tamburlaine said:

> Nature that framed us of four elements,
> Warring within our breasts for regiment,
> Doth teach us all to have aspiring minds.[10]

Sir Toby Belch in *Twelfth Night* says: "Does not our nature consist in the four elements?" In *Anthony and Cleopatra* the queen considers that she is fashioned of the purest elements of fire and air - "my other elements I give to baser life".[11] Presumably a well balanced person held the warring chemistry of the body under some control, but the position was not clear since there was argument about the power of the Will and about the relationship between elements and 'humours'. At times they seemed indistinguishable.

There was confusion about the links between the mind and the body. The work of the 'humours' was not well defined, and this meant that at times it was not easy to determine identity. These 'humours' rose like vapours within the body and they, too, had hot, cold, moist, and dry qualities. One view was that the elements taken in as food were converted by the liver into liquid 'humours'. However this may be, these 'humours' resembled the elements. There was a melancholy 'humour', which was cold and dry like the earth, and could produce in excess a black bile. There was a phlegmatic 'humour' which was cold and moist and might originate in the kidneys or in the lungs. There was a hot and moist sanguine 'humour' situated in the liver or kidneys, and a choleric

18

'humour'. The latter, being hot and dry in quality, corresponded to the element of fire and might be thought to be superior as a temperament, but it did not work out like this. Often it was regarded as indicating lack of control.

It is true that a melancholy person was for a time regarded as an inferior creature, since his qualities were, like the earth, inferior, but as respect for the individual grew and unusual temperaments became of interest this attitude changed. The melancholy temperament even became fashionable and much later John Earle, in the seventeenth century, held the view that such a person was intellectually superior. It was a view which Chapman held. His *Shadow of Night, The Tears of Peace* and *Eugenia* portray a solitary person, of melancholy disposition, contemplating in darkness; "Silence and night, do best fit contemplation".[12] On the other hand, Chapman portrays melancholy characters who need to be cured; for example in the play *Monsieur d'Olive*. There were contrary views about melancholy people in late Elizabethan times. One view, influenced by the Greek authority Galen, was that an excess of melancholy was a disease. It was caused by a burning up of 'humours' which produced black bile. Although noted for its cold, dry qualities it could in excess generate heat and cause fever. It therefore changed its quality, and when it became a serious disease was known as 'adust melancholy'. Whether a person was a sad, withdrawn, contemplative character or a crazed, unbalanced creature depended on one's subjective view of his nature.

Aristotle had remarked that melancholy people were often imaginative and reflective, and his view when set beside that of Galen meant that the ancient authorities could be said to support different points of view. Ficino[13] supported Aristotle's view and so did Sir Thomas Elyot in his *Castle of Health*. Bright, in his famous treatise on melancholy, mentioned that some melancholy people were witty. Much depended on the type of melancholy diagnosed, and diagnosis was not a medical science. Lawrence Babb, in his book *The Elizabethan Malady*, shows that there were many different types and that contemporary attitudes towards them were confused. The melancholy lover was a stock type in drama, and could be laughed at or sympathized with according to circumstance. He was not necessarily unmanly, although Sidney's

19

Pyrocles in the *Arcadia* was accused of modifying his previous manly identity. The love-sick Romeo was a masculine person, and his condition was understood. It was one of sensitivity and it was temporary. It was not that of the malcontent or hypochondriac. Confusion over 'humours' grew as time went on and new observation of behaviour altered attitudes; new perspectives of human identity became possible.

The choleric person, whose temperament was related to the purest of elements, fire - was often waspish and bitter. A superfluity of this 'humour' could be found in the gall, producing yellow bile, and this did not suggest a satisfactory personality. Perhaps the favourite was the sanguine person, who had a predominance of blood in the system.

Opinions differed as to where 'humours' were located and how they actually functioned. One view was that they were converted into 'vital spirits'[14] which were refined by the brain and sent out in the form of messages through the arteries and sinews of the body. They animated the body as well as the mind. A well balanced person had a satisfactory balance of 'humours', but since many people had a predominance of a particular 'humour' there were recognizable types. By recognizing types, identities could be roughly established. For example, it was thought that a choleric person would probably be somewhat bitter and over-hasty in judgement, but skilful with words. Such people were inclined to be active and courageous, but wilful. They tended to have reddish complexions. Phlegmatic people were somewhat lazy, although they could have active memories. They were pale in colour and careful in temperament. Those with an excess of moist 'humour' were usually short and stout, and not quick to react. All such types were not at variance with what a general observation of human nature taught the onlooker, and when there were contradictions these could be explained by other factors, such as the side effects of special circumstance, or planetary influence. As Ptolemy explained irregularities of movement in his ordered universe by elipses, so theories of 'humours' accommodated modifying factors.

Ben Jonson's well-known description of a 'humour' by Aspen in the play *Every Man Out of his Humour* is not an attempt to define 'personality' or to guide one in pinning down any human identity. Jonson was not dealing with normal people, but with those who were strongly idiosyncratic and had recognizable traits of character. He was dealing with people who had an excess of a particular 'humour'. Having described the fluctuating quality of 'humours' - their "fluxure" - Jonson goes on to say:

> . . . . . So in every human body,
> The choler, melancholy, phlegm and blood,
> By reason that they flow continually
> In some one part, and are not continent,
> Receive the name of humours . . . ."

But when a particular 'humour' becomes predominant, then it is recognizable, and it is this 'humour' which confers a special identity upon a person. It is in this sense that Jonson uses the word in the title of his play. He makes it clear when Aspen says:

> As when some one peculiar quality
> Doth so possess a man, that it doth draw
> All his effects, his spirits, and his powers,
> In their confluxions, all to run one way,
> This may be truly said to be a humour.

In other words, Jonson regards it as a person's dominant characteristic. If a person had no particular bias, or special characteristic, this did not mean, according to Jonson, that he was devoid of 'humour' but that the fluxion of 'humours' did not produce in him a readily noticeable identity.

It is of interest that Aspen will not accept that affected imitation is a true 'humour'. Playing a role, or acting a part, was an assumption of false identity. Adopted 'humours' were a frequent device of playwrites who wished to conceal identity. The wearing of special apparel, or an imitation of other people's habits, could disguise a person's true characteristics. Disguise is frequent in Jonson's plays, as it is in Shakespeare's, and was handled in different ways to highlight identity problems. This theme will be developed in a later chapter.

Theories about the operation of the 'humours' might seem to favour caricature in the hands of dramatists. If people could be

21

labelled as choleric, phlegmatic, sanguine - or as hot, cold, moist, and slow or quick to act - it could lead to the portrayal of characters as types. Sir Thomas Overbury's 'characters' suggest types, and so does Jonson in giving his characters names like Subtle, Face, Morose, Volpone and the like. There is some truth in this and one can pick out types easily enough in Elizabethan literature. Moreover, classical playwrites, such as Plautus, produced stock types which greatly influenced writers of the sixteenth century. But not all playwrites wished to exaggerate like Jonson, or to follow classical models. There were attempts to explore motivation and to present a variety of characters, some of which were subtly portrayed. The growing interest in individual identity went against caricature.

In any case, theories about the 'humours' were so complicated, and even confused, that they did not inhibit portrayal of character. It was accepted that many people had variable temperaments. 'Humours' could be affected by climate and geographical situation, as Hippocrates had recognized. These were some of the 'elipses', so to speak, in the general theory. People were influenced and formed to some extent by the places in which they were brought up and by changes in climate or locality.[15] Periods of the year could bring out 'humours' in certain people. Spring tended to cause surges of the blood, like rising sap in flowers, while summer with its sun drew out choleric qualities. As one might guess, autumn and winter could induce melancholy and phlegm respectively. Different times of day and different foods affected the balance of 'humours' as they were composed of elements. Age was also a factor. Youth was perhaps more sanguine than old age, and elderly people suffered from an excess of phlegmatic 'humour' which showed itself in white hair and rheumy eyes. Disease and pestilence had their effects on temperament, and so, too, had the influence of evil spirits, ghosts, magic and witchcraft.

An interesting perspective was explored when observation revealed the effects people had on each other. 'Humours' reacted to psychological situations. A dominant personality could influence the mood and action of a less dominant personality, and people could be encouraged or discouraged by their acquaintances. They could be led astray against their normal nature. In addition there was the turn of Fortune's Wheel - sheer chance - which could raise or depress fundamental character. Many believed in the power of Fate, although there was growing belief in the power of Man to determine his own destiny. Among the several influences which could form human dispositions and modify, even change individual characteristics, were the stars.

So far the links binding mankind within the universal scheme of things have been shown to be those of elements which affect the body, and in turn, the mind and personality. Man's composition, and that of the society in which he lived, was modelled on analogies in the surrounding universe. Man's development was, however, subject to non-material influences. Religion and the Church provided channels for divine influence which could affect character, as well as one's chances in the afterlife. Occult influence was also radiated from the stars, whose activity provided further links between Man and the macrocosm.

In spite of some doubts, there was general credence in the significance of astrology. Mention of the power of the stars is scattered throughout Elizabethan literature. Perhaps there is a psychological need to attribute to some external source the responsibility for one's destiny. Important though belief in free will and independence of spirit may be, it is comforting to believe in theories which take part of one's fate out of one's hands. Although belief in the power of the stars is widespread today, for many Elizabethans the stars did more than determine personal fate; they could influence the general direction of events on earth. They could provide warnings and indicate future trends. Robert Recorde in his *Castle of Knowledge* wrote that we must examine the heavens to obtain warning of dire events about to take place on earth. Disturbances in the heavens were frequently linked in some way with disturbances on earth, although often out of time sequence. In *Julius Caesar* the skies were troubled before Caesar's assassination and strange happenings occurred in the streets of Rome. Calpurnia felt that Caesar was in danger because of this. Similarly in *Hamlet* the ghost's appearance was thought to be an omen of some kind. Horatio recalled the omens before Caesar's death when "the sheeted dead/Did squeak and gibber in the Roman streets" and the stars seemed on fire. In *King Lear* the storm presaged the storm in

Lear himself as an audience would be quick to realize. Sometimes the omens could be trivial if they did not concern monarchs or great events. Byron in Chapman's *Byron's Tragedy* asks why the Captain of his guard should think he is in danger and is told:

> Judge by the strange ostents that have succeeded
> Your arrival here.[16]

He refers to the fact that Byron's wild duck died as soon as he left and that his horses went mad and killed themselves. The quarrel between Oberon and Titania in *A Midsummer Night's Dream* caused climatic disturbances on earth:

> Therefore the moon, the governess of floods,
> Pale in her anger, washes all the air,
> That rheumatic diseases do abound;
> And thorough this distemperature we see
> The seasons alter . . . .
>
> And this same progeny of evils comes
> From our debate, from our dissension;[17]

The Elizabethans were on the look-out for portents large or small.

It was not only one's natal star which helped to give one a special identity, but the modifying influences of other stars. If planetary aspects seemed to be bad for one at a given time it might be necessary to resort to counteracting magic or to orthodox prayer. The year's calendar was divided into periods of zodiacal influence. Fluctuating conjunctions involving one's own star caused complications. The stars, like 'humours' in the body, could work with or against each other. Pliny's writings were a useful source of information on such matters, but over the years so much was added, debated and modified that astral links with mankind became exceedingly complicated. Experts were needed to cast one's horoscope and the results might be as dubious as palmistry.

Towards the end of the fifteenth century doubts were increasing about the influence of the stars and these doubts, together with changing perspectives in the following century on the individual's place in the universal scheme of things, are reflected in writing in the age of Shakespeare. Ben Jonson makes occasional scornful references to the stars and so does Shakespeare through the person of Edmund in *King Lear*. Gloster considers that "These late eclipses in the sun and moon portend no good to us". Edmund, however, does not believe a word of this and his well-known comment is worth quoting in full:

> This is the excellent foppery of the world, that when we are sick in fortune - often the surfeit of our own behaviour - we make guilty of our disasters the sun, the moon, and the stars: as if we were villains by necessity; fools by heavenly compulsion; knaves, thieves and treachers, by spherical predominance; drunkards, liars and adulterers, by an enforced obedience of planetary influence; and all that we are evil in, by a divine thrusting on: an admirable evasion of whoremaster man, to lay his goatish disposition to the charge of a star! My father compounded with my mother under the dragon's tail; and my nativity was under *ursa major*; so that it follows, I am rough and lecherous - Fut, I should have been that I am, had the maidenliest star in the firmament twinkled on my bastardising . . . .[18]

Astrology is ridiculed and human destiny and individual identity are made the responsibility of the individual. This is the credo of the ego-centric man who lives on earth and is surrounded by the universe, but is not inextricably tied up in it. There is a common-sense flavour in Edmund's remarks which the audience would have appreciated. The speech is set in prose among other scenes set in verse, and as it is less declamatory in style it suggests a frank *tête-à-tête* with the audience; a revealing 'think piece'. On the other hand, there is a wry sarcasm about it which reminds one of those prose asides of clowns whose bluff humour expresses the sound common-sense of the common man who speaks the truth, but only up to a point; for his wisdom is limited and he cannot be taken entirely seriously. Edmund is wicked and not to be trusted, while Gloster is a good man, so that there is an ambivalence created in the minds of the audience. There is unease concerning the new perspective which Edmund opens up, but there are doubts about the old attitudes which he scorns.

There is a similar ambivalence in *Othello*. Iago is wicked, but does he not speak the truth when he says: "Virtue! a fig! 'tis in ourselves that we are thus and thus?"[19] He, too, speaks in prose. In *Julius Caesar* Cassius, another unsympathetic character, makes a similar point when he tells Brutus that the fault "is not in our stars,/But in ourselves". But Cassius is inciting unlawful rebellion and is not to be trusted. In some ways Edmund and Iago and Cassius represent the new renaissance man, but he is a disturbing creature and not on the side of the angels. In the 'brave new world' which Miranda hints at in the *Tempest*, the authority and healing power of Prospero are still needed, and Prospero believes in his friendly star:

> A most auspicious star, who influence
> If I court not, but omit, my fortunes
> Will ever droop.[20]

Old beliefs were not easily shaken off and existed side by side with notions about the freedom of the individual, which religious and political movements, encouraged. There were several ways of looking at things, and at people.[21]

Human identity presented problems of definition and of recognition when viewed from different angles, but it could be changed by material and spiritual circumstances. The effects of the elements, climate, and place on the 'humours' have been mentioned. Material things on earth might also form or change a person's disposition. Drugs could change personality, and we are given an example of this in *A Midsummer Night's Dream* when Puck sprinkles magic eye-drops and changes the emotions of his victims. The effects of magic potions are scattered throughout Elizabethan literature, and the use of poison is a frequent theme. Friar Lawrence in *Romeo and Juliet* has special skills in the use of 'medecines' and says:

> O, mickle is the powerful grace that lies
> In herbs, plants, stones, and their true qualities.

The work of Cornelius Agrippa on occult practices[22] and also on the use of potions, herbs and philtres was studied seriously, even if the witches' brew in *Macbeth* has a comic side to it. It was seriously believed that if only we knew how, we could use the blood of the bear to give us strength.

In addition to the many factors which shaped human personality, action and destiny, there was the work of spirits, good and evil. The impure air of the sublunary region was inhabited by ghosts and spirits, and they were often referred to in literature. They could lead one astray if they did not change one's temperament. "Be thou a spirit of health or goblin damned" says Hamlet as he prepared to follow the ghost. His companions are afraid that it may "draw you into madness". At the worst an evil spirit might so totally take over an identity that he or she could become insane. The aid of a priest might then be needed to exorcise the spirit. Under the influence of a spirit, a person was not his or her self. Necromancers or witches could manipulate people and damage their minds. It is interesting that the fear of witchcraft was particularly strong in the late sixteenth and early seventeenth centuries, and it is possible that as the importance of individual identity grew in people's minds this fear became stronger. The punishments meted out to suspected witches were cruelly severe. There were, of course, benevolent spirits - or those who were merely mischievous - and the fairies in *A Midsummer Night's Dream* were hardly evil!

If, as they believed, human beings were pulled one way and another by the elements and 'humours' within, and buffetted by the turn of Fortune's Wheel; and if they were also swayed by the influence of the stars and other external forces and pressures not to mention the effects of medicinal potions and magic spells, then it would seem that they were mere puppets on the world's stage. This was a possible view. It might be that Man had no real identity. If so, one could only hope for Grace, or perhaps cultivate a defiant and courageous Stoicism to stamp oneself as some kind of individual in a hostile and dominant environment. The early version of the *Mirror for Magistrates*[23] contains stories suggesting the dominance of Fate in which inner motives for self-destruction like guilt, are not evident. However, stories added at a later date admit to the possibility of human error in an individual's fall from high position.

Jack Cade asks himself in this work whether it was Fortune or his "forward folly" which caused him to rise and fall. He concludes that God gave human beings the faculty of reason to control their own destiny despite the strong pressures brought to bear upon them. The importance of Free Will and reason in human psychology was given greater stress during the time of Shakespeare's maturity than formerly.

Stoicism, the Calvinistic belief in predestination and the Protestant desire for freedom, provided a series of confusing perspectives on Man's identity and role in life. A stoic attitude is noticeable in drama, but this was partly due to the inherited influence of Senecan tragedy. It was also current because the image of a more than life-size hero, cast down by Fate or the malign influence of stars and the machinations of his fellow men, yet refusing to yield to destiny without a struggle (indeed sometimes dying on his feet), produced good, stirring drama. Such themes moved the audience and were not necessarily depressing. They underlined the courage and individuality of the hero; they evidenced that an individual was conscious of 'self'; and they allowed one to be thankful for one's lesser status in life. One finds stoic elements in Marlowe's *Tamburlane* and in the plays of Chapman and Marston. Shakespeare and other writers portrayed characters who were more responsible for their own destiny, even though outside influences were still present. Hamlet said that there was "a divinity that shapes our ends,/Rough-hew them how we will", but he uses this as an argument to rely upon our instincts. Free Will, Reason and Fate were difficult issues and they could not be clearly debated when theories about the working of the human mind were confused and obscure.

The movements of 'humours' affected the human mind as has been mentioned before, but the human mind itself was compartmentalized and different parts reacted, and inter-reacted upon each other, in various ways. The body affected the mind, but the mind affected the body and controlled it to a large extent. The playwrite Chapman is an interesting case of a writer who expressed varied and even contradictory views on human freedom and on the function and power of the mind. He is conservative in many respects and seems to believe in traditional ideas about the ordered universe and Man's place in it. There are several references to the influence of the stars in his plays and to the workings of the 'humours' and their effects on character. The stoic streak in his work has been mentioned. Nevertheless, he had a strong sense of individual responsibility and of the controlling power of the mind. He seemed to believe that people were motivated from within and could with effort control passions. He favoured the solitary, contemplative person - in some ways an outsider - and thought he had an important role in life.

> A man all centre is, all stay, all mind,
> The body only made her instrument;
> And to her ends in all acts must consent:
> Without which order, all this life hath none,
> But breeds the other life's confusion.
> Respect to things without us hinder this
> Inward consent of our soul's faculties.
> Things outward therefore think no further yours
> Than they yield homage to your inward powers
> In their obedience to your reason's use,
> Which for their order deity did infuse.[24]

Such an individual is ego-centric and in control. He has his own identity, in spite of external pressures upon him. On the other hand, some characters in Chapman's work express different views. In *Bussy d'Ambois* Bussy himself makes the point that an individual, however talented, can only achieve success if Fate provides a suitable opportunity - "so no man riseth by his real merit". But if the mind is in control, even if it cannot alter Fate or counteract strong astral influences, how does it operate? Has it an identity if it is compartmentalized?

What about the power and function of the Soul? Did it have a personal identity, so to speak, or was it a kind of spiritual radiation? Sir Walter Raleigh had his doubts about the Soul and its relationship to the mind and the body.[25] John Donne touched upon the connection between the Soul and the senses in the poem 'The Extasy', but is not entirely clear. The Soul was generally considered to be linked in some way to God, and was refined and incorporeal in a way that other organs of the body were not. But the manner of its sway over behaviour was debatable and its connection with the senses unsure. Donne seems to argue that as the senses rise like vapours to the higher faculties of the mind and to the Soul, so the Soul must strive to relate downwards and spread its influence - if not, its virtue is lost. Some considered the Soul to be etherial; a spiritual essence which mysteriously allowed us to receive Grace and which was significant after death. It was immortal. At times some writers seemed to be referring to a higher mental faculty, or to something which might be called our 'better instincts'. It was not even clear whether there were two or more Souls. Plutarch thought there were two - one spiritual and the other much simpler and linked to the senses. Another view was that there was only one Soul, but it possessed different qualities which were used for different functions. There was mention of a 'vegetable soul' which people had in common with plants and animals, and a rational Soul which belonged to Man alone. In other words, it was associated with the mind.

There were various views about the compartments of the mind and phrenologists mapped the brain out slightly differently. It was thought on the whole that the faculties of common-sense, imagination and memory were located in the brain and perhaps constituted what might be termed the 'sensitive Soul'. The faculty of common-sense was in the forefront of the brain and interpreted signals from the five senses, perhaps exercising some sort of judgement; although a more profound judgement came at a later stage in the mental processes. Messages from the faculty of common-sense were passed on to the imagination which shaped them into significant forms which could then be judged and acted upon or stored in the memory, which lay at the back of the brain. Considered judgement was thought by some to be exercised by the 'rational soul', which concerned itself with 'essences'. The 'rational soul' was given to human beings only, not to animals. It was concerned with choice, and the taking of important decisions, although one view was that the Will took over from the 'rational soul' in order to sort out good or evil factors and to make the final choice. The Will was referred to by Hooker as "appetite's controller". The picture of Man's mental processes was hazy and confused, but the power of the Will was generally recognized. It could, however, be corrupted. The 'sensitive soul', which was concerned with senses, imagination and memory, and the 'rational soul', which was concerned with reason and judgement (and possibly included the Will) were inter-related and could influence each other.

Several books attempted to describe how human beings were motivated, but these descriptions became more and more complicated as time went on and interest developed. Sir John Davies in *Nosce Teipsum* gave a somewhat old-fashioned account of human anatomy and the spiritual workings of the Soul, but Coeffeteau's *A Table of Human Passions*[26] was more helpful from a psychological point of view. Some thought that the heart welcomed, or rejected images and messages from the imagination. However this may be, there was a general belief that the heart was the source of emotion or appetite, and that emotion could overwhelm rational judgement and subvert the Will. A typical theme running through Elizabethan tragedy is that of the conflict between emotion and moral judgement, and the infirmity of the Will.

'Humours', as already mentioned, influenced the senses and could raise appetites or passions. These could sometimes be classified. For example, love was an appetite which operated in present time, while hope was an appetite which operated in future time. Appetites could be simple, superior, abstract or material; they could yearn for food or, say, money; they could be expressed in attitudes towards people - envy, hate, jealousy and so on. If 'humours' could affect the passions, so the latter could affect 'humours'. Newton's *Touchstone of Complexions* goes into questions of human bias and motivation in some detail.

In his play *The Revenge of Bussy d'Ambois* Chapman mentions the effect of sleep on imagination and memory:

> For as in sleep, which binds both th'outward senses,
> And the sense common too; th'imagining power
> (Stirr'd up by forms hid in memory's store,
> Or by the vapours of o'erflowing humours
> In bodies full and foul, and mixed with spirits)
> Feigns many strange, miraculous images,
> In which act it so painfully applies
> Itself to those forms, that the common sense

It actuates with his motion; and thereby
Those fictions true seem, and have real act . . . .[27]

In other words the rational part of the brain ceases to function properly, and memory works on imagination to produce fictions. When the imagination was not adequately controlled, or when the Will was defective, it was difficult to distinguish between what was true and what was false; between fiction and reality. These imbalances and distortions in the mind worried Shakespeare, who referred several times in his work to the false which seemed true. In *A Midsummer Night's Dream* imagination can produce shapes in the mind and ". . . gives to airy nothing/A local habitation and a name". The melancholy lover often suffered from uncontrolled imagination and, perhaps like some poets, his eyes were ". . . in a fine frenzy rolling". This was perhaps a case of poetic 'furor', and might be of divine inspiration.[28] It could, however, be a case of the mind running riot, and Shakespeare equates the lunatic and the poet in the above play.

Mention has already been made of an unhealthy excess of 'humour' which produced a burning, or possibly a putrefaction, within the body and this, being a serious disease, could obviously impair the workings of the mind. Uncontrolled memories could be stirred, and the imagination could work feverishly and without the control of judgement. The melancholy 'adust' described by Burton much later in *The Anatomy of Melancholy* produces instability of temperament and in such cases an individual can change, or lose, his proper identity. In other cases it was not a question of a lack of control by the common sense or a bodily fever, which produced strange, and perhaps evil, behaviour. There may have been an element of passion (i.e. hatred or envy) in Iago, but he gives the impression of someone who is in control of himself and has chosen his course of action. His Will was corrupt. How this might happen to people was not at all clear.

Theories about the working of the mind and body were varied and sometimes muddled. It was somewhat ironical that the more interest grew in investigating and enlarging individual identity, the more complicated and uncertain became theorizing about the operations of the mind and body. So much was added as individual behaviour was closely observed, so much was invented to provide explanations. In addition to the inheritance left by ancient Greek writers, there was the more involved writing of Coeffeteau, Newton, Bright and also the comments and portrayals by poets and dramatists. Theories became so widely embracing that they not only admitted the portrayal on the stage of stereotypes, which the audience could recognize and ridicule, but of strange new characters with subtle thoughts and motivations. The miser, the spendthrift, the old cuckold, the braggart, were still brought before stage audiences, and characters embodying particular 'humours' would often be given appropriate names. Jonson labelled some of his characters this way, and some of Shakespeare's characters - Dogberry, Andrew Aguecheek, Bottom - owed something to this view of types. However, there were many other characters who might have illustrated the more intricate theories about the human mind, and those of Shakespeare and Chapman come readily to mind. In some ways the theorizing about mind and body produced so many variables that writers were largely free to portray whatever experience and observation of life taught them.

Experience taught that people were not what they seemed to be, and that the underlying identity lay behind a mask. One has to keep in mind, of course, that playwrites took the audience into their confidence early in a play. The audience was allowed to know the inner thoughts, the underlying character, of strange people like Iago, or Middleton's De Flores, at the beginning of the action. But stage characters were unaware of the true nature of their acquaintances and were kept in ignorance until the denouement. The point can therefore be made that certain individuals were more complicated than appearances would suggest. Chapman's characters do not come 'alive' as do those of Shakespeare, and he often refers to the influence of 'humours' and the stars on behaviour and destiny, but he recognizes that a person can be complicated and portrays his characters as such:

> Oh of what contraries consists a man!
> Of what impossible mixtures! Vice and virtue,
> Corruption, and eternesse, at one time,
> And in one subject, let together, loose'.[29]

Playwrites were more constrained by literary conventions than by treatises on the 'humours', and on the way in which the brain controlled or was in conflict with the body. If Hamlet owed something to the 'melancholy man' he owed more to the tradition of the delaying avenger; but either way he is a unique figure. If Othello is wracked with jealousy, he is a character who transcends the stock idea of the jealous man. If Lear has something in him of the foolish, tetchy old man, he cannot be identified as a type.

The Elizabethan age was one in which several new perspectives were opening up. Advances of thought in one field opened up advances in other fields, and each change of attitude made other changes easier. But changes produced tensions and uncertainties. In this chapter it has been shown that while old concepts - of the universe and of Man's relation to it, of the social and political order, of the power of the stars and of Fate over destiny, of the working and the freedom of the human mind together with its relation to the body and to material things - continued to exist and to exert strong influence, these concepts were being gradually eroded. The early Renaissance package of thought, which contained views on an ordered and inter-related system, albeit often complicated, became too unwieldy, too frayed, and too loosely tied together by the end of the sixteenth century to be readily understood and acceptable. Too much had been added, too many insights had cast doubts on some of the contents. The individual became less trammelled by his cosmic and political surroundings, and by the doctrines of the universal Church, but was by no means entirely free. This meant that there were identity problems. What was an individual? The more one probed, the less certain one was of an established identity. There could be a 'persona' hidden beneath the surface; and the way in which the mind worked, and was influenced, was unsure. The identity of things could also be debated. Old labels were not satisfactory and definitions depended on perspective, and perspective depended on individual attitudes. Bacon asked himself what truth was in such an age,[30] and Shakespeare was concerned that falsehood often wore a "goodly aspect". Was truth relative?

If truth were masked, like personality, and had to be uncovered, it was worrying that revelation might create unwelcome situations and undermine beliefs which had stood one in good stead. Even poetry came under attack as being the art of 'feigning' and had to be defended by Sir Philip Sidney. It is not surprising that as new vistas were revealed, the vision was often uncertain, and that some held contrary opinions or practised 'double think'. It could be a dangerous world if one went too far, and concealment might be necessary. The use of disguise, and the assumption of false identity, fascinated Elizabethans.

The next chapter seeks to show how new perspectives led to tentative explorations and to ambivalence. Uncertainty about identities, and relationships in the widest sense, caused some writers to adopt shifting postures and to change their viewpoints. Attempts to uncover what lay beneath surfaces was counterbalanced by a tendency to dress up language and to veil meaning, just as people used costume as disguise.

II   Shifting Viewpoints

The age produced notable contradictions. Courage and flamboyance were Elizabethan traits, but so were furtiveness and equivocation. Some were tempted to seek the limelight and to wear elaborate clothes, to strut about on the world's stage; others favoured the shadows, cultivated solitude and dressed in sober attire. Authority did not always resolve contradictions, since authority itself could be changeable. The Queen's changing moods meant that courtiers had to make quick adjustments, religious authorities differed, and in literature classical authority was open to many interpretations. Plato could now be seen from so many angles that he seemed to be more than one person. There was the neo-Platonist angle for those concerned about the conduct of life and with the search for values, there was the mystical and occult perspective, but there was also the mathematical aspect. Plato was also an authority on religion, politics and on the structure of the cosmos. Aristotle was another authority, but he was sometimes under attack. The Ramists at Cambridge University were frequently opposed to him.

Classical influence in literature was varied and sometimes confusing. Senecan stoicism ran through some tragedies and reinforced the view that the passions could be brought under control. It encouraged individualism, on the one hand, but in emphasizing the power of universal forces over human destiny it also belittled human significance. Ovidian eroticism was a very different influence, and this was strong in romance and poetry. The playwrite Chapman was influenced by both sources and his poetic posture was changeable. Classical influence could stifle initiative for some - the drama of the public theatre was often more alive than the Senecan and Plautian imitations performed in more restricted circles - but for others it was a liberation from crude simplicity. In Shakespeare's early comedies classical devices were grafted onto the stem of native tradition to produce amusing comedy.

There was a tendency to shift angles of approach within existing conventions. This is noticeable not only in drama but in poetic allegory. The approach to tragedy from Marlowe to Webster varied considerably, and some playwrites were able to merge tragic and comic views. The porter's scene in *Macbeth* is often cited, and there are examples of comic relief in Shakespeare's other tragedies. In comedies, such as *A Midsummer Night's Dream* and *Twelfth Night*, there are crosscurrents of seriousness. The mixing of genres disturbed some and Sidney touched on this in his *Apology for Poetry*. Variations of approach were not simply due to technical experiment. The widening of perspectives, already mentioned, stimulated different ways of looking at things, and if there were precedents - the introduction of comedy within the serious theme of an early 'mystery' play, for example - these could be freshly developed. Variations of attitude in the convention of allegory are especially interesting.

Allegory was a form and manner of writing which reflected the basic idea that the universe was ordered, but mysterious, and that human life was integrated within the system. Meanings and equivalences had to be uncovered or reflected through comparisons and symbolism. Allegory had moral and didactic functions. In course of time, and as perspectives changed, the idea of equivalences weakened into notions of resemblances, and the concept of allegory shaded into that of extended metaphor. Themes developed from those of religious expression, and the expression of higher forms of love, towards more secular preoccupations. Moreover, the approach to metaphor also began to vary. At the end of the sixteenth century writers began to image disparate ideas, not to reflect the harmony and unity within the universe, but to show ingenuity, to create surprise and to produce tension. Some writers give the impression of forging what Dr. Johnson called "False conceits" and "unnatural comparisons".[1] Such comparisons could indeed suggest a disordered universe. There was a move away from the moral and didactic metaphor. One notices this in Chapman's *Ovid's Banquet of Sense*, although this is a poem with a didactic purpose. There are examples of strange imagery and of unusual comparison in this poem. Describing a maiden he refers to the "downward burning flame of her rich hair" and continues:

> She lifts her lightening arms above her head,
> And stretcheth a Meridian from his blood.[2]

Scientific analogy is used in Ovidian style imagery.

Marlowe, too, uses some startling conceits. In *Hero and Leander* he does not follow the Petrarchan convention of likening eyes to stars and tears to pearls. He writes of "translucent cisterns". His attitude to the lovers in this poem seems ambiguous, and not that which one would expect of an allegorical poet, or of a poet in the Petrarchan tradition. At times Marlowe involves himself in sensuous description, at other times he distances himself from the figures in his poem and seems to contemplate them with mild amusement. Chapman's stance, especially in the *Banquet*, is also curious. His similes and metaphors can be far-fetched, but he appears to believe in the inter-related nature of the universe. He is conservative in some respects, but he is idiosyncratic in approach and represents in many ways the new Renaissance man. Differences of viewpoint were such that poets could attempt to express a sense of order and harmony in the universe, like Sir John Davies in *The Orchestra*, or they could express the reverse. John Donne, whose comparisons could be disconcerting, complained about the loss of coherence in the world when to egocentric Man "Prince, subject, father, son are things forgot".[3]

The development of allegory from early forms created problems. It was a suitable form for an age which believed in universal correspondences, and therefore was not inappropriate in the Elizabethan age in spite of changing attitudes. In a commentary on the *Dream of Scipio* Macrobius[4] pointed out that Nature did not expose herself in obvious ways, and her secrets could not be understood by the vulgar masses. The 'veiled' nature of allegorical poetry expressed such a view. According to Boccaccio even learned people had to exercise their minds in elucidating allegorical correspondences.[5] It has also to be said that puzzle making and puzzle solving were scholarly addictions in Medieval and early Renaissance times. As time went on neo-Platonists complicated the use of allegory and often it had a mystical quality. Symbols and analogies became heavy with inherited values. They gathered encrustations of meaning and became more obscure. The Renaissance mind complicated allegory. By the time we come to Spencer's allegorical work the form and manner of writing had become so sophisticated and so personal that there was a danger of it becoming overloaded. If a poet changed his angle of vision the reader could become confused. This happens when one reads *The Faerie Queene*.

The problem had been there since Langland and Chaucer. Previously Dante's all embracing multiplicity of view had reconciled the real and the ideal, and he saw the earthly world *sub specie aeternatis*. In Chaucer's poetry the dichotomy was not so readily resolved, and in Langland's *Piers Ploughman* the real and the ideal are sometimes effectively and sometimes awkwardly related, while the poet moves in and out of his allegory - as did Spenser later. Langland moved from the abstract to the concrete and back again, and often addressed the reader directly in forthright colloquial language, thus abandoning the veil of allegory. Chaucer had changed posture when he introduced irony into *The House of Fame*, and when the allegorical poets sought to introduce argument, the conventional mould began to crack.

The background of chivalry in allegory began to change. Ariosto had made some wry asides about the gentle world he was depicting in *Orlando Furioso*, and when Spenser wrote *The Faerie Queene* the fashion for feudal revivals had become coloured with nostalgia. It became a cultivated attitude. The vision of earlier poets had been more universal and eclectic, and poets had high callings as teachers and possibly as seers. In the sixteenth century the view that poetry was 'feigning' and deceitful strengthened. Allegory might be a pseudo truth. When Spenser began *The Faerie Queene* he had confidence in his moral mission, but in the course of writing his long work his confidence began to waver. The fashion for chivalry, and for archaic language, was superficial. Gabriel Harvey, the Cambridge don, was concerned about Spenser's idealisation of the past and Jonson attacked his use of archaic words. Puttenham's *Art of English Poesie* referred to differences of opinion on whether poetry should be inventive or imitative, or something of both. Sidney in his *Apology for Poetry* was strong on the educative mission and the inventive quality of poetry. At one point he went so far as to say:

> . . . . lifted by the vigour of his own invention, (the poet)
> doth grow in effect into another nature, in making things
> either better than nature bringeth forth, or, quite anew . . .[6]

This suggested that the poet might even better nature. Sidney
drew back a little when he also made the point that one could not
reach perfection because of humanity's fall from divine grace, and
the resultant "infected Will".

When he wrote *The Faerie Queene* Spenser no doubt had these
arguments in mind. There were many perspectives he could take
into account, and perhaps his vision became kaleidoscopic and
over-elaborate. He had several aims and several models to follow.
He wished to entertain the reader with elegant romance, and there
was good authority for such writing in Europe. Ariosto and Tasso
were possible models. He had a didactic aim, too, and wished to
write a moral epic. For this Tasso's *La Gerusalemme Liberata*
might serve as a guide. Then there was the desire to glorify the
Queen and the nation, and here the stories of King Arthur could
be useful. Spenser had the additional aim of reflecting some of the
concerns of the age, while rising above ordinary matters into the
cleansing realms of the imagination. The models he had in mind
were diverse: Malory, Chaucer, European writers of the Renaissance, and classical authors. Aristotle, Plato, Vergil and Ovid did
not supply an easy mixture of influences; nor did Dante, Ariosto,
Castiglione and native writers. On the question of language and
style there were differences of opinion at home and abroad. In
attempting such an epic in allegorical form there was a danger of
losing poetic identity and of changing viewpoints, as different aims
had to be brought into focus.

There was also the danger of blurring the identity of the symbolic figures in the poem if the poet altered stance and changed
perspective. The tradition of symbolic obscurity in allegory was
not a precedent for losing control, or for confused vision; and a
case can be made out that Spenser shifted his viewpoints as time
went by. If one takes a long distance view of *The Faerie Queene* in
order to see it whole, it is possible to argue that Spenser blended

his aims and his authorities well, and that he achieved his primary aim of portraying ideal conceptions of conduct -

> . . . . to fashion a gentleman or noble person in virtuous and gentle discipline.

He describes the adventures of different knights, each standing for a particular virtue. They have to struggle to succeed and they have to be assisted. The active world of chivalry within the realm of fairyland was a reflection of ideal conceptions of conduct, and if Spenser did not imitate Ariosto's touches of humour along the way, this was obviously a wise decision. Irony would have been out of place.

The main themes emerge clearly in a general way, although the poem was unfinished. Prince Arthur, having seen a vision of Gloriana (symbol of the Queen), sets off on a quest to find her in fairyland. He has various adventures on his quest, is sidetracked by having to provide assistance to others, and from time to time also needs assistance himself. He has a hard and difficult journey and his task proves complicated. Arthur stands as a symbol of the nation. Unfortunately, the climax of his quest was to be reached at the end of the work with a description of Gloriana's court, and as Spenser did not finish the story Arthur was not fully to achieve his aim.

Side by side with these adventures are described the exploits of the Queen's knights. They were sent out on missions of aid from the court and embodied the virtues which Spenser had in mind and which were influenced by Aristotle's idea of the Magnanimous Man. A book is devoted to each knight who represents a special virtue. As the Queen's knights are not all-powerful they need Arthur's help in combatting enemies and Arthur's involvement adds to his education and to his development as a leader. Sometimes symbols occur which are relevant to contemporary affairs. Arthur slays a three-bodied monster and joins Artegall in slaying the Soudan. These evils represent in some measure the figure of Philip of Spain. Arthur himself might have been seen as Leicester, or possibly at times as Sidney, and he represented the qualities that a leading courtier ought to possess. The knights, like all human beings, are prone to temptation and need the support of other virtues besides those possessed by Arthur.

Spenser's allegory also depicts the darkness of the human condition, in which the light of truth is hard to find. There are, however, visions of beauty and of divine grace. In fairyland, clues are provided, enabling us to penetrate below surfaces and hopefully to reach upward to the divine, as the neo-Platonists taught. Parts of Spenser's poem have a strange, almost surrealistic quality, and an atmosphere of dream was, of course, in the mystic allegorical tradition; the tradition of "darke conceit". The elaborate tapestry of incident, and the intertwinings of the narrative serve symbolic purposes which have an ethical value. There are references to universal correspondences, and to the integrated world of Ptolemy as modified by neo-Platonist thinking. Spenser constructs a trellis of inter-related meanings which imply that complicated and obscure though the universe may seem to ordinary mortals, it is nevertheless planned by the Creator as an ordered structure in which each creature and thing have appointed places. There was an integral relationship between various patterns of life and states of being. Obviously allegory is an appropriate form to express such notions. It could present fiction to mirror truths, or mystery to create a climate of awe. Through metaphor and symbol a relationship between the material and the transcendant could be implied. Readers could be encouraged to relate the seen to the unseen worlds. Yet, in order to perform adequately on various levels and to create an effective symbolism the poet would need a standpoint, as indeed Dante had. If the poet were uncertain of his aims or of his relationship to his work, the use of allegory could cause confusion. Spenser's aims were no doubt clear at the outset but, as his great poem developed and time passed, mood and opinion may have changed. This would account for the lack of cohesion after Book II, and the occasional uncertainty of focus. Classical and Ptolemaic views about the form and nature of the universe, and its inter-related qualities, were becoming shredded, the old chivalrous ideals were unlikely to make a significant comeback in Elizabethan England, and Arthur did not represent the 'new man' of the age. The form of allegory as a poetic way of writing was also being modified to suit new needs.

When Spenser began to write, adventure in the romantic style was popular. Readers were accustomed to reading moral lessons into stories of victories or disasters. Vergil's *Aeneid* was read as an allegory of spiritual development. Poetic pageantry, stories of battles, monsters, love and of escapes were in fashion. Sir Philip Sidney was taking part in court tourneys. Later, fashion began to change and allegory became narrower in range. It also degenerated as a form when it was used as innuendo, or as a masque at court. By 1613 Beaumont and Fletcher were able to laugh at the old-fashioned love of romance in *The Knight of the Burning Pestle*.

Once one moves closer to *The Faerie Queene* one becomes less certain of its cohesion. One notices that some of the details do not fit into the overall picture as one was led to imagine it. There are contradictions which cannot easily be explained. The thread of narrative sometimes seems to become entangled or even lost. It is not easy to reconcile the aims, as outlined by Spenser, and the structure of the poem as it develops in detailed narrative from Book II onwards. Did Spenser have a firm standpoint one has to ask? Or did he alter his attitudes as time went on, as the fashion for chivalry cooled, the background of formerly accepted beliefs became less certain, and as his own hopes for advancement were not fulfilled? Gloriana's court may have become as elusive for Spenser as for Arthur!

Spenser's university friend Gabriel Harvey was not entirely happy about his trying to recapture a fictional, romantic past and resorting to linguistic archaisms. In a letter to Spenser he pointed out that the old world was not always a Golden Age, and that the present age had its values. He rejected the view that sensual pleasures should be brought under the control of reason as a matter of course, and he thought that the notion of viewing contemplation and imagination as superior to all other pleasures was naive. He went on to say that fashions and viewpoints changed as time went on. Harvey's letter is of interest because it indicates that viewpoints were shifting and uncertain, and he stressed the fact of change.

You suppose most of these bodily and sensual pleasures are to be abandoned as unlawful, and the inward contemplative delights of the mind more zealously to be embraced as most commendable.

Good Lord, you a gentleman, a courtier, a youth, and go about to revive so old and stale a bookish opinion, dead and buried many hundred years before you or I knew whether there were any world or no . . . .

To be short, and to cut off a number of by-supposes, your greatest and most erroneous suppose is that Reason should be mistress and Appetite attend on her Ladyship's person as a poor servant and handmaiden of hers. Now that had been a probable defense and plausible speech a thousand years since. There is a variable course and revolution of all things. Summer getteth the upper hand of winter, and winter again of summer. Nature herself is changeable, and most of all delighted with vanity; and art, after a sort her ape, conformeth herself to the like mutability . . .

So it standeth with men's opinions and judgements in matters of doctrine and religion . . . .[7]

Change, or 'mutability', had for long been recognized as a factor in the affairs of human beings, but it was a particular concern of the Elizabethans. The theme of passing time occurs in many poems, including those of Shakespeare, and it undoubtedly worried Spenser. At several points in *The Faerie Queene* he appears to doubt the permanence of art, the identification of absolutes and he ends his incomplete poem somewhat sadly in the Mutability Cantos. By then the tide of thought had begun to turn against the opinions of humanists like Sir John Cheke, Mulcaster, Ascham and others who thought, like Spenser, that there was a need to educate men for virtuous, public life, and in the ideals of noble action. Sidney, his friend, had been brought up in this tradition too, but became uncertain about some traditional absolutes.[8] New perspectives were hinted at by Harvey in his letter when he mentions the reading fashions at Cambridge. There was less stress on ideals and more stress on the empirical. Jean Bodin was being read as well as Castiglione and so, too, was Machiavelli. In Shakespeare's *Troilus and Cressida* one sees later how threadbare had become the old ideals of chivalry.

If Spenser was troubled about the role of the poet in the latter part of Elizabeth's reign it might well have caused adjustments in focus when portraying symbolic figures in *The Faerie Queene*. A change in perspective can create identity problems. Already in Book I of Spenser's poem there is a suggestion of the uncertainty of appearances. The knight in this book is unable to see Una for what she really is, and he does not recognize the true identity of the false Duessa who has the power to confer a "foule ugly form" on Fraelissa.[9] The role of seeming and the art of disguise, are indicated at several points in the poem. These themes were common in Elizabethan drama, too, and are examined in a later chapter. The notion of changing shapes, and of general flux, may also be attributed to the influence of Ovid's *Metamorphoses*. But this influence was strong because of the growing concern with identity.

Duessa's skill in changing forms and in deceiving people may have been an art, but it was harmful. At the outset, therefore, we have a hint of the worrying duality in art. Later some forms of art are represented as leading to fantasy, self-indulgence and even to self-destruction. In Book II in the Bower of Bliss, where "natures worke by art can imitate", and where art can overdress, the truth is discovered by those like Britomart who are not afraid to dismiss artifice. The Masque of Cupid is another example of delusive art. One would expect magic to be represented unfavourably, and so it is in general, but Merlin is a respected figure. He, however, exercises a 'lawful' kind of magic; he is an approved Magus. Even so he has a dubious identity, whatever his role, for his father was an incubus and his mother was a nun. One wonders what Spenser made of the Hermetic thinkers - of the Italian writers and of Dr. John Dee - who respected certain kinds of magic and the cultivation of Magus insights.[10]

The writing of allegory itself was a form of artifice and might perhaps work a dubious kind of magic in the minds of inexperienced readers. Spenser could have been somewhat insecure in trying to blend themes of moral education and fanciful romance in terms of sensuous description. The episode known as the Temple of Isis is a mysterious element in the poem, and it is difficult to know what to make of it. Possibly Hermetic influences are at work here, but the episode would seem to indicate a problem of relationship between art and the world at large. In Book VI Spenser broods over the limitations of the imagination, and one recalls Harvey's stricture on regarding this faculty as eminently superior.

In Books V and VI the poet's voice emerges more obviously and allegory somewhat recedes. Outside the land of fairy, there is political turmoil and a loss of innocence, and there is a noticeable nostalgia in the poet's voice. Values are not easy to establish or to achieve in a changing world in which empiricism is emphasized. The adventures of Calidore in Book VI raise questions in the mind. He represents courtesy and honesty, and may have been based on Sidney, but he has to take account of expediency. He has to lie to Priscilla's father to persuade him that the lady is innocent. He rescues Pastorella, but he has to disguise himself as a shepherd. He conceals his sword under a cloak before going into action.

Fortune begins to play a noticeable part in the way things turn out and this could be a complicating factor in the exercise of virtue. Sidney, and Sidney's heroes in the *Arcadia*, realize this. Nevertheless, simplicity, and the solid virtues of the "antique age", are held up for admiration. There is an incident when we are given a picture of the naked Graces dancing to the music of Colin Clout, who represents the poet. They are allegorical artifices, but they portray simple truths and virtues, such as kindness, sympathy and civility. They are not dark enchantresses who entice the crowd, and they vanish when gazed upon. When they are seen by those who are fit to see them then they -

> . . . . naked are, that without guile
> or false resemblaunce all them plaine may see,
> Simple and true from covert malice free.[11]

The curious allegorical figure of the Blatant Beast is retained in Book VI. It would appear to represent the enemy of the imagination and possibly of poetry. It can be defeated, but sadly it re-emerges and has to be fought again. Ironically it uses art to defeat art, but its skills are of the evil kind and not those of the true artist. But its identity is not sharply defined and it may have taken on different aspects in the poet's mind in different parts of the work.

The unfinished poem ends on a muted note. The figure of

Mutability claims victory over Nature on the grounds that every creature and every element is subject to change. Nature points out that change brings renewal and ultimately in God's good time "none no more change shall see".[12] This is not Harvey's bouncy attitude to change. The poem ends in a solemn prayer and a "repudiation of fictions and a confession of the human limits of imagining".[13] The tone and the viewpoint have altered since the time of the early Cantos of Book I. Spenser knew that time caused changes in attitude

> But eeke their minds (which they immortal call)
> Still change and vary thoughts, as new occasions fall.[14]

Fulke Greville, Harvey and others had made the same point, which was almost an Elizabethan commonplace, but Spenser strikes a note of personal melancholy. There is also the implication that ideas on relativity, brought about by new investigation and changing perspectives of the universe and Man's place within it, could weaken the old pillars of thought which were based on absolutes; and these were still valued.

During his long poem, Spenser keeps changing his stance with regard to the reader. Sometimes he remains hidden behind the allegory, then he partially emerges and may even speak directly. In Book II Guyon does not see Belphoebe arrive; she is brought in to break the theme so that the poet can speak to the reader. In the final Cantos Spenser moves out of the framework of the allegory to take up an attitude of prayer. The poet presents his figures and symbols from different angles. Una, Florimel and Amoret are allegorical figures and so are Gloriana and Belphoebe; although the latter also embody the idea of Queen Elizabeth. Calidore represents abstract virtues, but he also represents the actual qualities of friends like Sidney. The Red Cross knight is a symbolic figure on several levels. He relates to the legend of St. George, to stories of the life of Christ, and to memories of the Old Testament. On the other hand, Britomart seems to develop non-allegorical characteristics as the poem moves on. When one comes to Book VI there are humanized romance figures in the portrayals of the lost maiden, the shepherd, and the wild man. They are not figurations of universal truths like Una. They are more human in their actions than the knights, even when the latter are in combat. Often the knights fight like forms on a tapestry in a picturesque manner but hardly life-like.

The closer one moves in to view *The Faerie Queene* the more noticeable the alterations of vision, the changes of tone, the contradictions, the structural weaknesses, and the enigmas. Simple allegory changes into philosophical allegory, and occasionally the poet speaks directly. It is a possible argument that the models and influences were so many, the perspectives so varied and confusing, that Spenser was not always sure of his direction. Moreover, he was unable to digest satisfactorily the rich multiplicity of received ideas and retain his own role and identity, or indeed the identity of his symbols. Sir Philip Sidney and Sir Walter Raleigh had similar problems, and both, like Spenser, wrote long, incomplete works needing revision.

The use of allegory continued for a long time after Spenser wrote *The Faerie Queene*; it continued in poems imitative of Ovid, in pastoral poetry, and in court masques. These were, however, genres removed from the style of Spenser's great work. At the end of the 16th century the high-souled, moral expression of ideas in the form of figurative language, extended metaphors, symbols and emblems was no longer relevant. This form of allegory had become too sophisticated to hold together, especially if blended with romance. Shakespeare's *Venus and Adonis* was a different type of allegory, and so was Raleigh's *Ocean to Cynthia* - and in Raleigh's long unfinished poem one has the sense that the old-fashioned manner of relating himself to the Queen, and the hyperbole used, is often awkward. The trend was toward ingenious metaphor, and dramatic writing which expressed the strong contrasts in Elizabethan life and the growing sense of individual identity. Allegory continued in weakened forms throughout the 17th century and beyond. There was a curiously virile revival in Bunyan's work, and Milton made use of allegory in his own way. In general it became more of a poetic exercise, in which poets of refined sensibility became shepherds in the idealized landscape of Arcady, and classical figures represented themes and ideas. Allegory was also used in the 17th century to avoid direct political statement and to escape cen-

48

sorship. Milton's *L'Allegro* and *Il Pensero* are personal statements behind the allegorical mask and they are not on the epic or romance scale. Spenser had, of course, shown the way, but in Milton's age, allegory had become an elegant convention and, with the exception of Bunyan, had lost its visionary mystique.

The habit of moving the viewpoint is noticeable in other writers than Spenser, and in Ovidian type poetry. It is also noticeable in narrative poems on historical themes. Writers like Daniel had serious aims in writing historical narrative, and history was regarded as a mirror which could reflect moral lessons - the *Mirror for Magistrates* makes this clear. Daniel's *Civil Wars* aimed at teaching the reader, but it was not easy to decide how far one could go in using history for instructional purposes. Verse structure presented difficulties of presentation, and what attitude did one take towards a model like Lucan? How far should a poem be a kind of fiction based on history? Poets who chose to follow Ovid and write love poetry, may seem to have had an easier task in so far as their aims were not complicated; but this was not always the case. A poem such as Chapman's *Ovid's Banquet of Sense* was a difficult and thoughtful piece and expressed varied viewpoints. In *Hero and Leander* the attitude of both Marlowe and Chapman is at times uncertain. One has to bear in mind that the writing of erotic poetry was a way of reaching a wider public, if one did not write for the stage, and since there was an element of fashion in this, the attitude of the poet was not necessarily one of total commitment. Moreover, convention permitted different lines of approach in handling a love story. The poet could be sensual, ironic, detached, even at times philosophical. He might attempt to blend these attitudes.

Ovid was a popular source, being a poet of transformations. In the Elizabethan world of uncertainty about old, medieval and renaissance concepts, and enthusiasm for the individual approach, Ovid was relevant. His writing suited an age of uneasy change, which was fond of disguise and interested in protean, individual qualities but believed, at the same time, in an ordered universe in which everything was related. Ovid believed in this kind of universe too. He wrote of love, and in a franker way than some allegorical poets. In using his poetry as a model, the Elizabethans naturally sought to express their personal preoccupations in the context of their own society, and as one would expect there were several modes of approach. Even within the same poem there could be changes of perspective; a habit common in the latter part of the century. We see this in *Hero and Leander*.

Marlowe did not attempt, as did Spenser, to refer to moral issues. His allegory was slight, and his aim was to write a sensuous poem based on a known classical story. His reference to the lovers varies in tone. At times he regards his figures with wry amusement. At one point he describes love in terms of greed and in imagery of gold. At other times Hero's love is described in battle imagery. Some of the similes are oddly chosen and one wonders whether he took love seriously at all in the poem. The gods and humanity are not shown in a good light, and chastity (often idealized) is taken lightheartedly. Questions arise in the mind because Marlowe's dramatic work also presents some ambiguity of approach. His Tamburlane is a strange figure. He is created on a grand scale and one is induced to feel hero sympathy. Later, and particularly in Part II, he seems to diminish in stature and his cruelties cause alienation. Did Marlowe's view change? There are questions too about *The Jew of Malta*. How far can one take the villain Barabas seriously? If one turns to *Hero and Leander* with such questions in mind, one may admire the craftsmanship of the poem while feeling uncertain about the attitude to take over the theme.

Chapman took over where Marlowe left off, but again the poetic standpoint is uncertain. One knows from Chapman's other work that he could take a lofty Platonic attitude toward love, but he also accepted bawdiness and sensuality in society. This is seen in *The Widow's Tears* and in the sensuous descriptions in *Ovid's Banquet of Sense*. The sensuousness in his part of *Hero and Leander* is evident, but there is a note of detachment when he describes Leander in the ocean as "an empty gallant full of form". This does not suggest strong sympathy; and how serious was he when he declares that Neptune could not still the waves that drown Leander because the waves were lovesick for him?

> They loved Leander so, in groans they brake
> When they came near him . . . .[15]

Exaggeration and the frivolous touch were not out of place in Ovidian type writing, but the overall tones and attitudes need to be in harmony. One feels that Marlowe and Chapman were not consistent in their attitudes towards the subject of *Hero and Leander*. An element of the ridiculous sometimes emerges.

Marston's *The Metamorphosis of Pigmalion's Image* is a different kind of allegory. The title suggests the influence of Ovid and the imagery is sensuous, but Marston uses eroticism to convey satire. The Petrarchan type lover is viewed from a scornful angle, and the poem reveals the discrepancy between the ideal and the actual. Exaggerated similes hint at the absurdity of amorous rhetoric, and there is the hint that poetic language may distort truth and be turned to deceitful purposes. Beaumont and Fletcher's *Salamacis* is yet another case. The court of Astrea suggests a covert criticism of the royal court, and the poet hides behind a mask of anonymity. The onus of interpretation is upon the reader.

The fashion for writing erotic verse was followed by Shakespeare in *Venus and Adonis*, but again with a difference. The theme and the imagery are sensuous, but the climax of the story in the union of the lovers, is avoided. This is not simply erotic postponement. The debate on love is serious. The theme of lust is pursued, but it is contrasted with the pain caused by the death of Adonis. If Venus represents earthly love, Adonis represents personal integrity and the beauty which fades but is unsullied. Adonis retains his own identity, and is not changed, or lost, by the dominance of passion. His mind is in control over the body and its 'humours'. He is himself. Adonis does not need sexual intercourse to define himself and his role in life. Shakespeare's angle of vision is very different from that of the authors of *Hero and Leander*, and yet he is not untypical of his age in his concern for identity in times of eroding traditions and uncertain individualism. When we later turn to examine Sidney's *Arcadia* we shall find that he, too, was interested in personal integrity in a world of changing values and doubtful absolutes.

When one reads *The Rape of Lucrece* Spenser's form of allegory seems further away than ever. Again moral ideas are generated from a story of lust; and again personal integrity and personal identity are major concerns. This time sexual intercourse occurs, and the question arises (the more so since rape is involved) as to whether Lucrece has lost her true identity. She feels contaminated, and that although she is no more to blame than wax can be blamed for what is printed on it, people will continue to see "my loathsome trespass in my looks".

> . . . no more than wax shall be accounted evil,
> Wherein is stamped the semblance of a devil.[16]

She feels that she is a symbol of shame, and as a free agent must in some measure be guilty. Passivity, sometimes regarded as a virtue in women, may be a predisposition to rape. The problems of rape, which give us so much concern today, are touched upon in this poem, and the point made that suicide may not resolve the situation. In Shakespeare's time the Christian ethic was, of course, against anyone taking his own life, but there was a strong, classical, literary tradition in favour of the noble suicide. Sidney also brings up this question in the *Arcadia*.

Chapman's long poems are in the allegorical mould, but the spirit is markedly different from that of Spenser. However, he, too, changes viewpoint in his work. In his drama, as well as in his poetry, he seems to think through paradoxes and contradictions, and one is not sure that he was able to reconcile differences of viewpoint. In the poem entitled *The Shadow of Night* and its preface, he makes play with the idea that knowledge is best pursued in solitary withdrawal and by contemplation in darkness. There was nothing new in this idea. The mystic tradition that silent and solitary contemplation could bring one nearer to God and help to control the bodily senses, was an old and respected one, and in poetry Petrarch and Michelangelo had both referred to the pleasures of solitude. In the *Arcadia* Sidney mentioned the benefits of withdrawal:

> . . . solitariness perchance is the nurse of these
> contemplations. Eagles we see fly along, and they are
> but sheep which alway herd together.[17]

Chapman, Sidney and the other poets are not, however, concerned with the suppression of the ego, and with divine communion.

52

They are, on the contrary, concerned with the reinforcement of the ego. Darkness, according to Chapman, inspires the poet and contributes to his special identity.

> No pen can anything eternal write
> That is not steeped in humour of the night.[18]

But he is not always sure about the value of dark withdrawals. Monsieur d'Olive, in the play of that name, is spoken of as someone who had once withdrawn from society and he is not a very elevated character. Chapman was anxious about the *nox mentis* which had fallen upon mankind - this was, of course, a different kind of darkness, but it nevertheless implies that darkness can be a state of deterioration. *Eugenia* again stresses the value of darkness to the serious thinker - "silence and night, do best fit contemplation" - but in the *Epistle to Sejanus* he likens proud melancholy to darkness and is not in favour of it. Vandome, a man of reason in *Monsieur d'Olive*, persuades his mistress back into the world of light from her unhealthy retirement in dark seclusion, and in *The Widow's Tears* entombment is not implied as wise or healthy.

If we turn to *Ovid's Banquet of Sense* it is by no means easy to determine Chapman's standpoint. The introductory letter to his friend Roydon rejects affected or pedantic obscurity in writing, but accepts obscurity if the aim is serious. Poetry, Chapman considers, should reflect shadows as well as highlights, like a painting. He accepts the old idea that truth may lie in obscurity and "shroudeth itself". His Banquet has hidden significances, but some of them seem confused as well as hidden. He obviously had Plato in mind and Ficino's commentary on the Banquet, but Chapman's Banquet is not one of intellectual thought. It concerns the senses and involves the sensuous poet, Ovid. The angle appears to be occasionally that of irony. In the poem, Ovid makes a sensual tour of the scenery, of its sights and sounds, and comments on his experience. His sensuality achieves little, and in stanza 51 the poet abandons him for a digression on divine beauty, which is held up for praise in contrast to Ovid's "fancies storme". Ovid counters with argument, and although Chapman is not on his side, the role of devil's advocate almost runs away with him. The weight of the

poem rests so heavily on Ovidian description that it becomes unbalanced. Chapman becomes disorientated. Curious symbols are
set before us, such as Corinna's spring which disturb the reader.
Chapman is unable to use the narrative as a vehicle for expressing
the high ideals he strives for. He is also unable to elevate the poem,
as did Shakespeare in *Venus and Adonis*, into useful debate. One
has some sympathy with Marston, who thought little of this type
of obscurity, and wrote:

> . . . clothed a huge nothing, all for repute
> Of profound knowledge, when profoundness knows
> There's naught contained but only seeming shows.[19]

But Marston's own poems are obscure without clues to his
references, and Jonson criticizes him for his extravagant style. It is
not that Chapman and Marston are 'difficult' poets. The 'atmosphere' at the end of the sixteenth century, and at the beginning of
the new, was such that several poets faced problems in trying to
find their way. The strength of traditional concepts and examples,
the glimpses of new perspectives, the diversity of models, created
opportunities for initiative but equally for disorientation. Allegory
became a vehicle for political comment in Tourneur's *The Transformed Metamorphosis*, which indicated that Church and State
had changed for the worse and that there was a second metamorphosis in the development of a new age. Other poets used allegory
as a fashionable form of sophistication when writing masques.
    The court masque is a different order of allegory from that of
The Faerie Queene, although Spenser had indeed shown the way
in writing the masque. In Jonson's masques, however, one does
not sense beneath the allegory the mysterious interconnections
accepted by earlier poets. There is no mystique, in the sense of
spiritual vision, in Jonson's use of correspondences. By this time
allegory had become a method of writing pastoral poetry or experimental romance, and Jonson narrowed its function even further.
Indeed the term allegory is questionable here - symbolism may be
more appropriate. Figures in the masques stood for certain people
or ideas, and episodes represented themes with some topical relevance. Cynthia obviously stood for the Queen, and other masquers

stood for ideas such as virtue and depravity. The central idea was explained through the narration, or through the way in which the story developed. Sometimes there were separate parts - such as the anti-masque - but they contributed to the whole. Themes were illustrated by music, spectacle, and the wearing of symbolic costume. As in Jonson's plays there was a tendency to move from order to disorder, and back again to order. A common theme was that of compliment - to royalty, or to a family in a society marriage. There were underlying moral themes, but usually the main idea was to entertain in a lavish way. The pageantry in Spenser's allegory was changed into the presentation of a spectacle in a stage type performance, often with a surprise element.

A reference to two of Jonson's masques should serve to illustrate his method. *Cynthia's Revels* depicts the frivolity and the vanity of courtiers. The theme of self-love is emphasized. Amorphus, who "lost his shape" (i.e. his identity) by imitating the fashions of others, returns from abroad with a story about the miraculous waters he drank at the fountains of self-love. Servants are sent to provide draughts for the courtiers who soon become vainglorious. They disguise themselves as virtues in the form of a masque, but stand in reality for such qualities as 'frivolity', 'extravagance', 'voluptuousness', 'self-love', and so on. These false courtiers are unmasked in the presence of Cynthia and are handed over to a kind of poetic master of ceremonies for punishment. They have to drink from the well of truth at Helicon, and their pilgrimage is under the supervision of Mercury. At the beginning of the masque, this god was apparently sent by Jove, in disguise, to investigate and to help in purging the court. The masque was critical enough to cause some offence, although there was fulsome compliment to Cynthia as a goddess "excellently bright".

Hymenaei, as its name suggests, celebrated a noble marriage. The central theme was therefore 'union', and this allowed Jonson to pay compliments to the throne and to the union of England and Scotland. The masque presents to us a Roman wedding before the altar of Juno, with a song glorifying the King and Queen as well as the virtues of marriage. A specially constructed globe represents the small world of mankind and from it emerges a set of male masquers who perform a turbulent dance. They represent disordered 'humours' which have to be controlled by 'Reason'. After an oration on the mystical union of marriage, the heavens open to provide lady masquers. They join their male partners who have been brought to order. Together they form a perfect circle around Reason who speaks on the idea of union. Order emerges from disorder and the dancers leave singing the Epithalmium.

We find by the turn of the century that allegory, whenever it is used, is traced on a smaller canvas. It becomes more personal and more of a minor craft. Sometimes its exaggerated symbolism becomes the subject of mockery. Earlier on, Raleigh's reply to Marlowe's *The Passionate Shepherd* presents with some amusement the likely answer which the nymph would give to the Shepherd's unreal offers, and in Shakespeare's *A Midsummer Night's Dream* the "rude mechanicals" show amusement not only at country village plays, but at the ridiculous symbolism in masques.

> This lanthorn doth the horned moon present,
> Myself the man-i'-th'moon do seem to be.

Changing attitudes in allegorical writing are paralleled by changing attitudes in drama. Again we find uncertainty of direction, and sometimes a problem over poetic identity. Shakespeare lay behind his plays, but Jonson partially emerges. Chapman gives an impression of writing dramatic poems in drama form, in order to express his views or to think through his difficulties. Chapman and Jonson are very different characters and, naturally enough, their work is different, but it is interesting to find that both have a concern about the poet's identity and his role, and both have difficulty in handling perspectives from a sure standpoint. They were not alone in this, but they provide in their different ways interesting examples of the Elizabethan problem of shifting viewpoints and elusive values.

In Chapman's plays the main themes emerge strongly, but he moves towards their development like a mariner in a rough sea, tacking this way and that and almost facing shipwreck. Appropriately enough, rough seas and tempests form the basis of several images and metaphors in his work. In general his plays express the ideal of the wise contemplative man, as do many of his long poems, but he seems to have some early sympathy for the active hero. The Elizabethans were not sure about their attitude towards active 'outward' men, and authorities differed - Aristotle emphasized 'praxis', while Plato was interpreted as favouring contemplation. Fulke Greville, although a poet, came down on the side of activity as against artistic contemplation, and considered that "life is the wisdom". His friend, Sir Philip Sidney, emphasized the importance of the poet in his *Defence of Poetry*, but he went in for active pursuits and died a warrior knight. Sir Walter Raleigh at the point of death, referred to his active life and not to his work as a poet and historian. Chapman favoured the inward-looking man, the "intellective man", who was capable of subduing the violent 'humours' which were often the cause of individual undoing. He referred to the need for withdrawal sometimes into the world of darkness and isolation. Yet there is an uncertainty and ambivalence towards great leaders like Bussy, whose tragedy he portrays, and his support for calm, stoic characters like Cato, in his play *Caesar and Pompey*, did not go easily with his belief in the 'furor poeticus'. The latter was, after all, an excessive 'humour'.

Chapman held up wisdom as a power which could subdue the idea of war in the mind. This idea arises in *The Tears of Peace* and is reiterated in *Eugenia*, written in memory of Lord Russell, who is praised as a true nobleman, in contrast to the self-seeking egoists of Chapman's day. But Chapman is equally able to express with conviction a different viewpoint. In *Monsieur d'Olive* the main character, Vandome, is a man of resource and reason, and he thinks it best to persuade his mistress back into the world of light from her dark retirement. He cures his brother-in-law of a fit of melancholy (the intellectual's disease!) by high-minded reasoning. Yet it is not Reason alone which effects the cure. Vandome diverts his friend's passion from one woman to another, and it is the transfer of passion (the 'humour') which saves him. At the end of the play, the former recluse d'Olive reappears and is criticized for entombing his faculties.

Entombment is an image which recurs in Chapman's work and it is not a healthy one. It is central to the plot of *The Widow's Tears*, a comedy which does not have a definite moral standpoint. The play revolves round Tharsalio, but it is his brother's exploit in the tomb which is the core of the plot. The story, based on the Satyricon, is an amusing one and could give rise to subtle interpretations of human foibles and predicaments. But Chapman's handling is uncertain and his angle of perspective changes.

In the play Tharsalio believes in self-confidence; he is a contemporary egocentric man. He believes that an individual can turn fortune to good account if his Will is strong. He is a manipulator, and he creates a feeling of lack of confidence in his brother who then becomes suspicious and jealous of his wife. He persuades his brother to feign death and to assume a disguise in order to appear before his wife as a stranger, in order to test her fidelity and to woo her during her period of mourning. A crucial meeting takes place in his own tomb, where his wife, sincere in her grief, resists the wooing. Finally, however, she begins to give way.

Up to this point the verse has a serious rhetorical tone, but this changes and the play begins to develop almost along the lines of farce. The widow is informed in the nick of time of the plot against her and is able to turn the tables on her husband by saying that she knew his identity all along. One might expect a lesson to be drawn, or a general tidying up of the human situation. Instead, the play limps towards an unsatisfactory ending, and no interesting moral stance is taken. There is no Jonsonian vision of a balanced social community upset by a lack of reason, and by folly, pride, intrigue and corruption. At the end, the governor of the city makes a speech about clearing the city of its vices, but gives the impression that it is beyond him. He seems to be 'a Lord of Misrule' rather than a leader of men.

Chapman's tragedies also show uncertainties of balance. The author's voice is strong compared to that of some of his contemporaries, and his plays are in some respects, intellectual explorations towards a philosophical view of life. These explorations are uneven in quality and uncertain in attitude. We are presented with active heroes who fall because they cannot control their passions, or 'humours'. The distinction between noble-minded, inward-looking men (women play a secondary role) and the crude individuals who form the world of mass opinion are indicated. Bussy d'Ambois is such a man, in that he has a noble quality and is contrasted with the small men around him. Unfortunately, he is ambitious and hot tempered; and he is a man of action rather than a philosopher. He becomes "a falling star" that

> . . . silently glanced, that like a thunderbolt
> Looked to have struck and shook the firmament.[20]

Nevertheless, it is not easy to get Bussy in focus. He arrives before us in a state of poverty, inveighing against the hollow qualities of so-called great men who are adorned with riches. Nothing in his appearance leads us to anticipate what follows. Bussy readily accepts money to put on a good front in the court, where he aims to do good and to express his innate qualities. The idea of virtue in poverty fades away and does not return as a theme, although the faults of great men continue to be mentioned. We begin to see Bussy in various lights. He is a Hercules among men. The imagery and the classical allusions build up this view, but the ethical comments are at odds with this. If Bussy represents "noblesse", he is also seen as a man of uncontrolled enthusiasm and of pride. Seen from yet another angle he is a braggart and a seducer; a man of dubious morality.

The manner of Chapman's writing does not help towards a view of the play as an integrated whole. He begins with a few comic touches and references to court manners, and there is a vein of mock chivalry, but the weight of the play is serious. The blend of humour and high seriousness is not a good mix, and unlike the variety of moods in Shakespeare's plays it is not dramatically effective.

Bussy's brother Clermont, in the sequel play *The Revenge of Bussy d'Ambois*, is a different character altogether. He is a cautious, contemplative person; something of a stoic. He seems a strange hero for a revenge play, except that his hesitancy before revenge is in the tradition of sustaining suspense and withholding action. Clermont doubts the value of revenge, but since injustice has been done to his brother he feels obliged to take some action. Unfortunately this line of reasoning is not easily expressed. At one point the inevitable ghost of Bussy appears to move things along, and delivers a Christian type sermon which is not in character with his former self. In the end Clermont confronts his brother's murderer, but finds he is afraid to defend himself. Clermont therefore spends some time whipping up courage in his opponent by force of persuasion, so that a duel may be fought. Eventually a duel does take place and the contemplative Clermont kills his brother's murderer, providing him with a benediction at the same time. The situation is so unreal that it has an air of farce about it; an effect which Shakespeare avoided in *Hamlet*, which also presents an unreal atmosphere to a modern audience.

The two *Byron* plays are interesting because they develop the idea that active 'outward looking' men are deficient in certain qualities. Byron is eminent, courageous and active, but too easily flattered into doubtful alliances. He is proud and quick to take offence. He is trapped into a conspiracy against the ruler and is finally executed. He does not always carry conviction and we do not get the tortured doubts that trouble characters like Macbeth. His self-analysis is on the surface, and the author's voice seems to be behind his protestations in too obvious a manner. Byron is a grand figure and he is seen against a background of macrocosmic analogies which help to increase his stature. But it is difficult to appreciate how such a person could have achieved the heights while being essentially foolish and arrogant.

Byron has an excess of 'humour' in that he suffers from an "adust and melancholy choler". He also blames the stars for his misfortunes. Chapman's references to the stars would seem to support the view that mankind is subject to heavenly and other influences, and is something of a puppet on the world's stage. On the other hand, the importance of the inner self and of the faculty of free will is stressed. When Byron does not blame the stars he claims that he is of "a nobler substance than the stars". He makes out a case for the self-sufficient, self-centred, self-confident individual in a well known speech:

> Give me a spirit that on this life's rough sea
> Loves t'have his sails filled with a lusty wind,
> Even till his sail-yards tremble, his masts crack,
> And his rapt ship run on her side so low
> That she drinks water, and her keel plows air.
> There is no danger to a man that knows

What life and death is; there's not any law
Exceeds his knowledge; neither is it lawful
That he should stoope to any other law.
He goes before them, and commands them all,
That to himself is a law rational.[21]

The imagery is that of the material world, in the context of which
the hero is an active person, able to stand up to the elements. He is
not the pensive, withdrawn philosopher. He is not motivated by
astral influence. If the lesson one has to learn is that such 'outward
looking', active people eventually fall because of their qualities,
sympathy is drawn towards them by the style of writing and the
enthusiasm of the author.

Swinburne wrote an interesting criticism of Chapman, and he
thought that the Byron plays were "overlaid with so many touches
that the main outline is completely disguised". He found it difficult
to arrange parts of Chapman's drama in the mind so as to obtain a
single focus. One has to decide from what angle to view the development of the plays. Chapman himself refers to the problem of
perspective in *Eugenia*-

And till you stand and in a right line view it
You cannot well judge what the main form is.[22]

The reader of Chapman is moved from one position to another in
relation to certain characters. Sometimes characters make comments on the hero, or moralize upon the action in the manner of
the *sententiae* in Fulke Greville's dramatic work, but these 'statements' differ and can be confusing, rather than enlightening. The
king, who is set over Byron is seen, from one point of view, as wise
and good. From another, he is shown to be dubious. He was prepared to banish La Fin as a corrupt person, but later decided to
use him as an agent. Towards the end of the play Byron becomes a
changed character without noticeable development. There are hints
that he has something of a neo-Platonic view of life. One senses
that Chapman is speaking too obviously through his character.

If one stands back from Chapman's work, as one did for
Spenser's *The Faerie Queene*, there is little doubt about the main

stream of his thought. He was concerned to relate mankind to the universe in the traditional way, and he conceived of the universe on an Aristotelian-Ptolemaic basis. The neo-Platonic influences were also strong. Chapman favoured, on the whole, the wise, contemplative leader. He thought that reason and good judgement should control the passions, and he was aware of the problem of mixed and dominant 'humours'. He admired thoughtful men like Clermont and Cato in his tragedies. On the other hand, he believed in the individual and inspirational role of the poet in society and in the Homeric *furor poeticus*. Homer was a model in this respect, and his translation must have strongly influenced him. He was not a religious thinker, but he may well have been influenced by the individualism of the Hermetic thinkers. He believed in the importance of a quality called "noblesse", and in the need to rise above sensual desires.

However, the closer we focus on details in the plays the more confused we become. We begin to modify first thoughts and find ourselves in the task of unravelling themes and apparent contradictions. Chapman's thoughts and situations are often tempestuous and paradoxical. For a writer who believed in controlling the passions his verse is emotionally turbulent and moody, and many images are suggestive of struggle, and of courageous bids for freedom. The background is that of disturbed skies, rugged peaks and rushing torrents. Metaphors are frequently exaggerated and Chapman's poetic and dramatic struggles become so involved that they have sometimes to be settled by direct statement. The poet moves into focus instead of remaining behind his dramatic characters, and becomes another identity. He is in some measure the energetic, boisterous, individualistic Elizabethan, clothing his utterances in colourful and extravagant language. He is also the voice of the conservative past which expresses old notions in emotional terms unsuited to them.

The presentation of divergent views is, of course, inevitable in drama. Typical Elizabethan contraries and conflicts - passion and reason, ambition and resignation, authority and freedom, love and hatred, trust and jealousy, appearance and reality - are the very meat of dramatic tragedy. Some playwrights, like Shakespeare, are more in control of their material, and their minds do not necessar-

62

ily work like those of their characters. Ambiguity may then reflect deep insights, and one is not troubled by the lack of neat conclusions. Others, less in control, less sure, may be guilty of muddled conception. Even Shakespeare has had his critics over the moral standpoints in *Measure for Measure* and *All's Well that Ends Well*. In *Anthony and Cleopatra*, on the other hand, ambiguities express the nature of the play and of its characters. The lovers are united in opposing the outside world, but in their private worlds they keep altering position with regard to each other. They quarrel and make up, scenes change rapidly, there is a Roman viewpoint, then an Egyptian, and different judgements exist in parallel. All this is germane to the play. As the critic Danby says, the dialectic is "in the deliquescent reality that expresses itself through the contraries".[23] But whether changes in viewpoint are successful or not artistically, they were common in the Elizabethan age. And this is often due to the background of changing perspectives mentioned in the first chapter and to the growing need to question individual identity. The theme of mistaken identity will be examined in the next chapter.

Ben Jonson also had problems of perspective, although he took a different view of life from Chapman. He was not at ease in the society of his times and took the way of satire in his comedies. Like Spenser, Sidney and Chapman he believed in the noble calling of the poet. His models were Seneca, Juvenal, Horace and Cicero, but neo-Platonism was not a noticeable influence. His work was more narrowly focussed than that of Shakespeare, and he aimed to castigate and ridicule the follies he saw around him in England. His *Volpone* was set in Venice, but the characters have an English stamp to them. His other comedies were given English localities and they ridiculed English customs and English types. The satirical approach had been used by Nashe, Greene and Lodge, and by the pamphleteers in a rather rough-and-tumble way. At the turn of the century satire became more bitter, and its language more excessive. Attitudes narrowed and hardened, and new models were introduced from the continent which taught a more pointed and virulent form of writing.

Jonson did not approve of Marston's rough satirical approach. He aimed at greater refinement, and saw himself as the Horace of his age - although he, too, could be rough and sometimes crude. His Latinate and rumbustious Elizabethan qualities were somewhat at variance. He followed various models and his borrowings were so considerable that Dryden later said of him: "You can track him everywhere in their snow".[24] In this, Jonson was not untypical, for other writers were great borrowers and found it difficult to absorb a multiplicity of influences and present a coherent personal expression. The absorbing of sources was yet another reason for the Elizabethan tendency to shift ground. Some of Jonson's best comments are attributable to classical sources. In general he was on the side of Ascham, Sidney, and the humanists who wished to achieve a good, sinewy vernacular style that was neither coarse nor vulgar. "Pure and neat language I love, yet plain and customary"[25] he wrote in *Discoveries* - incidentally borrowing from Quintillian. He felt that language should "differ from the vulgar somewhat . . ." and that it should not "fly from all humanity with the Tamburlaines and Tamar Chams of the late age, which had nothing in them but the scenical strutting and furious vociferation to warrant them to the ignorant gapers".[26] Jonson wanted to employ language "such as men do use", and he censured Spenser for his artificial usages. If Jonson paid attention to language, he also paid some attention to structure. Again like many of his contemporaries he had problems with larger forms. Elizabethans, on the whole, were too untidy to produce carefully structured dramas, too full of ideas - but he did try to plan his comedies, and he observed the unities better than most. His plots move through order and disorder to resolution, and even a play like *Bartholomew Fair*, which may appear to be episodic and rather haphazard in development, is organized in its polythematic movement. After a series of incidents at the fair, the story moves through nodal points, and there is a climax at the end. In all his plays the characters are mainly clear-cut and verbally realized.

Closer examination reveals that Jonson was less sure of his ground than might at first appear. He does not achieve his linguistic aims when words run away with him. He can be verbose and crude. Sometimes words and images pile up in heaps, and he has a large vocabulary of hyperbole. This can be incantatory and achieve a comic effect, but it can also be tedious. At times his crudeness is adolescent. There are so many references to excretory functions in his plays that Edmund Wilson suspected him of anal eroticism. The earthy quality in Jonson does not always accord with the image of the moral educator, and the purifier of language. His approaches to art were also somewhat uncertain.

His critical statements are forthright, but he does not write from a determined critical standpoint. He does not appear to be concerned, as Middleton was in *The Game of Chess*, with contemporary political matters. He does not expose specific vices in recognizable contexts. The vices and follies he satirized were general, and when he touched on the subject of pretension and intrigue at court in *Cynthia's Revels*, he was careful to generalize through allegory, and counterbalanced criticism with fulsome praise of Elizabeth. Even so, this masque gave some offence, and one ought to bear in mind that Jonson had at one time been imprisoned. As he continued to write, his satire (and perhaps this is too strong a term) becomes even more general. After *Volpone*, his attacks are more relaxed. *Epicene* and *The Alchemist* are more concerned with follies than vices, and this shift of emphasis is continued in *Bartholomew Fair*. There is little pointed significance in the amusing ridicule other than an implied need for the operation of Reason in the workings of society. Jonson's comedy is really a comedy of manners or affectations. His posture as the Horace of his times does not hold for long.

If we query Jonson's view of his poetic identity, he in turn queries the identity of his characters. Disguise plays an important part in his plays and he makes much of it with reference to the distortion of truth and the confusion of personality. Volpone is a master of different roles, and is most himself when acting. Has he a genuine self? In wooing Celia he imagines himself in different shapes:

> Whilst we, in changed shapes, act Ovid's tales,
> Thou like Europa now, and I like Jove,
> Then I like Mars, and thou like Erycine;
> So of the rest, till we have quite run through,
> And wearied all the fables of the gods.
> Then I will have thee in more modern forms,

. . . .
And I will meet thee in as many shapes;
Where we may so transfuse our wandering souls
Out at our lips, and score up sums of pleasure.[27]

In *Cynthia's Revels* Amorphus has lost his own shape by aping
foreigners, thus losing his identity. Imitation, mimicry, and the
degradation of personality are themes in *Volpone*, and they are related to the wearing of clothes. Overdo, in *Bartholomew Fair*, disguises himself to discover the truth, and there is irony in the idea
that one must cover up in order to uncover other people. One is
reminded of the Duke in *Measure for Measure*. But Overdo does
not get the balance right. He misses the truth through faulty judgement. Disguise, and false representation, are themes in Shakespeare
too. The age was concerned with problems of identity when the
old backgrounds to life were changing.

Beneath the comic attitude, there is an undercurrent of unease in Jonson's plays. If one really respects the clothes and not
the person it is not always cause for amusement. The comedy of
Epicene touches on some raw points, and more than one person in
the play is epicene in quality. The college of women who shun
their husbands has somewhat masculine qualities. Truewit describes
them as an "hermaphroditical authority", and one of them had
the curious name of Centaur. Captain Otter is a rough, seafaring
man on the surface, but is weak underneath and his wife "commands all at home". He is seen to be a man of two natures: "animal amphibian". The stock criticism of women in the play is that
they chatter, but so do the uncourageous men Daw and La Foole.
The uncertain nature of sexuality is emphasized through disguise
and dressing up. Clerimont defends simplicity in clothes and com-
poses the verse - "Still to be neat, still to be dressed". Truewit pre-
fers "a good dressing". Mistress Otter "takes herself asunder still
when she goes to bed".[28]   The implications are more than sexual.
There is the constant notion that people and things are not what
they seem. People change attitudes, conceal their real selves and
put on false fronts. One finds oneself asking questions such as:
what does society expect in the way of social behaviour, and what
is the borderline between what is natural and what is artificial in
manners? What is the nature of sexuality? Is their a 'normal' sexual

66

role? Disguise distorts truth and confuses the definition of personality.

Jonson's unease provides a tension, and it gives his plays an astringent quality. His comedies succeed more than do Chapman's. But however different these two writers were in temperament, in general outlook, and in the use of language, they both exhibit the Elizabethan tendency to find it difficult to steer a straight course and to order their sources and individual inspiration within the large structural framework of drama. It was not easy to keep equilibrium in a changing and confused intellectual world. Among the many labels used by Jonson we find: 'Hermaphrodite', 'Androgyno', 'Amphibian', 'Epicene', 'Amorphus', 'Metampsychosis'. And there is no doubt that he saw the world around him as ambivalent at times.

Shifting viewpoints as illustrated in drama, allegory and in other poetry are also to be found in debates on language usage. The traditional study of rhetoric continued, but it had its critics. Rhetoric was still followed when it taught how to set out an argument. It also produced useful guidelines on the use of metaphor, antithesis, parenthesis, and so on. In writing, it taught the principles of decorum and the skills of imitation. These arts were not to be dismissed lightly, for in the hands of good writers they could produce ordered argument and elegant prose or verse. Ordered thought did not, however, come easily to the ebullient and individualistic Elizabethans, who were subject to so many new influences in their age of uncertain change. Unfortunately, the art of rhetoric had been taught for so long that the subject had become somewhat tired. At worst the practice of rhetoric had become pedantic, tortuous, tedious and even empty of solid meaning. In speech the art of traditional oratory was ill-suited to the drama of the public theatre. Shakespeare mocks old usages in *Hamlet*, not only in advice to the players, but in the Queen's criticism of Polonius: "more matter, with less art". Language scholars are ridiculed in *Loves Labours Lost* - although Shakespeare was sometimes given to the elegant, and tortuously skillful phrase himself. We have seen, too, how Jonson, who favoured plain speech, was often given to rich, literary vocabulary. But there was, in general, a mood in favour of plain and direct style, even if writers did not always follow their own views. Harvey thought that the archaisms favoured by Spenser might be justified on the grounds of decorum in rhetoric, but he did not like the idea. Sidney seemed to prefer a plain style in his *Defence of Poetry*, but his *Arcadia* was written in an elegant, and richly embroidered style - full of rhetorical examples and devices - although it was not as artificial as the style of Lyly's prose. Raleigh was another writer who could be both direct and plain, as well as following the old rhetorical structures.

Debate on style had sharpened after the pronouncements of the Pleiade group in France. Some thought that French poetry would be enriched by the emulation of classical and foreign models, and by the borrowing of foreign and old native words and expressions. Others argued against this. In England the poet Gascoigne wrote a treatise on verse. He was concerned about the poverty of the English language, and thought a moderate borrowing was necessary. Mulcaster was fairly tolerant towards the use of archaisms. Spenser was therefore in good company in his artificial use of words, but "E.K." still felt it necessary to defend Spenser's diction in *The Shepherd's Calendar*. The tide was soon to turn away from elaborately artificial writing.

The debate concerned the writing of prose; whether it should be enriched with rhetorical flourishes and with philosophical terms. Sir Thomas Elyot was all for enrichment. Others preferred a plainer style. Montaigne and later Bacon were opposed to what was called the Ciceronian style, and which was favoured by Ascham. But Bacon, perhaps on the principle of decorum, wrote in different styles in his work. He wrote the *Novum Organum* in a brisk, aphoristic manner, while in the *Advancement of Learning* he chose a 'magistral style'. In general, copious, embellished prose gradually gave way to a tauter, plainer style, but the debate went on and practices varied.

Writers felt the need to free themselves from slavish imitation, but did not want to run wild. A style was needed to express personal views, but authors were not always sure of their role or their literary identity. There was uncertainty about the function of language as there was about forms of art. Could the persuasive skills of language be deceitful and harmful? Did it persuade away from truth? Shakespeare became distrustful of language itself, as will be seen in the next chapter, and Spenser, too, was concerned.

The bad poet, Malfont, had his tongue nailed to a post, and the Blatant Beast, the enemy of true art, was skilled in the art of words. Chapman wrestled with language in what he called his "stifled verse", struggling through symbols to express and to order his thoughts. In time, bombastic declamation on the stage gave way to looser and more complicated rhythms and, in turn, these, too, became an imitated convention.

Word coinages became so common in the stretching of language to new uses that Jonson made fun of the practice of poets like Marston. In his play *The Poetaster* there is a scene in which a sick poet vomits ugly and unnatural words upon the stage. The surge of interest in the vernacular did not always produce plainer and more realistic forms of writing. Elizabethan and Jacobean dramatic writing created its own clichés and mannerisms. Drama, because of its scope, was able to embrace several styles. In *Hamlet* we are told that there were ". . . pastoral-comical, historical-pastoral, tragical-historical, tragical-comical, historical-pastoral, scene individable, or poem unlimited." Outside drama there were the styles of Eupheus, Petrarch, satire, aphorism, Cicero to be chosen and emulated. The attitudes and angles of approach were many.

In this chapter we have seen that viewpoints often altered, and expressed the contradictions and paradoxes in life created by a changing intellectual background. Medieval scholars were prone to produce paradoxes, and to set puzzles, but these were expressions of a belief in the ultimate harmony and overall unity of the universe. Towards the end of the sixteenth century this belief still held, but was less certain; and the existence of paradox and contradiction was to reinforce doubt rather than belief. Uncertainty about the nature of the macrocosm implied uncertainty about the nature and the function of the microcosm. The egocentric individuals of the age were sometimes difficult to know, and a knowledge of individual complexity is found in the drama of the day. It evidenced a variety of characters, far removed from older types, and different ways of seeing them. But most playwrights had in common Jonson's interest in idiosyncratic behaviour, in human disguise, and in problems of identity. Shakespeare, in particular, played on themes of mistaken identity, and this interest is examined in the next chapter.

III   Themes of Mistaken Identity
Shakespeare & Jonson

Since many doubts had been cast on accepted beliefs, some thinkers might well have asked whether anything was permanent. Elizabethan poetry touched on this worrying theme with its images of
fading beauty and the ravages of time. The eager, bustling, com-
merical world may have seemed, to those who were not involved
in its enthusiasms, temporary and insubstantial. It resembled a
stage, peopled with temporary players assuming misleading identities. Shakespeare's *A Midsummer Night's Dream* and *The Tempest*
reflect a dream-like world in which personalities and values change.
Basic values, depending on concepts of time and measurement, are
seen to be shifting values, and they alter with the angle of vision.
The Tempest creates an atmosphere of illusion and of relativity.
The action takes place on an enchanted island and Prospero tells
the audience that we are made of the stuff of dreams. As the terms
of reference shift in this play, the line between what is objective
and what is subjective is blurred. Within the enchanted world of
pretence there is a masque of pretence. Actors pretend to be
spirits, and these spirits pretend to be goddesses and rustics, and
later the audience is told that it, too, has a part to play. In such a
world how can one define identity? What does Prospero represent?
What does he mean in the Epilogue? In *A Midsummer Night's
Dream* reality is also uncertain. There is an "out of joint" fairy
world, and the whole play evokes images of mist, "wicked and dis-
sembling glass", and of translated reality, which make it impossible
to rely on definitions. Characters are 'drugged' by Puck, so that
they change their perceptions and their sense of values.

The Elizabethans and their successors were conscious of the
problem of defining identity. There was, however, concern about
the individual within the confusing macrocosm surrounding him.
Shakespeare was not alone in dwelling upon problems of identity,
but he highlighted them with more subtlety than his contemporaries and they constitute themes which run through many of his

70

plays. His interest moves from a superficial interest to a deeper preoccupation.

The word 'identity' (Latin root 'idem') has, broadly speaking, two meanings. It implies, as its Latin root suggests, 'sameness'. Identification is made by analogy, by comparison with similarities; and one can speak of things being 'identical'. The word also means 'individuality'; the special quality by which we recognize a person for what he or she is. We seek therefore to underline differences as well as similarities. Identity may be categorized by an external label; the name perhaps or the costume worn. But it can also re present the more complicated ingredients of personality and the workings of the human mind. Shakespeare plays upon the different meanings of identity. He may underline the idea of sameness - although in the case of identical twins it is only to show that they are different beneath the camouflage of appearances - but he also emphasizes the differences between people through character portrayal. He occasionally draws attention to names and to other personality labels, but more frequently he suggests that the establishment of identity is elusive. "You know me by my habit", says Mountjoy, and King Henry V replies: "Well then I know thee; what shall I know of thee?". The answer is deliberately vague, for Mountjoy's identity is assumed. He is a herald, and is acting not for himself but for the King, his master. Later Henry returns to the question of identity: "What is thy name? I know thy quality". More usually the question is put the other way round, for a name implies little. "What's in a name?" said Juliet. But names and labels were important to the Elizabethans.

Shakespeare develops the theme of dubious identity on several levels. There is the level of plot - and here he uses the old device of the mix-up of identical twins or the use of simple disguise to create amusement, suspense and surprise. Important people disguise themselves as beggars - a frequent ploy in Elizabethan drama. The part played by coincidence in life is brought out. He also develops the theme through character portrayal, and people are shown to be not what they seem on the surface. They mask their natures as well as their bodies, or else they change from what they were. Thirdly, on the level of thought and of language the question of defining identity is brought before us. We learn that identity is elusive and that language may serve to conceal truth or to mislead. Words themselves often lack definition and may mean different things at the same time. Shakespeare was, of course, fond of punning and of using double-edged phrases.

It was not unusual for writers of verse or drama to present an enigma, to engage in oblique reference, or to use code. Convention demanded the use of pseudonyms in satire. It would have been easy enough to guess who were the objects of Jonson's satire in *The Poetaster*, but more difficult to know the models in *Love's Labour's Lost*. It would have been even more difficult, for those not in the know, to elucidate the references in *Willoughby His Avisa*.[1] In a society which showed a growing interest in idiosyncracy, it would have been natural for some to disguise character traits and to refer to others in an oblique manner. Linguistic games, such as punning or the use of nicknames, were popular. There was a fashion for using fancy names in Elizabeth's court and Sir Walter Raleigh and others had special names given to them by the Queen. There were games of hide-and-seek in literature.

One has to bear in mind that the allegorical tradition of obscuring meaning to make it more significant, and of using representational figures in narrative, still exerted an influence. When allegory became somewhat trivialized it became a poetic game, and in unskilled hands, the device in pastoral poetry of speaking through shepherds and shepherdesses could become hackneyed. These devices were, however, accepted ways of obscuring identity in the interests of discretion as well as of enriching meaning. Identity achieved another dimension through symbolism. This was also true in painting. The Queen's picture in Hatfield house, known as 'the rainbow picture', was enriched by symbols to heighten effect. A person's costume could have social or private significance, and we have seen how Jonson deliberately confused personality with clothes. There were, too, political dangers in being direct. The Queen looked for her hidden identity in *Richard II*, and Jonson got into trouble over hidden meanings in the play he wrote with Nashe called *The Isle of Dogs* in 1597. The authorities ordered copies to be destroyed.

If the ethos of Elizabethan England encouraged the use of masking and disguising, one must remember that disguise had for long been a dramatic convention. It was also employed in story telling. It was used in Oriental as well as in Western cultures, and the comedies of Plautus were powerful models in Shakespeare's time. Shakespeare's originality lies in the way in which he worked upon these ancient devices and presented themes of mistaken identity on a more significant level than that of plot. He had before him the somewhat different models of early English plays, which sometimes linked the idea of disguise with character. The figure of Vice had often transformed himself. In Lyndsay's *Three Estates* the figure of flattery disguised himself in the robes of a friar and discussed his disguise openly. The play of *King John* by Bayle presents several changes of identity with suggestions of character deceit. The use of disguise, with intimations of immorality as well as comedy, was a technique ready to hand when Shakespeare began to write.

Theories about 'humours' helped to define identity by categorizing characters: the hot, choleric person, the pale moist creature, and so on. But, as mentioned in the first chapter, it was not as simple as this. Special situations could upset the balance of the 'humours' and characters could change. A timid, inactive type might develop, in certain situations, active and choleric attributes. Therefore, an imaginative writer was not prevented from producing rich, changeable characters and from confusing superficial concepts. Shakespeare may have owed a debt to theories on the 'humours', but he was not trammelled by them. The portrayal of characters was based on life experience as well as on models in literature. It is not possible to define Shakespeare's characters by labelling them, and we are shown that people should not be taken at their face value.

In the early plays of Shakespeare, the theme of mistaken identity is developed on the level of plot. The story in *The Comedy of Errors* hinges upon errors of recognition, like a comedy by Plautus. A pair of identical twins, who have lost each other, and who happen to have a pair of identical servants who do not know of each others presence in the same city, come together after a series of amusing mistakes. A woman locks her husband out under the mistaken idea that he is someone else, and cannot understand why he is later angry with her. She also makes the mistake of thinking that he is enamoured of her sister, again mistaking his identity. Masters mistake their servants and there are comic confusions causing wrongful beatings, false arrest, and unexpected love scenes.

> Dromio: "I am transformed master, am not I?"
> Antipholus: "I think thou art in mind, and so am I."[2]

It is worth noting that some of the devices used in this play - shipwreck, identical twins, the handing over of money to someone who later refuses to acknowledge the fact because of an error of recognition - are also used in the later comedy of *Twelfth Night*. They were stock gambits in the drama of the day. In the plays *The Two Gentlemen of Verona* and *The Taming of the Shrew* the theme of mistaken identity is again present. In the first play the girl Julia (acted of course by a boy) pretends to be a male page. In speaking to Sylvia she/he describes Julia (i.e. herself) as being someone very like himself. She explains that she/he knows because she/he once wore Julia's gown when acting a part in front of Julia herself! Illusion and reality mingle to confuse perspective. In the second play, Shakespeare seems as interested in the characters as in the situations. Has everyone been mistaken in Catherine? It would seem that she fashioned a new identity for herself in serious marriage. When one comes to *Love's Labour's Lost* the theme of mistaken identity is pursued in plot and through character. One is led to ponder the concept of human identity. Is appearance everything? Are our ideas as transient as human relationships?

A bachelor Academy, which seems to run on lines indicated by the French academies of the 16th century, is invaded by a group of beautiful women. The members of the academy abandon their assumed role of scholars in secret, and become secret lovers. They try at first to hide their new romantic roles from each other, and to conceal the fact that they have betrayed the ideals, somewhat monastic, of the academy. They do not succeed and eventually have to reveal themselves for what they are. They decide, nevertheless, to conceal their true identities from the ladies they love by disguising themselves in Russian costume. However the women see through these disguises, although they pretend to be ignorant. In turn they, too, play the disguise game. They mask their features and exchange with each other what are nowadays called 'accessories', but which might here be more appropriately called 'identity kits'. The result is that the men mistake their lovers and are misled by their acting skills. They go by outward appearances and woo the wrong women. It is at this point in the play that one detects a serious undertone - a hint that danger could occur if one mistakes the outward show for the inward reality. One is reminded that people and things are not what they seem.

In *A Midsummer Night's Dream* the chemistry of human nature does not work well and 'magic' is brought in to alter the balance of the 'humours'. Briefly the situation is as follows:

Lysander is in love with Hermia
Hermia is in love with Lysander - Her father opposes the idea.
Demetrius is in love with Hermia - Her father favours the idea.
Helena is in love with Demetrius - He rejects her.
Oberon and Titania have quarrelled in fairyland.

Oberon, through the agency of Puck, dispenses magic eyedrops which change the characters' views of each others identity. He does this to punish Titania, who will be made to dote on the first earthly creature she meets. He also decides to intervene to help Helena by changing Demetrius' view of her. Like the stars in the heavens the non-human Oberon is able to influence human beings and to change their destiny. However individual and idiosyncratic a person may be, he or she is in some measure subject to outside influence. This view, one remembers, was not held by everyone in Shakespeare's age, and was not held by some of his characters.

The weaver, Bottom, is changed into part-ass, and owing to the effect of the eyedrops Titania sees him as an attractive lover. Puck mistakes the identity of Demetrius and works magic on Lysander instead. Lysander's outlook undergoes a radical change and he falls out of love with Hermia and into love with Helena. Demetrius, too, is made to love Helena, who becomes distraught with her change of fortune. The situation becomes dangerous as well as comic and a fight takes place between the two men. Tragedy is only averted when Oberon learns that Puck made a mistake. In the end the characters become themselves except for Demetrius, who presumably spends the rest of his life under the influence of Oberon's chemical magic. This light-hearted comedy has serious undertones, and dark shadows fall from time to time. One is perhaps led to feel that the human condition cannot be entirely contented in a world of shifting realities, of misty definitions, of confused identities, and of irresponsible interference from outside. Illusion may be amusing, but it has worrying implications.

In *Romeo and Juliet* errors in judging character and situations have tragic results. They do not depend on disguise, as in the early comedies, for the theme of mistaken identity is presented through character and through expressed opinion, The idea that people are not what they seem emerges. The Montagues and the Capulets misjudge each other, and the 'lie' by which Friar Lawrence causes Juliet to lose identity in a pretended death brings on the final tragedy. Imitation death is the most dangerous disguise of all, and Friar Lawrence refers to it as a form of disguise. He calls it "the borrowed likeness of shrunk death". Identity labels, in the form of names which have a more than nominal importance, are called in question by Juliet. Does it really matter that Romeo has the Montague name?

> What's in a name? That which we call a rose
> By any other name would smell as sweet.

If one turns to *The Merchant of Venice* one finds that the mistake is not so much that Portia is in disguise and is mistaken for a man; it is that people misjudge each other. Shylock misjudges his adversaries and his cause, and is in turn misjudged to the point where he feels bound to exclaim: "Hath not a Jew eyes? Hath not a Jew hands, organs, dimensions, affectations, passions?" He is regarded by the Christians as if he had a special identity which separates him from the rest of the human race. The relation between identity, disguise, and surface appearance is brought out in such questioning lines as:

> A goodly apple rotten at the heart.
> O! What a goodly outside falsehood hath.[3]

and

> So may the outward shows be least themselves;
> The world is still deceived with ornament.
> In law what plea so tainted and corrupt,
> But, being seasoned with a gracious voice
> Obscures the show of evil?[4]

In other words, what one identifies as Justice may be falsified by a form of disguise, by painting over the false to resemble the true. As Shakespeare matures as a playwright the theme of mistaken identity becomes less important on the level of plot and more important on the level of character portrayal. This is noticeable in the History plays, but it is not to say that Shakespeare abandons the use of traditional disguise. Disguise is used in the final plays.

In *As You Like It* and in *Much Ado About Nothing* the theme is again represented in the course of the plot. Rosalind disguises herself as a boy and meets her lover, Orlando, in the forest. Orlando does not recognize her. In order to test his love she asks Orlando to pretend that she (in disguise as a male) is his love, Rosalind. Thus one is presented with disguise upon disguise, and a double masking of identity. As the part of women on the Elizabethan stage was played by boys, a boy actor assumes the identity of a girl called Rosalind who disguises herself as a boy and asks Orlando to pretend that she is a girl! Only at the end of the play does the true stage identity emerge.

In *Much Ado About Nothing* the mistake over identity is nearly serious. It will be remembered that Duke Claudio has an enemy who causes him to suspect the fidelity of Hero, by a trick of disguise. Claudio rejects Hero, who disappears and is later believed to be dead. One recalls the death trick in *Romeo and Juliet* and in *The Winter's Tale*. Hero only feigns death. The Duke then learns that he was mistaken in his judgement of her and goes through a period of intense remorse. Eventually Hero is brought in masked and then reveals her identity to the Duke, who is overjoyed. The sub-plot provides the witty characters of Beatrice and Benedict, who are stamped as being against marriage. They prove to be mistaken in each other.

The play of *Twelfth Night* develops the theme of mistaken identity on different levels. The story uses the same devices which are used in *The Comedy of Errors*. Viola is washed ashore after a shipwreck believing that her brother, who closely resembles her, is drowned. As she is in a strange country she disguises herself as a boy. This leads her later to be mistaken for her brother, who was not drowned and turns up in the same town as Viola. He takes money from his friend Antonio to keep safe for him. His sister Viola assumes the identity of a youth and calls herself Cesario. She enters the service of Duke Orsino, who is in love with a lady called Olivia. This lady does not respond to the Duke's advances, but finds herself strongly drawn to Cesario (the girl-boy) who speaks to her on the Duke's behalf. Viola-Cesario is troubled by Olivia's attitude towards her and says feelingly:

> Disguise, I see thou art a wickedness
> Wherein the pregnant enemy does much.
> How easy it is for the proper-false
> In women's waxen hearts to set their forms.[5]

The dialogue between Cesario and Olivia is interesting because of its play upon words and meanings which are relevant to the theme. Olivia enters veiled and Viola-Cesario begins the conversation:

Viola: The honourable lady of the house, which is she?
Olivia: Speak to me; I shall answer for her.
Your will?
(poetical compliments follow and Olivia then says . . .)
Are you a comedian?
Viola: No, my profound heart; and yet by the very fangs of malice I swear I am not that I play. Are you the lady of the house?
Olivia: If I do not usurp myself, I am.
Viola: Most certain, if you are she, you do usurp yourself; for what is yours to bestow is not yours to reserve.
(Olivia then comments on the way in which rhetoric may disguise the truth, and having taken a fancy to this

78

personable youth, asks . . .)

Olivia: What are you? What would you?

Viola: . . . What I am and what I would are as secret as maidenhead.[6]

The scene harps upon the idea of disguise, false presentation and usurpation of identity. Is beauty only skin deep, or perhaps the art of skilfully applied cosmetics, Viola seems to ask when Olivia draws back her veil - "Excellently done, if God did all". In a very different situation Hamlet also pondered on the nature of beauty when gazing upon the skull of Yorick.

As the play develops Viola and her brother are mistaken for each other by Sir Toby Belch and his friends. Sir Andrew Aguecheek is encouraged to fight Viola-Cesario who seems weak and timid. He decides to do this, but owing to an error in identification he ends up fighting her formidable brother instead. Sir Toby Belch fights the brother, too, and is soundly beaten. He is taught the lesson that it is unwise to play upon people and to paint them in false colours. The Lady Olivia, who has fallen in love with Viola-Cesario, similarly confuses the identities of brother and sister and pledges to marry the brother. Confusion ends when Viola reveals her true identity. The Duke decides to take her as his wife, and Olivia marries Viola's brother. Meanwhile the brother's friend, Antonio, deciding to ask for his money back speaks to Viola-Cesario by mistake, and is rebuffed.

The theme of mistaken identity is played subtly through the sub-plot in which Malvolio appears. Malvolio is deceived by people and in people. He is led to cast himself in the role of a lover and equal of Lady Olivia. He mistakes others and he mistakes himself, and plays a ridiculous role. This results in his losing sympathy and being cast into a dungeon as a madman. During his confinement he is plagued by the Clown, Feste, who pretends to be a parson. Malvolio, therefore begs his help. Identity is confused to the point of causing cruelty. Malvolio does not know who is who, or what is what. Finally he is forced to recognize himself for what he really is, but when the masks are off, reality is hard to accept. In this play, as in *King Lear* the audience does not find it easy to define Feste's identity.

The identity theme is expressed on the level of thought and of linguistic usage, as well as through character portrayal. Malvolio is not only deceived by people; he is deceived by words. Several times Shakespeare uses language to suggest double meanings, and to deceive. He expresses a distrust in words, for they may disguise meaning and mask truth.

> Viola: Save thee, friend, and thy music! Dost thou live by thy tabor?
> Feste: No, sir, I live by the church.
> Viola: Art thou a churchman?
> Feste: No such matter, sir; I do live by the church; for I do live at my house, and my house doth stand by the church.
> Viola: So thou mayst say the king lies by a beggar, if a beggar dwell near him; or, the church stands by thy tabor, if thy tabor stand by the church.
> Feste: You have said, sir. - To see this age! A sentence is but a chevril glove to a good wit: how quickly the wrong side may be turned outward!
> Viola: Nay, that's certain; they that dally nicely with words may quickly make them wanton.
> Feste: I would, therefore, my sister had no name, sir.
> Viola: Why, man?
> Feste: Why, sir, her name's a word; and to dally with that word might make my sister wanton. But indeed, words are very rascals since bonds disgrac'd them.
> Viola: Thy reason, man?
> Feste: Truth, sir, I can yield thee none without words; and words are grown so false, I am loth to prove reason with them.[7]

Later in the course of this dialogue Feste says of his occupation in Olivia's household:

> "I am, indeed, not her fool, but her corrupter of words".

In the History plays, it is history itself which provides the plot, and the theme of mistaken identity is pursued through the portrayal of character; although disguise is sometimes used. Prince Hal disguises himself to catch out Falstaff, and as Henry V he cloaks himself to mingle with his troops. In character portrayal ambiguities are brought out and one is led to ask the question: "What is true identity? Does it exist?" Richard III is seen from more than one angle, and he plays more than one part. He becomes persuasive in his wooing of Anne. In *Henry VI* (part III) Richard stands on the stage and announces his ability:

> Why, I can smile, and murder whiles I smile;
> And cry 'content' to that which grieves my heart;
> And wet my cheeks with artificial tears,
> And frame my face to all occasions.[8]

As an actor himself, Shakespeare knew it was possible to assume an identity and, with art, to persuade people that you were other than you were. He often compares the world to a stage, and his contemporaries also did this. The critic, Miss Richter, in *Shakespeare and the Idea of the Play* points out that Edward's *Damon and Pithias* reflects the notion that the world was populated by people playing roles. Yet if the world were like a stage, the stage had in turn to present the real world, albeit through illusion. The actor had a particularly difficult part to play in History plays, since the characters represented real people from the past. He was not acting out a simple comedy role. He had to pretend that he was an historical personage, and to convince the audience of the temporary reality of his assumed identity.

In *Richard II* once the mask, or disguise, of title and ceremony has been removed the frail human being is exposed:

> . . . Throw away respect,
> Tradition, form, and ceremonious duty:
> For you have but mistook me all this while;
> I live with bread like you, feel want,
> Taste grief, need friends . . .[9]

Richard seems at times to lack identity because he lacks position. He has no role to play in society. He says that he does not know "what name to call myself" and resorts to fantasy role playing:

> Thus I play in one person many people
> And none contented. Sometimes I am a king
> Then treasons make me wish myself a beggar
> And so I am . . .[10]

Names and descriptions were important in society, in spite of Juliet's remark. Adam had conferred identity upon the animals in the Garden of Eden by giving them names, and ever since, the naming of things had been of significance. Without a word image, it was difficult to conceive of existence. Words, things and creatures, through a sort of transubstantiation, were linked together. Feste joked that they could change the nature of his sister's character. Words worked magic, too. By naming and calling spirits, one could, if one new the technique, summon supernatural influences. The Cabbala had mysterious and powerful words. Yet Shakespeare began to question the basic function of language, as did others of his age. The old perspectives were doubtful. The arguments in Europe and in England about the use of language in poetry and prose, perhaps added to distrust and uncertainty. Spenser, Harvey, Sidney, Jonson and Bacon were among those who were concerned. Bacon worried about laxity in word usage and thought that most discourse led to misinformation. Discourse was one of Bacon's idols - the 'idol of the market place' - and he stressed the need to pay attention to the things themselves rather than to the words which described them. In *All's Well That Ends Well* the King is puzzled over questions of identity, and Helena says to him: "'Tis but the shadow of a wife you see,/The *name* and not the thing".[11] Although Shakespeare was addicted to word games, he also reacted against his own skills. After *Richard II* one finds a growing element of scepticism in the power of words to convey truth.

Feste knew that words could be traded like commodities, and so did Falstaff. "I would to God thou and I knew where a commodity of good names were to be bought".[12] Falstaff ponders the concept of honour and concludes that it is only a word. "What is honour? a word. What is that word honour? air." Style could be arranged and put on like a costume to express personality, or to

82

conceal identity. Pistol uses language to create an impression and also to confuse people. Shallow is not sure of him: "Honest gentleman, I know not your breeding". Fluellen is at first taken in by Pistol's bold talk. But there is a sense in which Pistol's style of speech is not misrepresentation, for it is expressive of his real character; and this is as false, pretentious, and ridiculous as his speech. Ultimately words do not help him. They do not help King Richard either, nor Falstaff.

If character may be portrayed through a personal style of speech, it is also portrayed through attitudes and actions. Important people, like kings, sometimes seem to have two personalities: one for public presentation, and one for private expression. Dramatists often comment on the special identities of kings and of those in official positions. Prince Hal's personality is not the same when he becomes King. He plays one part to prepare himself for another:

> For God doth know, so shall the world perceive,
> That I have turn'd away my former self.[13]

This transformation would have been understood, whereas we find it difficult to accept today. The manipulation of people by those who are cool and calculating - Iago, Edmund and others - was also observed. No matter what the 'humour' was, it could be changed by the influence of personal relationships. This had long been appreciated, but it was an idea which was given a stronger psychological emphasis in the sixteenth century. It was one of the new perspectives. In Sonnet 94, Shakespeare refers to those who are "the lords and owners of their faces," and who keep their natures under control. But there are those, like Othello, who are stimulated by others and who may appear to change under their influence.

In the play of *Coriolanus*, the hero has difficulty in maintaining a set of attitudes for public presentation. He does not wish to appear as an ordinary human being, who is subject to ordinary emotions and weaknesses. It may be the tradition for a victor to show his wounds to the populace, but this is distasteful to the proud Coriolanus. When he has to consider human pleas for mercy, he is uneasy and feels "like a dull actor" and that he has "forgot my part". He is only at ease as a soldier, an active leader; but not as a politician who has to assume popular identities. In another Roman play, that of *Anthony and Cleopatra*, there is a problem of defining identity. In a world of deliquescent attitudes and movements the Protean characters of Anthony and Cleopatra are not obvious stereotypes. Anthony is seen in a different light by different people, and his past reputation conflicts with his present behaviour, while Cleopatra possesses "infinite variety". In *Julius Caesar* we see the personality of Caesar, as we do of Anthony, in different lights. He is spoken of as a Colossos, but appears as a man given to epileptic fits. At times easily persuaded, even weak, but not without courage of a sort. He is obviously a leader because of the opposition and enmity he provokes.

In the later so-called comedies, *Measure for Measure* and *All's Well That Ends Well*, the device of disguise is again used, but it is no longer a light-hearted game. Disguise is more intimately related to the problems of human relationships and to the expression of ideas. Disguise sometimes provokes the thought, as with Jonson's plays, that one may have to cover up in order to reveal, and this is one of the paradoxes which interested the Elizabethans. As always, it depends on the viewpoint.

In *Measure for Measure* the disguise of the Duke is central to the plot. He discovers and uncovers much by putting on a disguise. But it is not simply costume which deceives; it is character. Actors put on a performance, and so do people in real life. Angelo, the Deputy, is not what he is supposed to be, and Claudio, when put to the test, proves to be flawed. In *Troilus and Cressida*, too, the theme is one of human frailty. Idols prove to be hollow, as Troilus discovers. Cressida is false and Achilles, the renowned hero, cuts a poor figure. Ideals of chivalry are debased. People, in general, and the myths they have created, are not what they are often claimed to be.

Does the theme of mistaken identity continue through the Tragedies? Macbeth smears the faces of the grooms to mislead, soldiers disguise themselves as Birnam Wood, Edgar disguises himself as a mad beggar in *King Lear*; but it is human performance which disguises reality rather than costume, and yet again language is used to deceive. Macbeth changes because of the pressure put upon him by his wife. Duncan realizes that true identity is often hidden and remarks that: "there's no art to find the mind's construction in the face". Hamlet also changes in the sense that he is different from the reported Hamlet of the past, and throws "words" at Polonius and, in another way, at Ophelia. Hamlet becomes suspicious of friends and of outward tokens of identity. He doubts the nature of his former companions, Rosencrantz and Guildenstern, and even that of his mother. He doubts the King and has second thoughts about the Ghost. "Seems, Madam! May it is; I know not seems". But it is seeming which obsesses him. He has more than one self - the Prince as known formerly, the controlled madman, the impulsive person who lies underneath the surface appearance.

In his book *Shakespeare's Doctrine of Nature* Danby says: "In bringing up the problem of the true and the seeming true the machiavel posed a dilemma which obsessed Shakespeare for fifteen years".[14] Machiavelli had, of course, suggested dissimulation for political ends and Cortegiano had accepted that a good courtier had to act a part. Identities could be assumed and people could be mistaken in each other. Hamlet begins to identify Ophelia with all frail women. He re-names women, re-identifies them: "frailty, thy name is woman". The goodly world is now identified as a "sterile promontary", and what was once seen as noble man becomes the "quintessence of dust". Hamlet considers that the devil is a master of disguise, and that he has "power to assume a pleasing shape". When one turns to the play *Othello*, it is also shown that people are subject to change and that appearances are often false. We are all authors of each other's identity in many ways, and Desdemona saw Othello's "visage in his mind". Othello's temperament, one is led to believe from previous reports, changes when the passionate 'humour' of jealousy is kindled by Iago. Iago is seen from different angles by Othello and by the audience. In *King Lear* one finds that the king is mistaken in his daughters, and this mistake is parallelled in the mistake which Gloucester makes in his sons. In this play one has to ask oneself about the identity of the Fool.

Both King Lear and Richard II lose identity in their own minds, and they both lose it because they no longer have a position. Changes in human relationships cause confusion, and then there is a need to re-define identities. Lear begins to ask himself what the true nature of Man is, and in this he is not unlike Hamlet. In his despair he regards mankind as bestial: "Down from the waist they are Centaurs/Though women all above".[15] Malformations, masculine women, feminine men, interested the Elizabethans. Ben Jonson's plays contain abnormal figures, and Bacon's Pan was what he called a "bi-form" creature. Bacon thought that persons have two faces which reflect interior and superior identities, and these were often in conflict. Thus it could be argued that people have divided selves. Hamlet is divided and so is Lear. When Lear has to consider what he is in exile he asks:

> Doth any here know me? - Why, this is not Lear:
> Doth Lear walk thus? speak thus? Where are his eyes?
> Either his motion weakens, or his discernings
> Are lethargied - Ha! waking? 'tis not so.
> Who is it that can tell me who I am?[16]

Earlier in the play Regan had commented that he was a person who "hath ever but slenderly known himself".

We have seen that Shakespeare indicates in several plays that language is an uncertain way of expressing the real needs of individuals in complicated situations. Cordelia in *King Lear* admits that she does not have "that glib and oily art/To speak and purpose not".[17] If one goes through *Measure for Measure* one finds many phrases suggesting falseness. There are coin metaphors suggesting counterfeiting, and normally incompatible ideas are yoked together in phrases like "foul redemption", "charity in sin", and so on.

In Shakespeare's last plays, physical disguise is used as in the comedies to further the plot, but it becomes a serious matter. In *Cymbeline* there are complicated and sudden revelations of identity. Dream and reality become confused and behind fantasy lurk sinister elements. In *The Winter's Tale* dream and reality intermingle. Leontes is confused and his wife says to him:

> You speak a language that I understand not,
> My life stands in the level of your dreams.[18]

Even on the level of innocent masking, disguise may do more than simply conceal. When Perdita acts as a Whitsun Queen she remarks:

> . . . Sure this robe of mine
> Does change my disposition.[19]

Unaware of her real identity, Camillo advises her to disguise herself in order to "disliken the truth of your own seeming". In the masque within the play illusion grows upon illusion. Finally Perdita's identity is discovered and Hermione, who had used the disguise of death like Hero and Juliet, presents herself as a statue and then returns to life. In *The Tempest* magic is used to restore justice, and true identity is only revealed through the careful work of Prospero.

The relationship between clothes and personality has already been mentioned in regard to Jonson's plays. The Elizabethans were fascinated by dress. The colourful and fanciful dress at court, with its ruffs, pinched waists, and other exaggerated features indicates a special interest in clothes. Puritans went to the other extreme and dressed in sombre black, but almost equally noticeably. Costume could both conceal and express personality; and, of course, it could enhance sexual attraction. Comments on dress are common in the literature of the day. Sir Philip Sidney mentions dress and disguise frequently in his *Arcadia*, and Sir Walter Raleigh was fond of dressing up.

In *Cymbeline* Posthumus' clothes have special significance. In some ways they suggest a relationship between truth and seeming. Imogen sees the headless corpse of Cloten, but since he is dressed in her husband's clothes she identifies the body as that of her husband. Why was Cloten so dressed? The strange reason is that he wished to enjoy Imogen in her husband's clothes and then to cut the garments to pieces before her face. Somehow to Cloten the clothes possess the spirit of the original owner. Earlier in the play Cloten had said to Guidarius - "Knowest me not by my clothes?" and the latter had replied:

> . . . No, nor thy tailor, rascal,
> Who is thy grandfather: he made those clothes,
> Which, as it seems, make thee.[20]

Posthumus himself changes clothes. When he allied himself to the Italian cause he wore Italian clothes. When he was back in England he decided to put on the clothes of a poor English peasant. He claimed that he would show more valour than his clothes would suggest:

> To shame the guise o' the world, I will begin
> The fashion - less without and more within.[21]

In *Henry IV* Falstaff tells us what Justice Shallow was like without his clothes:

> . . . like a man made after supper of a cheese paring: when a' was naked, he was, for all the world, like a fork'd radish, with a head fantastically carved upon it with a knife; a' was so forlorn, that his dimensions to any thick sight were invisible . . .[22]

But much depends on the view of the beholder, for we know that Bottom's donkey-like appearance endeared him to Titania. Clothes and appearances alike have strange effects on people. There is a curious passage in *Henry IV* part I when Douglas rushes into battle in pursuit of the king and is confused by soldiers wearing the monarch's clothes as decoys. He kills one soldier in mistake for the king, and when told that the king was still alive he angrily imagines himself murdering a whole wardrobe of false kings in order to find the real one.

Ben Jonson's interest in clothes and in disguise is worth looking at in some detail. He makes reference to the effects of dress upon society as well as on individuals, but he fears the loss of identity which goes with false creation. Disguise could cover up one's inner nature, and the use of pretentious language was sometimes seen by Jonson as a form of dressing up. The Vice figures in his *Epigrams* are given type names because they have no faces - only vizards. The frequent changes of wardrobe in his plays suggests the evanescent quality of the world of fashion and the lack of a genuine sense of personal identity. For example, Chloe in *The Poetaster* takes on so many qualities that she is no longer herself:

She is a Venus, a Vesta, a Melpomene; come hither little Penelope; what's thy name, Iris?[23]

In *Timber* Jonson refers to the loss of self. ". . . we so insist on imitating others, as we cannot (when it is necessary) return to ourselves".[24] In the *Masque of Augurs* Vangrose loses his own language as well as his apparent identity. "He is no Dutchman, sir, he is British borne, but hath learned to misuse his own tongue in travell and now speaks all languages in English".[25] In such a world mirrors distort the truth and fantasy may be substituted for what is natural. Yet Brainworm in *Every Man In His Humour* remains himself even when in disguise, and another perspective is provided through the puppet show in *Bartholomew Fair*. The puppets only exist because they are dressed up and because words are provided for them by ventriloquists. They display a life which is reduced in size and quality. It is reduced to crude basics, but is recognisably almost human. Action is trivialized and language is a mere babble; love becomes lechery and individual identity is travestied.

Confidence tricksters display a fantasy world before us in *The Alchemist* - a world of mirrors and costume changes - and yet we recognize it as a world we know. Subtle changes his manner to suit each dupe, and Face is a captain one moment and an assistant the next. *Volpone* provides many superficial identity metamorphoses. Sir Politic and his lady imitate the actions of others, and she apes the dress of fashion which is created to seduce. Cosmetics, too, are a form of disguise.

When one turns to Jonson's *New Inn*, the story of lost children and multiple disguisings is so weird and complicated that one has difficulty in knowing how to take the play. The Inn represents a closed world in which the Host, a disguised runaway, creates a sort of holiday world for himself. His guest, Lovel, refuses at first to co-operate in parlour games and acts as a solitary. However, when Lady Frampul arrives (and she is in reality the Host's lost daughter) he is drawn into things, for he finds himself in love with her. She, however, lives in a world of make-believe and decides to set up a pretence form of a Court of Love. She persuades her maid, Prue, to act the part of the Queen of the court. Playacting and speechifying follow, and one is not quite sure whether Lovel is entirely serious when he produces a high-minded speech on true love in such a context. However, he actually moves Lady Frampul through his oratory, and she finds herself serious for once. However, neither Lovel nor Prue knows whether she is acting a part when she declares her views. Earlier in the play she had said that she would be acting and Prue had said:

> But how do I know, when her ladyship is pleased
> To leave it off, except when she tell me so?

Disguising and playing games make serious relationships unreal and uneasy.

There are some strange exposures in this play. The Host turns out to be Lord Frampul, and his daughter is 'discovered'. His so-called 'son', who has been made to disguise as a girl, turns out to be a girl after all - a discomforting fact from a sexual point of view. The frequency of clothes changes in this, and other of Jonson's plays, is evidence of his concern for human identity and sometimes it has sexual overtones. In *The New Inn* one hears of a tailor who fornicated with his wife while dressed in other people's clothes, and the scene when Prue has to put on her mistress' gown makes her feel uncomfortable:

> I had rather die in a ditch with Mistress Shore
> Without a smock, as the pitiful matter has it . . .

When she asks Lady Frampul how she can treat with Lovel without a commission, she is told "Thy gown's commission".[26] In *Epigram XI - On Something That Walks Somewhere* - there is a sub-human who walks and talks, and presumably dresses, like a man, but who has no real identity. He is a facsimile. In *The Staple of News* Pennyboy Junior is transformed by his tailor, for ". . . clothes do much upon the wit, as weather does upon the brain". Man, in Jonson's eyes, is a creature of clothes and made up of insignificant 'elements'.

One has already noticed that Mistress Otter in *Epicene* is a collection of parts - "she takes herself asunder still when she goes to bed, into some twenty boxes; and about next daynoon is put together again, like a great German clock".[27] In *Mercury Vindicated* creatures are created from sugar, nutmegs and tobacco. In *Bartholomew Fair* Cokes seems to be like a puppet. He has no brain, only detachable parts "If a leg or an arm on him did not grow on, he would lose it in the press'. Human beings at the fair are sold as if they were cattle. Their identities are often washed out. If they are inner motivated, the strongest urges are lust, money and superstition. In *Epicene* there is sometimes no distinction between man and beast, and between male and female. Sexual ambivalence is at the core of *Epicene* as the title of the play suggests.

Jonson and Shakespeare were not alone in emphasizing the theme of mistaken identity, with its undertones of seriousness and of sexual uncertainty. It is a common theme in drama. Middleton's *Changeling* provides an interesting example of the way in which identity problems fascinated the Elizabethans; and in Sidney's *Arcadia* the theme is pursued with subtlety in romance form. Sidney's concern is discussed in a later chapter. As a background to the presence of identity problems one has to keep in mind the religious and political atmosphere of the time. It was often dangerous to declare oneself openly. It was wiser, in certain situations, to hide one's thoughts, to plot in secret, and to use oblique reference instead of straightforward speech. The age was fond of linguistic disguise, of the enigma, and of the maze. The maze caused confusion where before there was order. One might consider, too, the idea of the typical, large Tudor garden. It was a private and secret garden in so far as it was hidden behind high walls. It was not formal in the Continental sense, for within the design there was an opportunity to grow in liberal confusion. In such a garden there was a certain lack of definition, and sometimes one might come upon the unexpected.

IV   The Dramatic Identity

Interest in human identity, in the person behind the mask, enlarged the role of individual characters in drama. Shakespeare's later plays moved away from concentration on the plot, as performed by recognizable types, towards portrayal of character. The plot did not diminish in importance, but it became more subtly integrated with the expression of individual psychology. This is not to say that characters were portrayed with great psychological insight. The 19th and early 20th century tendency to exaggerate the importance of Elizabethan character portrayal was corrected by such critics as L.C. Knights, Stoll, and Bradbrook who considered that judgement of Shakespeare's plays based on concepts of characterization could lead to critical distortion.

The view that character interpretation was essential to any dramatic critique was a reaction to previous views, for Shakespeare's move towards more expression of individual character was not much noted in the 17th and 18th centuries. The trend in drama towards character portrayal was reversed when confrontational politics highlighted certain issues and induced people to make up their minds and to take sides. Characters in drama reverted to more universal types, or became the embodiment of ideas or themes. There was less call for multi-faceted characters like Falstaff, or complex personalities like Hamlet or Lear. Attitudes hardened, and before and after Dryden there was a tidying-up process in literature. Shifting viewpoints and problems of identity were not in fashion.

It is interesting to remind ourselves how late 17th and early 18th century views on character changed. Rhymer concentrated on plot and saw *Othello* as an unnatural drama. On character he stated that "in framing a character for tragedy, a poet is not to leave his reason, and blindly abandon himself to follow fancy, for then his fancy might be monstrous, might be singular, and please nobody's maggot but his own; but reason is to be his guide, reason is common to all people, and can never carry him from what is natural".[1] Johnson was also concerned about the improbabilities in some of Shakespeare's plays, but considered that in general his portrayals of character were true to nature - "a faithful mirror of manners and life . . .". He thought that "His persons act and speak by the influence of those general passions and principles by which all minds are agitated, and the whole system of life is continued in motion". Johnson went on to say that "In the writings of other poets a character is too often an individual; in those of Shakespeare it is commonly a species".[2] This is as if to say that although Shakespeare was skillful in depicting special traits he was in general portraying recognizable examples or types. Johnson does, however, draw a distinction between early creations, which he regards as artificial or contrived, and whose set speeches were "commonly cold and weak", and later, more natural characters. Morgann, however, in his well known essay on Sir John Falstaff in 1774, recognized that Shakespeare's portrayal was more than that of a type. He saw Falstaff as an individual in his own right. Morgann notes the incongruities in Falstaff's make-up, but regards the creation of the character as an act of artistic genius by one who "so well understood the uses of incongruity".[3] In the nineteenth century critical judgement of the plays depends more upon interpretation of character. The critical perspective changes from that of the 17th and early 18th centuries. The individualistic performances of great actors playing Shakespeare's characters as star roles would, of course, encourage this change of view.

It is obvious that Elizabethan and early Jacobean playwrights were not versed in individual psychology in the sense that we know it today. It is also evident that they were influenced by traditional conventions and attitudes. Many of Shakespeare's characters lack adequate motivation. Some act according to the convention of love at first sight, or to an accepted pattern of sudden repentance. Some make set speeches which Bradbrook describes as having the "detachable quality of an operatic aria".[4] Some inconsistencies are no doubt due to the imperfect realization of character, or to the influence of old models. On occasions, the behaviour of Hamlet can be attributed to the conventions of revenge tragedy, and that of Falstaff to the influence of the old stage 'Vice' or the classical 'Braggart Soldier'. Characters are often in the end what they were in the beginning; villains remain villains and virtuous heroes or heroines remain virtuous. Even when characters are fleshed out to seem real, and are given individual expressions of speech, they have a static quality compared with, say, the creations of novelists of the 19th century.

Yet within an intellectual world of changing perspectives and of variable viewpoints, when there was concern about the individual's place in the universal scheme of things and within society, where there was concern, too, about human identity, it is arguable that in some respects the age of Shakespeare has closer links of interest with our own age than with that of Dr. Johnson. We can discern that although some of Shakespeare's characters were unrealistically motivated, and were as contrived as figures in early romance tales, others were instinctively portrayed as individuals. As Shakespeare moved on through the History plays he became more absorbed in individuals; more interested in their relationships and in their effects upon each other. Plots and situations were used to set off individual characters.

One does not find that Shakespeare is entirely at ease in his early comedies when developing the main lines of plot with the economy of Plautian models. He tends to crowd plays with minor incident and with entanglements to show off his characters, and sometimes he dwells on those whose temperaments create new situations. Such characters are not always strictly subordinated to the demands of the plot. For example, *The Two Gentlemen of Verona* is a fantastic and wonderfully amusing story, but the figures in it are more than traditional comic types. They are not always funny, and they have the air of contemporary human beings. The movement away from Plautian comedy is to be seen in *A Midsummer Night's Dream*, where individual characters have a significant role and express personality traits. Incident may still be important for its own sake, and the lovers are entangled in situations brought about by the external interference of Puck, but the comedy exists in our perception of the characters themselves; in their reactions, emotions, and in their manner of speech. Bottom is more than a clown or a recognizable type. In *As You Like It, Twelfth Night*, and *Much Ado* there is plenty of comic incident, plenty of witty dialogue. There is an element of farce, but there is also a strain of seriousness, and a concern for characters in their dilemmas. The sunlight of romance is shot through with darker shafts of reflectiveness, and this is caused by the characters themselves and by what they say. Jaques is not always a comic figure, the gulling of Malvolio is not simply farcical, and Feste is not an ordinary clown. In the other-world of romance, Shakespeare allows the real world to emerge from time to time. Sir Toby Belch and Touchstone take us momentarily away from the fairy world of make-believe into the real world of the tavern and of rude speech. In a blend of romance and low comedy, individual characters are frequently as important as the plot.

Following old models did not necessarily mean that playwrights were confined to producing stereotypes for the stage. In the Morality plays there was an occasional glimpse of real life, and if classical comedy focussed on stock figures of fun it could produce quirky individuals who would be able to come alive through the skill of a good actor. Classical tragedy may have been concerned with ideas, rather than with character study, but even then it emphasized the importance of individual choice; and in an age which was concerned with individualism this was a dramatic factor of psychological significance. Every age produces its noteworthy individuals, but the Elizabethan age produced particularly colourful and varied examples. It is not surprising, therefore, if contemporary drama before the time of Shakespeare's maturity, produced characters which were richer, and more individual than the accepted stereotypes. There was a growing egocentricity in thought and in life-style which later led the poet Donne to warn that no man was an island and to himself alone.

Men like Sidney and Raleigh were strongly individualistic, and so were writers like Marlowe and Jonson. It would be natural if an age which produced individual characters, and was interested in personal heroism, evidenced a preoccupation with unusual personalities on the stage. There was, as has been mentioned, confusion over the influence of the stars, and of other external forces upon the lives of human beings, but there was a greater awareness than before of the existence of a unique self and of the possibility of carving out at least a part of one's own future. People were not always seen as puppets who had little responsibility for their own actions. In Elizabethan drama there was a noticeable concern for problems of responsibility, and especially in those who were in positions of leadership. If some still believed in the dominance of outside forces, others felt differently. Machiavelli (and later Bacon) tried to teach techniques to master the play of Fortune; and so, too, in their different ways did the Hermetists. Puritans gave an impetus to causes of self-expression and self-mastery, and in drama there was a recognition of the contradictions in achieving self-realization and self-control. Renaissance Man may have felt that he was more liberated than his predecessors, but he recognized that in many ways his freedom was an illusion. It was understood by writers that a person could be a compound of different selves; sometimes divided selves. Bacon suggested that if one gained power over others one might lose power over oneself.

Shakespeare's interest in character grew out of his work in the History plays and out of Comedies which had their sour side. Elizabethans saw history as being largely shaped by distinctive personalties. If Fortune played a part in the affairs of nations, and Time was a destroyer of the best laid plans, individual leaders had a strong hand in shaping events, and their actions affected others. Fate hovers over Shakespeare's history; nevertheless, leaders like Henry V, Richard III or Brutus do influence events. Even in the early Henry VI plays there is a sense that human frailty is behind several disasters. J.R. Wilders in *The Lost Garden*[5] notices that as Shakespeare developed his skills through the history plays he paid more attention to "the psychological origins of political change and paid much greater attention to creating full and complex characters". Human nature became corrupt after the Fall and was complicated. Individuals were frequently untrustworthy and strange; drama presented them as such.

Men and women in the post-lapsarian world have difficult choices to make. In *Julius Caesar, Anthony and Cleopatra*, and other plays, there are situations which call for individual choices. Sometimes the paradox is revealed that while human beings exercise their free Will, they are also destined by their temperaments to a fate which is basically determined. Shakespeare's tragic characters, and those of other playwrights, seem fated at the outset to end up in tragic situations, although it is arguable that the precise situation is one of their own making and of the people they have influenced. Whatever view one takes, the tragedy of the late Elizabethan period is largely centred on personality. People struggle against people, against destiny, and against themselves. If destiny defeats the great, their individuality and their vitality shape and colour the flow of events and are the causes of our dramatic concern. People act, choose and fight according to the sort of people they are. Richard II and Bolingbroke are different and they act in different ways. Their personalities interest us. But personalities are found to be more complicated than a general knowledge of 'humours' would imply. The identity of the outer-motivated person was easier to understand than that of the inner-motivated person.

Strange facets of character are shown by revealing the personality behind the mask or the disguise. They are also seen from different angles. Richard II attempts to look at himself from different viewpoints. He sees himself as a wronged king and then as an ordinary man. Viewpoints change in *Anthony and Cleopatra* not only because Cleopatra is volatile, but because Anthony has changes of mood too. We also see both characters through the eyes of others. Elsewhere, Lear is viewed from different angles, and so is Shylock. The person behind the outward front can be a dramatic discovery, at least to the other characters in the play. A new Cressida is revealed to Troilus, and Lear discovers a self which he did not previously know.

Outside the world of drama writers also focussed interest on the individual. Montaigne may have disparaged the nature of Man, but in studying him he stressed his significance. In Florio's translation of the *Apology*, Man was described as "a wonderful, vain, divers, and wavering subject". He was seen to be complicated psychologically. Towards the end of the 16th century there was a series of books on aspects of the individual. Bright wrote *Of Melancholy* in 1586 and Sir John Davies wrote *Nosce Teipsum* in 1599. On the continent there were several studies and Juan de Dios Huarte Navarro's *Examen de Ingenios*, translated in 1594, was a popular work. In the *Arcadia* Sidney showed an interest in the workings of the mind.

In such a context, writers of drama would naturally focus on the stranger aspects of individual character. Marlowe, Marston and

Dekker, in their different ways, emphasized peculiarity. Sudden conversions like that of Bellafront, in Dekker's *The Honest Whore* (part I), or of Bertram in *All's Well* may seem crude today, but could be explained by one passion driving out another and becoming dominant; and life was sometimes like this. Preoccupation with strong passions and perverted motivation, which produced exciting drama, led to the creation of the monsters of Jacobean tragedy. Marston's characters may seem unreal besides those of Shakespeare, but he, too, was interested in what appeared to go on beneath the surface, and he studied the effects of 'humours' on temperament. He was notably interested in madness.

The mad, the society outcasts, the introverts, were subjects for dramatists. The interest in melancholy and solitary people has already been mentioned. Petrarch had written on the subject of the solitary person in *De Vita Soletaria* and in *Secretum*, but it was not until about 1570, as Janette Dillon[6] points out, that literature in praise of solitude began in England. Once it began, the subject became popular and Bacon noticed this. Singularity both fascinated and repelled, and the solitary person could be regarded either as selfish or selfless. Solitude could release imagination; it could also degenerate into the sin of self-love. It depended on the person and on the way of looking at the situation. What was seen as a retreat from responsibility by some, might be seen by others as a religious retreat which was of value to society. Some Hermetists emphasized the importance of the cultivation of a special identity, formed through contemplation and withdrawal, in order to reach God.

Dillon comments that the word 'self' was in frequent use at the end of the 16th century, and it was used in poetry as well as in drama. It occurs in Greville's poetry and notably in Shakespeare's sonnets. In sonnet 9, Shakespeare is not in favour of cutting oneself off from society in the form of a 'single life', but elsewhere he infers the value of self-completeness. One is shown that people can be seen in various ways, and viewed from different aspects. One learns that the human face does not represent true identity. Sonnet 94 expresses something of the advantages and the disadvantages of self-control and self-withdrawal.

> They that have power to hurt and will do none,
> That do not do the thing they most do show,
> Who, moving others, are themselves as stone,
> Unmoved, cold, and to temptation slow:
> They rightly do inherit heaven's graces
> And husband nature's riches from expense;
> They are the lords and owners of their faces,
> Others but stewards of their excellence.

The sestet argues that those who live alone thrive like summer flowers, but die for themselves alone and if infected fester like others. The best may seem more tainted, when infected by sin, than the worst.

> For sweetest things turn sourest by their deeds,
> Lilies that fester smell far worse than weeds.

Shakespeare, like others before and after him, was troubled about the nature of 'self'.

Elizabethan characters were not always weak on motivation and the ability to develop, although as has already been pointed out, writers were limited in their knowledge of psychology. But we have only to compare early plays with those at the turn of the century to realize how far the Elizabethans had moved in the direction of creditable motivation. Characters no longer 'represented' passions, as in plays like *The Thrie Estaitis* by Lyndsay in 1540; the passions actually moved them. Sometimes these passions mingled to produce complications. The theories of the functioning of the 'humours' permitted a degree of flexibility in portraying character, but obviously much depended on the writer's attitude and on his observation of real life around him.

Sometimes new passions were added to the stock list, such as the feeling for duty (as in Henry V), or idealism (as in Brutus). In *Hamlet* there is a portrayal of several forms of grief, and of the contrasting attitudes of individuals. Hamlet was once the "glass of fashion, and the mould of form", but he comes before us as a reflective person. On the one hand, the king thinks his behaviour is due to grief over his father's death, but Polonius thinks it is due to love sickness. People see Hamlet from different angles. In *Othello* the Moor's actions are shown to be due to the passion of jealousy, but he himself believes he kills Desdemona almost out of a sense of justice to humanity, and even to Desdemona herself. The surface view of his character is shown to change, and as he becomes more infected, his language changes and becomes coarser. In *Macbeth*, too, one is presented with variant angles of viewpoint. He is seen to be overwhelmed by ambition, but his wife thinks that it is fear which drives him on. It is not cowardice in the military sense, but the mental, guilt-ridden fear of an imaginative person, given to hallucinatory dreams.

Some of Shakespeare's characters, unlike Richard III, do not understand their motives, and Lear is a notable case. "He hath ever but slenderly known himself" says Regan. Cordelia, on the other hand, is more self-aware. Motives, and the knowledge of self, become polluted in *Troilus and Cressida*. The springs of idealism and of love, which should at the outset be the motives for action against the Greeks, become tainted. Values are shown to be relative, and individuals lose their moral bearings and something of their original identities. Hector informs Troilus that his ideal of honour runs counter to everyday life.

> The reasons you allege do more conduce
> To the hot passion of distempered blood
> Than to make up a free determination
> Twixt right and wrong.[7]

In this play one sees how individuals may be viewed from diverse standpoints, and how they change. One can see Cressida through the eyes of Troilus, or Diomed, or Ulysses, or Thersites. Montaigne held that people alter as time moves on and that they remake their personalities. Some playwrights were aware of this.

Focus upon individual personality creates a problem in the Henry IV plays. Falstaff, Mistress Quickly, and to some extent Prince Hal, are somewhat apart from the main theme which is historical, and as Falstaff grows upon us he threatens the balance of the historical narrative. It might be argued, as a structural point, that it was necessary to remove Falstaff if historical values were to be emphasized; but when Shakespeare leaves the chronicles of history to write stories of personal tragedy there is no problem in emphasizing individual personality. The background to the Roman plays is historical, and to a lesser extent so it is with *King Lear* and *Macbeth*, but the main theme is that of personal tragedy. Other themes do not conflict with the presentation of individual character. Themes and personalities grow out of each other.

This is not always the case in *Measure for Measure*. The issues which are raised in our minds are determined by the ideas and by the actions of the characters in the play. But one has the feeling that the characters are contrived for the context. The Duke is not easy to believe in. He is in part realistically treated, but he is in part a symbol. He is sometimes involved in detailed happenings, and sometimes he lingers behind the scenes in an unreal way. Isabella, too, is not easy to accept as a rounded, flesh and blood character. Her motives are stated, but she is not sympathetically conceived. *Measure for Measure* is a thoughtful and disturbing play, but it is not one which illustrates a realistic presentation of individual character. But because it is a play which provokes ideas it causes us to think about the way in which individuals behave and how they react to each other. In some ways the play questions moral motivation. Isabella's virtue (which Angelo admires) leads to his fall, and strong, enduring virtue may seem like an inhuman quality. Justice and legality may not always go hand in hand, as one knows from *The Merchant of Venice* and from Sidney's *Araadia.*[8] In *Measure for Measure* and *Troilus and Cressida* human values are questioned and motives appear dubious.

Shakespeare's portrayal of individual character varies so much that it is impossible to generalize; some characters are more static than others. If there is little to suggest that individuals develop in a modern sense, they are pictured in such a way that one is made to realize that they change, mature, or degenerate. Macbeth changes when worked upon, and Lear is a different person at his death, although he retains the traits of his earlier personality. The egocentricity of several characters is brought out, especially in tragedy and in the Roman Plays. They crave for the satisfaction of their faculties, and they need fully to express themselves. Sometimes they appear to ignore the world around them.

Individual expression, in the form of personal speech, was used more and more from the middle of the 16th century onwards to distinguish characters on the stage. Different characters used different 'languages'. It is, of course, true that the schools of rhetoric recognized the principle of 'decorum', but this had not created a realistic approach to speech on the stage. Oratory was not the same as verbal interchange, and the distinctions between a high style and a low style, did not go far towards producing a language which expressed individual personality. One is aware of the problem of dialogue in Sidney's *Arcadia*. He delineates differences in personality and creates contrasting characters, but their speech is unreal in the sense that they often speak alike, and sometimes they speak like Sir Philip Sidney. When, however, one turns to playwrights it is noticeable that they make attempts to make speech fit the character. Early Elizabethan plays evidence crude techniques, and the rhythms of dramatic poetry create problems. But it was not long before dramatic verse became flexible and poetic language became a more appropriate vehicle for individual expression. The five beat line was not strictly adhered to, and ordinary words and expletives were used.

Jonson's concern to write in language "such as men do use" has been mentioned. He was not entirely successful in this aim, and at times piles up his imagery beyond the demands of real situations. He may have found it difficult to represent strong critical themes in the form of real characters speaking in real terms. He recalls on occasions the old Moralities, although he dresses up his Vices as men and women 'o the time'. Jonson attacked modern vices from the stage as preachers attacked them from the pulpit, and his characters can resemble grotesques rather than real people. If, however, their language is excessive, it is language which suits them in their exaggerated forms. They are distinguishable by their speech. In *Epicene*, Morose's talk is egotistical, cranky and foolish. Mrs. Otter indicates her language when she plays a part. Underneath one knows that she is a coarse railer. Phraseology and vocabulary are used to emphasize individuality and to express idiosyncracy. Some people are able to manipulate others by manipulating language in order to deceive or to impress. Such a person is Volpone, and his exaggerations are in character. Some of Jonson's characters are professional people, and they use professional turns of phrase to suit their styles of life. In the busy, commercial city of London a playwright could draw upon rich and varied material if he had a good ear.

Even in Shakespeare's early plays there is an attempt to suit language to personality, and when one arrives at *Love's Labour's Lost* artificial speech is mocked.

> Taffeta phrases, silken terms precise,
> Three-pil'd hyperboles, spruce affectation,
> Figures pedantical; these summer-flies
> Have blown me full of maggot ostentation:
> I do forswear them . . .[9]

Such is the aim of Berowne, and yet he finds himself slipping back into old linguistic habits which are growing out of fashion. He has to admit to having "a trick of the old rage." And despite Berowne's criticism of artificial language, the play itself continues with witticisms, puns, oxymorons and other rhetorical devices. In the History plays there is, however, a noticeable movement towards a more natural style in spite of the declamatory speeches and the 'arias'. Henry V's soliloquies, the talk of Falstaff and of different soldiers, have the effect of individual utterances. Richard II's profuse expression of inner feelings reaches the point where words seem almost to have lost meaning, but his battle with incomprehensibility reveals a side to his character. In *Henry IV* Hotspur does not speak like a stage general, or leader; there is an attempt to get inside his mind as an individual. Elsewhere, Pistol, Bardolph, and Fluellen indicate through their forms of speech the sort of people they are. Writers had moved a long way since Gorboduc and Sidney's *Arcadia*.

Two further aspects of the focus on individualism in drama need to be taken into account. Authors, too, were becoming more conscious of themselves and of their roles; and so were actors. In spite of plagiarism, and the tendency of companies to alter texts, authors were becoming known as such, and Jonson published his writings under his name with the title of 'Works'. By then the times were not like those in Sidney's youth, when authors did not vaunt their personalities. In times gone by Kyd's name did not appear on the title page of his *Spanish Tragedy*, and nor did Marlowe's on *Tamburlane*. If writing was an art, it was not necessarily an expression of personal emotion. However, as time went on the author became less of an 'artificer' without a face, and more of a personality with a view of his own. Spectators of drama responded to authors as well as to players. But it was the players who excited the major interest.

The popularity of leading actors, and the use of elaborate costume on the stage, increased the focus on individuality. Even if an audience saw through a disguise, a good actor could make a character seem individual and alive. Theatrical posturing, and the habit of declaiming a speech - and these were faults which Hamlet criticized when speaking to the players at court - may suggest a world of unreality, but audiences were used to the conventions and were willing to be taken in. They accepted boy actors in the role of women, and when these 'women' disguised themselves as boys there would have been little sense of the ridiculous. Once in the theatre good actors would make scenes and individuals seem real enough. In *A Midsummer Night's Dream* the players are worried that the courtly audience might take everything they see on the stage for reality, and that they might be carried away by their feelings. They felt it necessary to explain in advance that the lion which would attack Thisbe was only an actor in disguise, and that their whole play was only make-believe. Dramatic characters were temporarily regarded as real individuals on the stage of life. Costume helped in the illusion, but disguise did not have to be sophisticated. It was the actor who made the play.

The actor's histrionic qualities, the way in which he took on different characters, his skill in deceiving the audience underlined the question of human identity. From yet another angle, appearances were deceptive. What was the true nature of an individual? What was the persona behind the mask?

> Why, I can smile, and murder whiles I smile;
> And cry 'content' to that which grieves my heart;
> And wet my cheeks with artificial tears,
> And frame my face to all occasions:

I'll drown more sailors than the mermaid shall;
I'll slay more gazers than the basilisk;
I'll play the orator as well as Nestor;
Deceive more slyly than Ulysses could;
And, like a Sinon, take another Troy:
I can add colours to the chameleon;
Change shapes with Proteus for advantages;
And set the murderous Machiavel to school.[10]

This is the 'actor' Gloster in the third part of *Henry VI*. The skill which actors assumed another person's personality could sway an audience, and even an ordinary actor seemed able to convince himself that he was another person. "What's Hecuba to him, or he to Hecuba/That he should weep for her? . . .". Hamlet was amazed that players could so enter into the spirit of the characters they were playing that their tears and emotions seemed genuine.

One has, of course, to recognize that Elizabethan playwrights only give as much of the character of an individual as the play requires. Portraiture, as Professor Sewell points out in *Character and Society in Shakespeare*, is subordinate to the needs of the play as a whole, and so often they are used to develop themes. They may be used to indicate that there are different aspects to the experience of others. Thus Gloucester shows us another aspect of Lear's experience, and Iago provides a contrast to an Othello. The way one looks at things depends on the way one is made, and this sense of the relativity of values is noticeable towards the end of the 16th century. One finds it emerging in Spenser and in a later chapter one will find it in Sidney. There is often an individual point of view, but equally the individual may be changed and influenced by others as *Troilus and Cressida* suggests.

There are diverse qualities in Elizabethan plays and character development is not often a main theme. At the same time one should not play down the interest in individual character in dramatic writing. It is there because the mood of the times demanded and created it. It was reinforced by the thinking of religious nonconformist movements, and Hermetic thought. Hermetists may have sought to move back to earlier times, but they emphasized the significance of individualism in their approach to divine revelation. Their attitudes contributed to the atmosphere of the times, and were in turn a response to it.

V   Darkness and Light

A strain of mystical thinking inherited from the Middle Ages, continued and developed during the early Renaissance. The developments owed something to the neo-Platonists, to Nicholas of Cusa and to the Italian scholar, Ficino, who translated Greek texts attributed to Hermes Trismegistus. Those whose mystical thinking relied upon the texts as sources were often known as Hermetists, although there was no school under that name. The so-called followers of Hermetism are difficult to identify, for they were sometimes secretive and did not all accept the different views expressed in the Greek texts. Some writers were influenced by Hermetic thinking without adhering to any school. There are traces of Hermetic influence in the work of Sir Philip Sidney, although he could hardly be described as a follower. Giordano Bruno, who figures in the next chapter and who was known to Sidney, was undoubtedly influenced by Ficino and the Greek texts, but he went his own way and was not an adherent of any school of thought. Yet Hermetism was a pervasive influence in the 16th century and would have been discussed in the Italian and French academies,[1] which in turn had an impact on visiting scholars like Sidney.

It is a paradox that while many Hermetists stressed the importance of the sun, and of light generally, in their views of the universe, writers on the subject tended to express themselves darkly in obscurantist terms, through arcane symbolism, and sometimes in partial secrecy. The light of Hermetic knowledge was often concealed in darkness. John Dee was following precedent when he stated that he did not want his knowledge to be revealed to the unlearned. Both he and Bruno were difficult to understand. Both influenced students and acquaintances in private coteries, and revealed more of their thinking in semi-secrecy than in public debate or in published work.

Raleigh touches on Hermetism in his *History of the World*,[2] and one wonders what he discussed at those private meetings when he was absent from the court.[3] Sidney raises issues in the *Arcadia* which might well have been influenced by Hermetic thinking, and which he might have picked up when travelling in Europe as a young man. Hermetism developed in the shadows, and it produced its own contradictions and inconsistencies. Some Hermetists held to basic Christian beliefs, but gave them a Platonic slant, while others focussed on occult practices. Bruno wished to point the way forward by going backwards into ancient history and by special reference to the religious practices of the ancient Egyptians.

The Renaissance habit of respecting ancient authority led Ficino (1433-1499) to take the Hermes Trismegistus texts seriously. They were comprised of a set of writings in Greek attributed to the legendary figure of Hermes, who was thought to have lived long before Plato and Moses. It was said that Plato had imbibed the wisdom of Hermes when travelling through Egypt. There were tenuous connections between Greek philosophy and the wisdom of the Middle East, and the Greek Hermes was also identified with the Egyptian god Thoth, who was a priest-god. Some believed that Hermes had been a priest in ancient times, possibly in Egypt, and that like Moses he had experienced a divine revelation. His wisdom and his vision had been handed down through the Greeks and was eventually written down in the texts known collectively as the *Corpus Hermeticum*. Hermes was even coupled with Zoroaster in a confused way. The *Corpus Hermeticum* referred to ancient Hebrew and Egyptian views, and this reinforced the notion of early origins. The texts came to be regarded by many as an expression of the earliest fount of true religion.

A particular text called *Pimander*, which was translated by Ficino, caused much speculation. It provided a description of the origin of the world which closely resembled *Genesis*, although it was more mystical. It described how Hermes had received a revelation from God, and it mentioned God the Father as in the later Scriptures. There was reference to the Son of God in the form of an abstraction of the luminous and creative Word. *Pimander* was regarded as an early statement of Genesis, and seemed to be pointing the way to the much later birth of Christianity in that Hermes had foreseen the birth of a new faith and the coming of Christ. Like Plato after him, Hermes taught how to rise above material things and to strive for communion with the divine. He taught that if an individual were to prepare himself properly, he could receive the divine spirit which would flow into his soul. This spirit pervaded the universe, and human beings had to train themselves to 'tune in' to the divine radiations in the cosmos. It was claimed that Hermes' views were handed down, possibly through Orpheus and his followers, to Pythagoras and eventually to Plato. In his turn, Plato had begun to formulate the essence of the Christian faith and the religious path to be followed before the coming of Christ. Such views were readily acceptable to neo-Platonists like Ficino, who was the head of the Florence Academy which specialized in Platonic studies.

Because Ficino translated the *Pimander* text before he began to translate Plato it probably coloured his view of its antiquity. He found correspondences between Plato's ideas and those of Hermes, and was convinced that Plato had been influenced. The *Pimander* text was published in 1471 and went through many later editions. Its influence was strong and continued in the 17th century, long after its authenticity was questioned by the scholar Casaubon. In 1554 the French scholar Turnebus published an edition which was frequently referred to, and this was followed by another edition twenty or so years later. Protestant writers also interested themselves in the Greek texts. One of these was Phillipe du Plessis-Mornay, who touched on Hermetism in his book *De la Vérité de la Religion Chrétienne* in 1581. This was a book which Sir Philip Sidney contemplated translating; he had started on the work before leaving for the Low Countries.

Side by side with these Greek texts was a text called the *Asclepius*, which had been known in the Middle Ages, and was also thought to be of great antiquity. It dealt with occult practices and with the magical experience of the ancient Egyptians. In turning to the East and to ancient magical practices it reinforced the magical core of Hermetism, for some of the Greek texts were more concerned with astrological matters and with the occult than with the philosophical mysticism of *Pimander*. They touched on ancient Egyptian magical rites, on sympathetic magic, and on techniques for using the powers of the stars and for absorbing the divine radiations in the universe. But if they encouraged belief in magic, it

108

was not witchcraft or so-called 'black magic'. The ideals were religious and could be related to a Platonic view of Christianity. Magic was to be used for good, and to enable individuals to rise above material restrictions.

Ficino's translations and commentaries inspired Hermetism. He helped to make respectable the old magical treatise *Asclepius* and the traditional notions about religious magic and mysticism. Although he believed in the ability of the individual to manipulate nature for good or for evil, he held strongly to the Catholic faith. He accepted the Aristotelian and Ptolemaic concept of the universe, but he Platonized it and his ideas had a strong mystical slant. He believed in magical powers, and that the magical properties of certain symbols and talismans could be used as aids to religious experience and to control supernatural forces.

In 1614 the scholar Casaubon proved that the texts were written long after Plato, by several writers between the years 100 and 300 A.D. Far from influencing Plato, they had borrowed from him. They had also borrowed from other Greek sources, from Hebrew and Arabic texts, and from the Bible. They were a hotchpotch of mystical ideas. In spite of Casaubon's exposure the influence of these ideas continued for some time. The English Hermetist Fludd did not seem perturbed that the *Corpus Hermeticum* had been discredited, and the Cambridge Platonist Henry More (1614-1687) considered that the ancient Egyptian and Cabbala type mysteries were revelations from God, and that Plato had brought much out of Egypt. So strong was the hold of the new mysticism that later movements, such as Rosicrucianism, may have had Hermetic roots.

Throughout the 16th century Hermetism was an intellectual current, even if it flowed in the shadows and produced its own inconsistencies. It influenced writers in different ways. Bruno was inclined to a mystical view of the universe, but he was also interested in promoting religious views which could unite nations torn with strife. He had a political side to his nature. Dee, on the other hand, was more concerned with the development of the individual through learning, and the practice of occult skills, into a Magus who could manipulate nature and achieve a secret spiritual knowledge. The mystical side of Hermetism did not appeal to everyone, nor did the more outlandish magical rituals. St. Augustine had paid tribute to Hermes, but objected to rituals in the *Asclepius* which aimed at producing living idols. Cornelius Agrippa, however, was attracted to the magical learning in ancient texts and wrote his *De Occulta Philosophia*, which in turn had a considerable influence in the 16th century.

Agrippa, in common with several thinkers of his time, was able to shift his intellectual position. His treatise on the *Vanity of Knowledge* contained an attack on occult sciences as vain forms of activity, but he became a leading authority on magical experiments. It is true that he did not wish those who were not learned to indulge in magical experiments, and he might have been concerned to safeguard himself from accusations of sorcery - a fate that pursued Dee later. He refers in his work to Hermes, Zoroaster, and Orpheus as priestly leaders of men who aspired to do good, and practised magic in a religious sense. Agrippa believed that there was an occult virtue in all things, for they were penetrated with radiations from the upper world. Magical incantations could enable the wise and the good to attract these radiations. On a practical level Agrippa wrote on poisons, fumigations, philtres, and the effects of talismans. He was attracted to the Cabbala and claimed that it could be used to bring one into touch with Angels of Light. He probably had a strong influence on Dee, who at one time maintained that he was in touch with angelic forces.

Before Agrippa the writings of Pico della Mirandola had also dwelt on the magical aspects of Hermetism. Like Ficino he believed in the efficacy of certain forms of natural magic and also thought that there was hidden magic in the Hebrew Cabbala. He believed that the ancient Hebrew language had a special power, and that combinations of Hebrew letters could be used like talismans to invoke angelic influences. He was fascinated by letter combinations and by the mystery of numbers, referring to the work of Raymond Lull on the significance of patterns of thought.[4] Pico believed, too, that with training, self-discipline and devotion, an individual might be able to invoke angels and perhaps attain a state which permitted revelation of the divine. This he was convinced had been the experience of Hermes and of Moses.

Pico's enthusiasm for the magical element in mysticism got him into trouble with the religious authorities, and he went to

Rome in 1486 armed with a set of theses taken from different philosophies to prove in debate that seemingly divergent views on religious matters could be reconciled. Bruno was to make out a similar thesis much later. The debate did not take place and instead Pico produced, more than a decade afterwards, his famous *Apology* with its oration on the 'Dignity of Man'. Some of his views were regarded as heretical. His *Apology*, which could be taken to imply that Man was almost divine in essence (a concept implied in *Pimander*), troubled the Church. The Pope condemned his statements. Pico had to retract and fled to France where he was imprisoned for a time in Vincennes. In France, however, his views gained some sympathy in academic circles, and eventually he returned to Italy with a royal commendation. He settled in Florence as a respected religious man, although still somewhat under suspicion.

His influence was considerable, encouraging the belief in the importance of the individual and in his unlimited potential, given the Grace of God. It emphasized reliance on the Will, and what Sidney was to call the 'erected wit'. According to Pico, Man retained elements of his divine origin despite the Fall. Such a view is consistent with the *Pimander* text, in which Hermes sees Pimander in a dream and Pimander reveals the origins of life. Hermes is made aware of a blinding vision of light which is succeeded by a profound darkness. Out of darkness is born a strange celestial fire and the mysterious Word, symbol of the Son of God, is made manifest. Out of fire and air God creates spirit forms and a human in his own image. Humanity is both mortal and immortal, and Pimander sends Hermes to teach how to attain immortality. The *Asclepius* also refers to Man's divine origin. All the texts encourage the individual to look into himself. There is no reference to the need for institutions like the Church, for each individual is, in a sense, his own priest; or, if not, he could rely upon those who, through superior knowledge, became Magi. It is understandable that the Church, while allowing tribute to be paid to the *Corpus Hermeticum*, was uneasy about the direction certain 'followers' were to take. If it took Pico della Mirandola to task, it was even more concerned about the attitudes of men like Bruno in the 16th century.

Ambivalence towards Hermetism was an aspect of the changing perspectives of the Renaissance, and of uncertainty about Man's place and stature in the universe. Problems of identity were not only the concern of dramatists. They were the concern of thinkers in philosophy and in religion. The humanists were dubious about some of the mystical ideas that were generated in their time, distrusting occult mysticism as akin to medieval barbarism and superstitious ignorance. Erasmus had not taken to some of these ideas and was doubtful about the authenticity of mystical work like that of Dionysius the Areopagite. Some, like Sidney, were able to vary their viewpoint as the need arose. At one point in his *Apology for Poetry* he seemed, like Pico della Mirandola, to suggest that the poet had almost divine qualities.

Shifting viewpoints were noticeable among those who were most influenced. For example, Pico had to retract some of his views, Agrippa seemed to contradict himself, Dr. John Dee insisted that he was not a heretic or sorcerer and Bruno tried to effect a reconciliation with the Church. The Spanish Dominican priest, Campanella, who was born in 1568 wrote a book called *The City of the Sun* which presented a mystical view of Utopia. In his new world the sun was dominant, and it was worshipped as in Ancient Egypt. If Hermetists did not necessarily believe in a heliocentric universe, the sun (and light generally) played a significant part in their thinking. Campanella was eventually accused of heresy like Bruno, but tried to make his peace with both religious and secular authorities by variously proposing that the Spanish monarch and/or the Pope should lead the world to ensure a global, religious unity. In the next chapter we shall see that Bruno, too, envisioned a universal religion under a great leader. Such ideas, in a time of growing religious strife, might have grown out of discussions in the European academies, and may have owed something to Dante's *De Monarchia* with its vision of a world united under one Emperor and one Pope. Sidney, at one time, seemed to favour the notion of a League of Protestant Princes under Elizabeth to lead Europe. Eirenicism was a Hermetic tendency, but it was not a tenet. Dee was more concerned with individual, spiritual development, and with experimentation.

All the Hermetic texts had in common the idea that human beings could be linked with the divine, and that through intuitive striving the learned could communicate with God. The picture of the universe was in general Ptolemaic, and while the lower world was penetrated by the influence of the stars, the stars were under the control of spirits. Unlike the picture presented by Dionysius, however, these spirits resembled more the gods of ancient Egypt, and they were similarly numbered. The main message was how to avoid baleful influences from outer space and to attract, and use, the forces of good. As Plato also indicated, there was a divine spirit which pervaded the universe, and it was possible to 'tune in', as it were, by various methods.

An enlightened individual could escape evil influences and communicate with higher beings by elevating himself. Contemplation, as well as the use of magic, could induce a trance-like state which suited higher communication. Some of the Greek texts were concerned with Pythagorean and Cabbalistic methods of working, or with the use of mathematical formulae to manipulate the forces of nature. Since human beings were in part divine, the intuitive nature of their psychology was stressed. In focussing on the individual, on personal resources, on the use of magic as an experimental technique and a possible path to discovery, and on Platonising Medieval notions, the Hermetists were in the Renaissance current. Man need no longer seem passive, awaiting the turn of Fortune's Wheel, but could be an active operator in the universe. His mind was his own, and not subject to the dominance of the Church. There were also political as well as religious implications in the spread of Hermetism.

But this is only one way of looking at Hermetic thinking. In some respects, it was medieval and obscurantist, as Erasmus implied, in so far as it plunged into the occult and made use of talismans. Magic may be seen as the beginning of experimental science, or as a retreat into ignorance. It depends on the way it is regarded and practised. If, on the one hand, Hermetists wished to move forward, they also moved back into the remote past to seek their inspiration. In attempting to spread the light, they also wished to keep their knowledge to a select few, and they tended to move into the shadows from time to time. Their work was often muddled and unclear, as one sees from that of Dr. John Dee and Giordano Bruno.

John Dee was undoubtedly influenced by Hermetism and must have influenced others, even if they did not go all the way with him. He was accepted in Court circles and Elizabeth showed him favour. He was tutor to several people and was known to Sidney and to Raleigh. John Aubrey commended him and he was respected abroad. The other side to the picture is that his strange ideas, and his fascination with the occult, caused suspicion and distrust among some of his contemporaries, and on one occasion his house was attacked by a mob and ransacked. He was accused of sorcery. Towards the end of his long life he was neglected and suffered some poverty. King James did not show him the favour that Elizabeth had granted, and may well have regarded his ideas with antipathy.

John Dee was born in 1527 and died at the age of eighty one. He was a strong individualist, and his curiosity and knowledge were wide-ranging. He was a philosopher, classicist, mathematician, geometer, and generally knowledgeable in the science of chemistry. He was well versed in geography, navigation, optics and mechanics. In some ways he was the model of the new Renaissance man; the *uomo universale*. He was knowledgeable, too, in the arts, especially in music, painting and architecture. He had read widely and possessed one of the largest libraries in Europe. As a collector of books he played a great part in saving several old manuscripts from oblivion. Although he was interested in new ventures in philosophy, he was also conservative, if not old-fashioned, in many respects. He held to old notions about the historical and legendary origins of England, and he looked back into remote and uncertain periods of history to formulate his ideas. He was romantic, rather than scientific, in many of his attitudes and thought that his ancestry might, like the Tudors, have noble Welsh origins.

Since he was under attack as a dabbler in sorcery he stoutly defended himself in his *Compendious Rehearsal*. He refuted the charge, and gave the outline of his life in a style of prose which suggests a personality given to defensive arrogance. He was undoubtedly full of a sense of his own unique importance, and proud of his court connections. It appears, however, that his merchant father had served Henry's court and might have given him a back-door entrée. He married three times and his third wife was a daughter of a lady-in-waiting. But it was his learning and his strong personality which kept him in court circles.

114

One learns that he studied at St. John's College, Cambridge from 1542 to 1545, and that he was strong in Greek. He would also have studied the 'trivium' - grammar, logic, and rhetoric - and gone on to take arithmetic, the sciences, and some philosophy. During his time at Cambridge he was good enough to obtain a Fellowship as a Junior Reader, and it was while he was there that he apparently caused a stir by his production of *Pax* by Aristophanes. The story is told that his mechanical skill was so good that he was able to make a stage beetle, with a man on its back, rise into the air. This produced consternation in the audience, and the incident was later recalled as an example of his conjuring abilities and held against him!

He left Cambridge to obtain more specialized tuition in the Netherlands. Perhaps, too, he wished to turn away from the growing humanist line of thought at the university which may not have appealed to his innate conservatism, and romantic nature. Possibly neo-Platonism, stemming from earlier roots, began even then to attract him. The practical side of his nature was evidenced when he brought back to England on his return, a set of new navigational instruments. In 1554, he refused a stipend to lecture at Oxford and set off once again to Europe, continuing his mathematical and scientific studies at Louvain. It is likely that his studies at Louvain would have been more theoretical than practical, and to some extent related to older Platonic and Greek philosophical traditions. He travelled much during his stay and eventually left for Paris.

In his *Compendious Rehearsal* he states that he lectured in Paris on Euclid, and that his lecture was a great success. He was then only 23 years of age, and proud of his attainments. P.J. French[5] considers that he then expounded a theory of numbers based on work in Agrippa's *De Occulta Philosophia*, and expressed views related to Hermetism. He could well have been influenced at that time by Pico della Mirandola, and his lecture could have been a Hermetised version of Euclid, for one notes that in his 'Mathematical Preface' to Euclid written in 1970 he referred to the function of numbers in the religious or celestial world.

Dee's work shows him to be both practical and imaginative. His mechanical skill, demonstrated at Cambridge, his use of instruments to make calculations, and his chemistry experiments reveal the practical side; but geometry and mathematics were for him not only of value in the material world of building and navigation, but aids to determine mystical values. He accepted the Ptolemaic universe, in which the stars influenced the lower world. He believed that God channelled powers through the stars, and that if one understood which bodies, or materials on earth were sympathetic to certain planets one might be able to attract their energies. This could be done by appropriate magical exercises. However, he was careful to explain in his 'Preface' that he did not favour what he called 'light practices', by which he probably meant the use of magic for ignoble purposes. One is reminded of Agrippa's caveat.

He may have been boasting about the success of his Paris lecture, but it evidently drew the attention of scholars like Crontius, Professor of Mathematics at the College de France, the famous Ramus, and others. Ramus spoke well of him, although his line of thinking was markedly different. He thought highly of him as a scholar and kept in touch. Dee's reputation was growing, and when he was back in England he was introduced at the court of Edward VI. His father's previous connection may also have been known. He presented the king with some treatises which he had worked on and was rewarded with a gift of 100 Crowns. This he apparently later exchanged for the benefit of two absentee rectorships which produced a small annual income. The Duke of Northumberland was impressed with him and engaged him as a tutor to his children. At this time he tutored Robert Dudley, who became Earl of Leicester, and who was known to be interested in the sciences. Such contacts would eventually have brought him into the circles frequented by Sir Philip Sidney and his friends during Elizabeth's reign.

In expressing his strange ideas he would have made both friends and enemies, and when the Duke of Northumberland fell from power Dee would have lacked support. His fortunes varied somewhat. He was accused at one time of trying to enchant Queen Mary, and had some difficulty in clearing himself. He was in prison for a brief period, expiating any faults he might have committed by serving as a chaplain to Bishop Bonner. In the middle period of his life he became interested in preserving the many valuable manuscripts which were endangered when Catholic institutions were being plundered. He had hoped that Queen Elizabeth might help in preserving works of scholarship in the form of a large library, but when his pleading failed he began to hunt down and to collect such works himself. Thus he began his very considerable library.

If Dee's fortunes drooped after the fall of Northumberland they rose again when the Dudley family gained influence under Elizabeth. He began to perform small services for the Queen. He acted as the Court astrologer and advised on propitious dates for certain functions. He traced the Queen's ancestry back through Welsh nobles into the misty past, producing a praiseworthy lineage which owed more to imagination than to historical scholarship. He also tutored the Queen in the interpretation of mystic symbols. He suggested the reform of the Julian Calendar, although no action was taken on this. He was a man of considerable energy, and busied himself with several projects as well as his teaching work. He was knowledgeable in the lore of legends, and supported the romantic versions of the part played by Brutus and Arthur in English history against Polydore Vergil.

As time went on he turned more and more towards Hermetic views of the universe, as his *Monas Hieroglyphia*, and his comments on the Hebrew Cabbala, reveal. The *Propaedeumata Aphoristica* provides 120 aphorisms on the magical principles which operate in the universe. Such works attempt to look forward to a new learning, but they plunder old notions and myths. At times the style of writing recalls medieval argument. The *Monas* is difficult to comprehend, but the main theme is that all is ONE, in what appears to be a changing and complicated universe. By preparing the mind for a mystical ascent it may ultimately reach and apprehend the divine unity.

Dee believed in the active role of the individual imagination. He thought that intense contemplation, which was necessary to achieve the trance-like state in which one might receive divine radiations, could be induced by the use of incantations, the gazing at hieroglyphics, and the use of other magic materials. He designed a special hieroglyph himself. This aimed at expressing in symbolic form the unity which lay hidden behind the multiplicity of relationships within the universe. The *Monas* explains the meaning of certain lines in his design, and the use of the cross and circle in

terms of astral significance. The hieroglyph was meant not only to
'embody' his ideas, but to be an aid in the contemplation of the
divine.

In previous chapters one has been concerned with the search
for the real identity behind the mask - the mask of personality or
the mask of allegory. In the searchings of Dee, and other Hermetists, there is an attempt to express the feeling (or perhaps the need)
for a core identity in a bewildering and sometimes apparently disordered universe. The question also arises as to the identity of the
individual. Man, according to Dee, should try to rise above his
mundane, ordinary self. One has the impression that a Magus, in a
state of trance, might even leave his body and return to the aether-
ial and divine nature of his origin. The Magus had a role to play in
life; his identity was special. It was unfortunate, to say the least, if
he were often mistaken by the multitude for a sorcerer.

Dee continued to travel extensively in Europe. He was in turn
in Antwerp, Zurich, Italy and Hungary. One might note in passing
that Sir Philip Sidney, as a young man, visited Hungary and other
places frequented by Dee and might well have been in touch with
the scholars that Dee knew. The *Monas* was published when Dee
was in Antwerp, and was dedicated to the Emperor Maximilian.
He did not neglect to praise the Queen at a later date and to thank
her for defending him when he was attacked by critics. One knows
this from a comment made in the *Compendious Rehearsal*. If the
Queen did not reward him much financially, she seemed to grant
him her favour and protection.

In England he settled at Mortlake in a large house in which he
housed his vast book collection, his instruments, and his laborat-
ory equipment. According to French[6] his books varied widely in
subject, covering mathematics, science, Aristotle, Plato, other
Greek writers, Lull's work, medieval scholarship, Hermetic works
(including Ficino, Pico, *Pimander, Asclepius*), Agrippa, Paracelsus,
and various grammatical and Humanist studies. In addition there
were works on poetry, drama, architecture, and music. All forms
of knowledge were covered in his library, and since he gave tuition
one wonders if his house became a kind of academy - on the lines
of those in Europe, although on a small, private scale. Certainly he
was visited by many people, and once the Queen herself visited

him at Mortlake. Sidney, Lord Russell, and Alasco - the Polish Prince Albertus - went to see Dee after their attendance at the university of Oxford. Alasco's visit to Oxford may have drawn Giordano Bruno there at the time when he became involved in angry debate.[7]

Dee continued his practical and scientific work in England. When the supernova appeared in 1572 he published a method of calculating the parallax of circumpolar objects. He also wrote on maritime matters and some time in 1570 he produced a treatise on supplies of men, timber, and other materials needed to maintain an efficient navy. He then calculated the tax needed to support it. He advised Frobisher to try for a N.E. passage to the New World, and the Muscovy Company actually attempted this but had to abandon the venture when their ships got stuck in pack ice. Dee wrote a lot on astrology, too.

In 1581 he was again in Europe, and it was at this time that he claimed to have been in touch with angels. The story is curious. It seems that a strange character, called Edward Kelley, had impressed Dee with his powers as a medium. He had previously worked as an assistant to Thomas Allen, a respected scholar and astrologer, but he also had a more dubious background. He had been in some sort of trouble at Oxford and was pilloried in Lancaster for forgery. When he visited Dee he claimed to see visions in his glass crystal. Dee was impressed and took him abroad when he went to call on the Emperor Rudolph. It was Kelley who assisted Dee when he claimed to have got in touch with angels, by acting as a medium and relaying Dee's enquiries. It seems that Dee did not himself speak directly to the heavenly spirits, only through Kelley. This suggests that Dee was completely taken in by a charlatan, but it is possible that Kelley genuinely believed that between them they had communicated with celestial spirits. Since Dee used various aids to induce trance it might have been the case that intoxicants produced a genuine hallucinatory state in which Kelley really did have visions. However this may be, Dee was convinced that he had talked to angels, although the messages he received were either commonplace or Delphic. He may have had Hermes in mind when he wrote that he had asked God to give him the wisdom to get in touch with his 'creatures', and that this experience was his reward.[8]

In Poland Dee travelled to the university town of Cracow, where his portrait hangs to this day in the Collegium Maius of that city. There he had talks with Dr. Hannibal, who had written a commentary on *Pimander*. In Bohemia he was given an audience with the Emperor, who was addicted to occult matters, and in May 1586 he and Kelley left for Leipzig. Their departure was timely, for the Papal Nuncio had just sent a note to Rudolph accusing Dee and Kelley of 'conjuring' and requesting their arrest. They were wanted in Rome for questioning. Dee avoided this and later returned to England. He had been away six years on the continent, and during this time he had discussed his views with many scholars and had tried to influence important people to his ways of thinking, including Stephen Batory of Poland.

It was the Queen who commanded his return, and throughout the attacks upon him she continued to favour him. It is interesting that in the first edition of Foxe's *Acts and Monuments* Dee was referred to as a 'conjuror'. This work had a wide circulation and Dee felt called upon to protest. His complaint was noted and critical references were omitted from the 1576 edition. However, his reputation was not enhanced by the episode of the angel seance with Kelley. His strange companion stayed in Europe after Dee had left and tried to regain Rudolph's favour. Rudolph became more than irritated when he failed to produce gold by alchemy and he was imprisoned. He later died of a fall when trying to escape.

In 1593 Dee's house was broken into and plundered by a mob, and in the following year he was sufficiently under attack to write to the Archbishop stating that he was a devout Christian and not a necromancer. His situation resembled that of Bruno, who was also accused of heretical practices and of undermining the Catholic Church. Bruno also stated that he was a true believer. Hermetists obviously had a problem in reconciling themselves to religious authority. However sincerely they believed in the Christian faith, they did in a sense, by-pass the need for the Church in emphasizing the direct individual approach to God. The Magus was his own priest and he expressed the idea of God's identity, and of His modes of operation in the universe, in different terms from those of established religious authority. When forced to make a choice and to submit to the Church's rulings, Hermetists sometimes seemed to look several ways at once. Pico, Campanella, Dee and Bruno found themselves in intellectual dilemmas.

Dee gradually fell into neglect, and complained to Sir Edward Dyer that few would listen to his views. He lost support when Leicester died in 1588, and when Walsingham died a few years later. The Queen had given him a gift in the Wardenship of Christ's College, Manchester, and this was important to him. However, when James came to the throne he had little time for Dee and probably regarded his views as anathema. On one occasion Dee actually appealed to the King to have him tried so that he could have the opportunity to clear himself in public of accusations of sorcery. He insisted that he had no dealings with demons or other spirits; only with God's angels. He made the same point in his *True and Faithful Relation*, when describing his interview with the Emperor Rudolph. His defence did not appear to win people over, and as he grew old, complaints about him increased. In 1605 he had to give up his Warden's post and he returned to Mortlake after his wife's death. There he lived in some degree of poverty and in ill health. The King ignored him. And it was at Mortlake that he died in 1608 at the age of 81 years.

It is difficult to assess the extent of Dee's influence, and it is difficult to judge the influence of Hermetism in England. Hermetism did not take root as it had in Europe. But one has to remember that the academies in Europe which discussed a range of contemporary ideas were visited by scholars and eminent visitors from England. Dee had been a teacher, and in his maturity he had held a place at Court. He knew people of importance, and for years he was respected as a scholar. His work on geometry was said to be popular and he furthered the study of arithmetic. He may well have been a stimulating teacher, and had he opened the minds of men like Leicester and Sidney his influence would have been significant. It is possible that he played a part, as no doubt Bruno did, in combatting the more arid elements of Humanism which existed in Oxford. Certainly Sidney thought that strict adherence to Aristotle had gone too far, and Ramus wished to purge Humanism of conservatism. Ramus respected Dee, although he could hardly have been sympathetic to many of his ideas. Thomas Digges, a former student of Dee, spoke well of his old tutor, and so did Gabriel Harvey in his *Marginalia*. Mercator took his ideas on charts seriously, and Dee's new edition of Robert Recorde's *Ground of Arts* was a popular introduction to arithmetic.

Dee's life and work illustrate the way in which changing perspectives could highlight questions on the status and function of Man. These perspectives also produced some contradictory viewpoints. If Dee did not consider that his attitudes were in any way inconsistent, he may have induced inconsistency in others. Hermetists before his time had difficulty in reconciling their outlook with the demands of Church orthodoxy. Dee's contemporaries were also faced with problems. Were men like Sidney and Raleigh, who asserted their belief in Christianity, moved towards unorthodox speculation by men like Dee? As Sidney's tutor, he cannot have been without influence. It is interesting to note that he was an adviser to Humphrey and Adrian Gilbert who were related to Raleigh. Sidney's family knew the Gilberts, and Sidney's sister, the Countess of Pembroke, was taught chemistry by Adrian Gilbert. Dee's influence on Sidney's circle may well have been considerable.

Giordano Bruno, the subject of the next chapter, was also a disturbing influence. Like Dee, he speculated along the lines of the Hermetic thinkers, although his thought had stronger political implications than that of Dee. Both men challenged established views, and straddled partly the Medieval world and partly the world of the Renaissance. They contributed to the tendency to shift viewpoints, to merge the old with the new, and to focus on the significance of the individual in society and on his unique identity in the universal scheme of things.

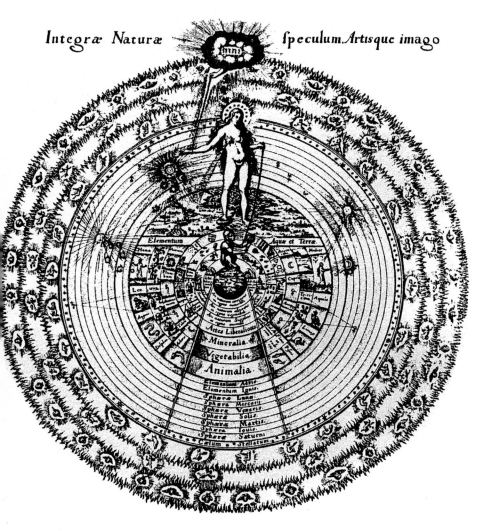

'Anima Mundi' - the Soul of the World - as a female whose right hand is con-nected to God and whose left hand holds a chain which controls the Ape of Nature (in Man). The Universe shows the earth in the centre, surrounded by spheres and the elements. From Robert Fludd's 'Utriusque Cosmi Historia'.

Elizabeth I (1533-1603) by an unknown artist c. 1575.

William Shakespeare (the Droeshout portrait)

Wilton House, Wiltshire (c. 1829) drawn by J.P. Neale. Engraved by J. Redaway.

Sir Philip Sidney (1544-86). Oil on panel by an unknown artist.

'St. George and the Dragon'. Facsimile of the woodcut from the 1590
edition of Spencer's 'Faerie Queene'.

A LETTER,

Nine yeeres since, written and first published : Containing a most briefe Discourse Apologetical, with a plaine demonstration, and feruent Protestation, for the lawfull, sincere, and very Christian course, of the Philosophicall studies and exercises, of a certaine studious Gentleman : a faithfull Seruant to our late Soueraigne Lady, Queene *Elizabeth*, for all the time of her Raigne : and (*Anno* 1603. *Aug*.9.)sworne Seruant to the King his most excellent Maiestie.

Dee and his Enemies. Title-page of Dee's Letter addressed to the Archbishop of Canterbury, 1604 (written earlier).

Sir Walter Ralegh (1552-1618). Engraving by C.H. Jeens after the portrait by Zucchero at Longleat.

VI   The Dissidence of Bruno

Although Giordano Bruno, an Italian scholar who visited England in 1583, was regarded as an extremist and was burned at the stake for heresy, his unorthodox views were not unfamiliar in the 16th century. Behind the walls of orthodox thought, there were areas of revolutionary speculation and the Church was sometimes tolerant of unorthodoxies. It would be mistaken to regard Bruno as a thinker who was ahead of his time in reaching towards modern concepts of the universe, or as a man of science who proved that Copernicus was right, that the earth moved round the sun, that the universe was infinite, that there was possible life on other planets, and that there was no central point in the cosmos (such as the earth) since all depended on the position of the observer. He expressed these views with originality and force, and he displayed a view of life which combined them in a rambling but generally cohesive way. Nevertheless, the elements of his philosophy were borrowed and he was in some ways in the Hermetist tradition. He was a man of his time, even if his thinking was strange and his style individual.

Bruno's heresies were tolerated for years before the religious authorities decided to try him before the ecclesiastical court. His wildest ideas were born out of the ferment of the period. His views on the structure and operation of the universe were not the result of a new scientific approach, but rather of an imaginative development of Medieval and early Renaissance thought. He was something of a Magus, although he was not so steeped in occult lore, and as far removed from reality, as his contemporary Dee. It is likely that his views were shaped to a large extent by the discussions held in the Italian and French academies of the day. Some of these discussions were unorthodox, wide-ranging, and far-reaching.[1]

Bruno represents, in an extreme form, the intellectual plight of those 16th century thinkers who found themselves facing several ways. They reveal the contradictions of their age. Some talked over their views in coteries, and were partially secretive. We are not sure what Raleigh and his friends discussed outside court circles, and we know little about the intellectual sessions held by Sidney at Wilton. Bruno, however, was a propagandist for the causes he held dear. In the end they led him into confrontation with the religious authorities,

He was born in 1548 in Nola (and was called Bruno 'the Nolan') of respectable but humble parents, who sent him to Naples to study. At an early age he seemed destined for the Church, and when he was seventeen years of age he entered the monastery of San Domenico in Naples. There he was known as Giordano. He apparently studied widely and voraciously. He was well acquainted with the work of Aristotle and Aquinas, continuing to respect them in later life even when his views diverged from theirs. He may have been led through studies of the Arabic and Hebrew commentaries on Aristotle to look into the philosophies of the semitic world, and his later writing showed a knowledge of Semitic scholarship. He mentioned Averroes favourably, and had probably read Avicenna. Like some of the Hermetists he had an interest in numbers, and in numerical and mystical relationships. The Alexandrine school might have appealed to him. He was certainly steeped in the classics - especially in Plato, whose *Timaeus* he was often to cite - and classical mythology permeates his work. In addition to classical philosophy he would have interested himself in astronomy, for he knew about Copernicus and for a time he taught astronomy at Noli, in 1576.

Without strict guidance in his studies a widely read young man, fed on such a varied intellectual diet, might have found it difficult to establish his bearings. When older, he drew upon medieval notions of magic, on the work of Ficino, Pico della Mirandola and Cornelius Agrippa. Like Dee, he favoured the neo-Platonist thinking rather than the Humanist, but he was very much aware of Erasmus. During his time at the monastery he was accused of reading dubious secular works, and of concealing the writings of Erasmus in the monastery privy. He also took up the fashionable study of mnemonics, and was so good at it that when he was a priest he was summoned by Pope Pius V to explain his system. He establish-

124

ed a reputation for having a prodigious memory, and was therefore thought to have invented an efficient mnemonic system.

If he showed early promise, he also showed a tendency to unorthodoxy. It was not just that he concealed dangerous reading material; he was accused, too, of casting aside the images of Saints and of speaking disparagingly about them. This was in 1576. He then moved to Rome and it was there, at the headquarters of his order, that he learned of the accusations against him. It was felt wise to abandon, at least temporarily, his monk's habit. It may have been in this period of his life that the seeds of his later views were growing in his mind, and that he was searching for a view of life which would reconcile religious conflicts. If not, his subsequent attachments to Italian and French 'academies' would have made known to him that there was considerable interest in ideas on the reconciliation of contraries.

From 1576 to 1581 he wandered as an itinerant scholar throughout northern Italy, Switzerland, and southern France. This way of life was in the medieval tradition and Bruno was not in any way original in following it. He earned money where he could, mainly as a tutor and a proof reader. He taught astronomy at Noli and also grammar, moving on to Turin, Venice and Padua. For a time he resumed his monk's habit and crossed the Alps on his way to France. In 1579 he had reached Geneva where he was patronized by the Marchesa de Vico of Naples, who was then assisting refugees from Italy. Many of these refugees were Calvinists and Bruno must have learned something of their doctrines and general attitudes. At one point he got into some quarrel with local academics and was briefly denied the sacraments. He was a forthright, not to say tactless, individual when it came to dealing with uninspiring senior academics and his criticisms may have been unwise. Again he seems to have abandoned his monastic habit. Perhaps he no longer felt wholeheartedly committed to his order, as he travelled and his mind broadened.

He moved on and after a time ended up in Toulouse, which was a Protestant stronghold. There he proved to be popular with the student population and was elected by local scholars, whom he must have greatly impressed, to a vacant post in the university as a lecturer in philosophy. The university environment was liberal and any unorthodox views he may have expressed may have aroused interest rather than occasioned dismay. His skill in memory recall may then have been on display for it was about then that he wrote a book - unfortunately now lost - on mnemonics. The work of Raymond Lull on numbers and systems had become popular in France and Bruno developed some of his theses. His reputation as a scholar with a remarkable memory grew and he was eventually sought out by King Henry III, who was interested in the unusual. It may have been Henry's influence that got Bruno a place in what is often referred to as 'The Palace Academy'; a recognized discussion group, with themes and courses of study, rather than a formal university institution. It had, as its members, leading thinkers and poets, and was to some extent modelled on the earlier Italian 'academies'. It is likely that in such a milieu there would have been an interest in the possibility of reconciling divergent religious views, and of bringing Catholics and Protestants closer through the exercise of intellectual good will. This would have been of interest to Bruno, who later wrote on the idea. Francis Yates[2] comments that before the massacre of St. Bartholomew several ideas on reconciliation were current. King Henry, himself, may have thought to use Bruno, when he went to England, as a special ambassador to put forward enlightened ideas on such subjects in London. However this may be, Bruno was given letters of recommendation to Nauvissière, the French Ambassador in London. The Ambassador took Bruno into his household, and at his residence there were discussion sessions with leading people in the form of cultural salons.

His stay in Paris must have taught Bruno much. He would have heard of the views of Ramus, who had dared to criticize Aristotle and certain elements of Humanism. Bruno later indicated that although he was impressed with Aristotle as a thinker, he did not go along with him altogether. He would have heard, too, of the academy's Professor of Greek who died in 1577, and who made the point in his *Douze Livres de la Vicissitude ou Variété des Choses de l'Univers* that in philosophy as in life contraries tend to balance each other. Bruno was to make this point also, when he wrote about what he called the 'coincidence of contraries'. In Paris he may have met Jean Bodin (1530-1596), the political thinker, who, although befriended by Henry and a staunch supporter of authority against rebellion, considered that sovereignty belonged to the people as a whole. There were many unusual ideas for Bruno to ponder and, of course, many interesting people to meet.

Bruno's early reading was influential. Nicolas of Cusa (1401-1464) had rejected many Ptolemaic concepts and had taught that the earth moved round the sun. He also hinted at the relativity of all human knowledge, believing that in a world of conflicts and bewildering contraries one could only achieve understanding and freedom by rising above human concerns and seeking a knowledge of God. According to Cusa, God alone could unify contraries, and this view is echoed in Bruno's work. Bruno paid homage to Cusa, who in his time had come close to a Pantheistic view of nature, and had developed his line of thought. Cusa believed that the spirit of God existed even in material things, and with Bruno this became almost a magical concept. He linked the Platonic view that the universe was permeated with the divine spirit with the occultism of medieval scholars.

In Milan, Bruno would have heard of Sir Philip Sidney, for Sidney had travelled in Italy and talked to leading thinkers there. It was therefore natural that Bruno should try to seek out Sidney when he went to England and perhaps try to influence him. By this time, Bruno had published some minor works, some of which have been lost. He already had a reputation, and with the help of Nauvissière it would not have been difficult to meet influential people in London. Sidney would have been interested in ideas on the reconciliation of different religions, and in Bruno's views in general, for he had a lively and curious mind.[3] In works which Bruno dedicated to Sidney, he refers to the idea of reconciling contraries, and of achieving unity through the acceptance of multiplicity. He considered that one ought to take stock only of religious essentials.

Bruno was in England from 1583 to 1585 and stayed mainly with the French Ambassador. Nauvissière himself believed in religious tolerance. He had earlier been used by the French king to plead with the Normandy Parlement to spare the lives of Huguenots, and to try to pacify Queen Elizabeth after the massacre of St. Bartholomew. The massacre was, of course, an enormous setback for those who aimed at resolving religious strife in one way or another. Nauvissière was appointed Ambassador in 1575 and remained ten year in the post. During that time, he ran a sort of intellectual salon, and one can only guess the kind of people Bruno would have met at the Embassy.

London was a busy, cosmopolitan city, full of Flemings, Huguenots, Italians and others. Bruno must have been stimulated by it, although he once described the ordinary inhabitants as uncouth, and the streets and climate as undesirable.[4] In London he met John Florio, whose Jewish, Italian father had become a Catholic, and later changed his views to follow the Protestant faith. Florio's edition and translation of Montaigne did not appear until 1603, but he was well known, especially in the Nauvissière circle. It was Florio who introduced Bruno to the poet Sackville. In London, too, Bruno could have had discussions with Dyer, Gabriel Harvey and those who had leanings towards the Ramist school, and who brought up the name of Copernicus from time to time.[5] Bruno might have been given introductions to the university of Oxford while in London. He went to Oxford on the occasion of the visit of Prince Albert Laski, and while he was there he was engaged in a dispute on the views of Copernicus with university scholars. One learns from *The Ash Wednesday Supper*[6] that the debate turned sour.

One does not know what happened at Oxford in detail. Bruno might have been criticized for inaccuracies in his statements on the theories of Copernicus. Equally, it is likely that he in turn criticized old-fashioned views held by some Oxford scholars. He may have cited Ficino's views, or mentioned the importance of astral 'magic'. Arguments may have become over-heated. Certainly, Humanists would not have gone along with Bruno's views of the universe and of Man's place within it, especially in a religious context. Man's identity and function would have been viewed from very different angles. Something of the quarrel emerges from *The Ash Wednesday Supper* when Bruno pours scorn upon his adversaries and on the lack of true learning at Oxford university. Bruno, though angry, seems to have regarded the episode as a personal triumph.

Bruno was not, of course, alone in England in doubting some elements in the Ptolemaic system. These doubts have already been mentioned. Robert Recorde had raised questions on the earth's movement, and Leonard Digges had decided in 1576 that the universe was infinite. He thought that the earth rotated daily and that the sun was most likely to be at the centre of things. William Gilbert (1540-1603) stated in his *Magnet* that the concept of 'fixed stars' was pure speculation and not proven fact. He knew Bruno, and so did the mathematician Hariot. The changing ideas on the nature and structure of the universe, as expressed in Europe, were known to English thinkers. Bruno's views were therefore not original in essence, and many scholars would have given his views on Copernicus a sympathetic hearing. But one does not know how far he went in expressing his particular brand of Hermeticism, and what his manner of expression was. At Oxford it was probably forceful, if not fiery.

By 1585 there were signs that the French were becoming un-popular in London, especially owing to their ties with Mary Queen of Scots. The French Ambassador had at one time been in touch with Mary and his position may have become a little insecure. He was recalled in 1585 and Bruno left with him for France. As he could no longer support Bruno, the latter set off on further travels.

Bruno's stay in England had produced works of speculative philosophy and he had dedicated two books to Sir Philip Sidney. As he moved across Europe he continued to write and to lecture. He also continued his habit of quarrelling with local authorities. His stay in Paris had not been all that smooth and he found his way to Wittenburg, which had a reputation for tolerance of unorthodox opinions. Even here, he could not resist criticism. He had complained about the crudeness of London citizens and about the filth of the city's streets. In Germany, he complained about drunkeness and gluttony, although he later found virtues he could praise. It was perhaps typical that when he gave a farewell address in Wittenburg he made a passing tribute to Luther. This may have been in line with ideas on reconciling contraries and on emphasizing the essentials common to all religions, but he was a Catholic in the Benedictine Order and his remarks would not have gone down well in the Catholic community. At a later date in Prague he gave a funeral oration for Duke Julius, who was a Protestant, and dedicated one of his books to him. This action was quoted against him when he was examined by inquisitors. In Helmstadt he got into further arguments and left for Frankfurt and Munich. During his wanderings over Europe he wrote several poems in Latin.

From 1591 to 1592 he was in Italy, in Padua and Venice. He was invited to Venice by a noble Venetian called Mocenigo, who was interested in Bruno's system of memory training. It is possible that Mocenigo thought that Bruno was a Magus, skilled in the arts of magic, and that he would be able to learn occult techniques from him in return for hospitality. Bruno's extant work on mnemonics is illustrated with diagrams and sets of magical images which, together with incantations and other formulae, are part of the training course for the cultivation of memory. One is reminded of the work of Cornelius Agrippa, and of Dee's hieroglyph. In common with some Hermetists, Bruno seems to conceive of training and study as a means of creating a sort of priestly personality, a new identity. The magical elements in his thesis are there for religious purposes only.[7]

Bruno was Mocenigo's guest for some time, but resisted his importunities. It is not surprising, in view of Bruno's reputation and his published work, that Mocenigo thought he could learn something of the art of magic from his guest, and, knowing Bruno's irascible temperament, that quarrels would result. Mocenigo began to threaten Bruno with exposure. Curiously unaware of possible danger, Bruno took no special evasive action, staying where he was. Mocenigo then reported him to the church authorities as a man with heretical opinions, and soon afterwards he was arrested and asked to give a full account of his life and ways of thought.

Under arrest, Bruno was obviously under pressure. Several witnesses appeared who testified that he had expressed heretical views, and others said that he was a man who had no religion. He eventually confessed to certain misdemeanors, sought absolution, and said that he wished to be accepted by the Church. Formal trial was postponed for two months, and during that time, Bruno again pleaded for reconciliation. There followed a period of indecisive waiting and finally it was decided that the case ought to be considered in Rome.

Up to this point, Bruno had a good chance of acquital. The Doge of Venice and the Senate had the privilege of giving ecclesiastical judgements independent of Rome, and normally they might have wished to keep Bruno in Venice. But as time went on, evidence against him began to accumulate. His writings were examined and a number of contacts, which seemed dubious from the Catholic standpoint, came to light. It was claimed that Bruno had written against the Catholic religion, and that some of his actions were anti-Catholic. The charges became more and more substantial, and as Bruno was not a Venetian, it may have been felt that he could be sent for trial in Rome without loss of local privilege.

In Rome his trial became protracted. He was placed in prison where he lingered for many years while his case was discussed and rediscussed. He was, no doubt, well treated, and while in prison he carried out his own defence as if he were engaged in an academic disputation. As one might have expected, his skill was notable, but his manner sharp and at times arrogant. He did his cause little good by clever argument, especially at a time when heresy was causing growing concern. Italy had been moving towards closer ties with Spain, and in Spain there was a strict attitude with regard to religious dissidents. Campanella had been censured and Bruno's views would have been strongly in focus. There could well have been pressure to find Bruno guilty, and as time passed by, the scales against him began to tip. The formal trial began and the evidence against him accumulated. His writings were quoted against him, his dubious contacts were mentioned, and his attitude towards important people, who were unbelievers like Queen Elizabeth, was also criticized. Finally, he was condemned to death for heresey and led to the stake in the year 1600. It was said that he faced death with dignity and that he refused the crucifix when this was offered to him.

Like John Dee he was a wandering scholar whose influence would have spread through his pupils. He wrote more than Dee, however, and his work would have brought his views to the notice of leading thinkers of the day. He would not have been condemned to death had the Church thought that his work was of little importance, and during the course of his trial the extent of his writing was eventually realized. If many of his ideas were borrowed from other sources, he marshalled them in his own way and presented them with the unique flavour of his strong personality. While staying in London, it is possible that his views, together with those of Dee (who was away when Bruno was there), formed an influential element in the intellectual climate surrounding contemporary English writers. The Queen was fairly tolerant of unusual intellectuals, provided they were not dangerous politically. Bruno flattered the Queen in an introduction to one of his works, and seemed to see her, at one point, as a leader in his 'Commonwealth' of religions. He may well have been sympathetic towards Sidney's idea of a league of Protestant leaders against Spain, although Bruno claimed throughout that he was of the Catholic church. Eirenicism may have appealed to Sidney, and although on his side he was a convinced Protestant he was not averse to discussing matters of moment with Catholics like Campion. Sidney's student days in Italy must have brought him into contact with unorthodox views on politics and religion, and he would have been aware of Hermetic thinking. Some of Bruno's ideas, notably the concept of relativity which Bruno inherited from Cusa and others, would have intrigued Sidney, whose *Arcadia* indicates that there were problems in determining a scale of absolutes.

It is useful to know something of Bruno's life and travels to appreciate the extent of his contacts and the likely impact of his strange personality. He was a forceful character and this quality is expressed in his writing. Like Dee he stressed the importance of the individual, of human identity, but he was also concerned in bringing together disparate personalities and views by concentrating on essentials. While he, himself, was an awkward, combative individual, he was anxious to promote peace and unity through intellectual tolerance, and by recognition of the identity of one God in the manifold expressions of different religions. Both he and Dee represent the Hermetic dimension, as against the Humanist, in the many revealing perspectives of the age. Bruno was particularly concerned with relationships and with the problem of recognizing core identities.

The Ash Wednesday Supper[8] reveals much of Bruno's thought. It is written in the form of dialogue, and the style varies from magisterial prose to that of colourful burlesque. In the first dialogue, he describes how he came to visit Fulke Greville, Sidney's friend, and to hold a seminar at his house. This was the evening of an intellectual supper. In it, he compliments and criticizes the English, and has some harsh words to say about the crudeness of the ordinary citizens of the city and the filth of its streets. He then touches on the quarrelsome debate at Oxford, pours scorn on his adversaries, and concludes that he had a triumph at the university. In the third dialogue he formulates some of his philosophical views. He accepts Copernicus' theory on the earth's movement, and states his admiration for the thinking of Nicolas of Cusa. The fourth dialogue is concerned with the arguments at the supper and as one nears the end of the book there is revealed a belief in an infinite universe, the notion of relativity of values, ideas on what he calls 'innate necessity', and some thoughts on motion in space. The book is discursive, at times rambling, and refers to arguments mentioned in his other works. There are also occasional flashbacks to previous views.

It is interesting that during his trial in Rome, Bruno stated that he had held these discussions at the house of the French Ambassador and not at Greville's house. It is possible that he thought it might be safer to claim that unorthodox discussion took place in the home of a leading Catholic rather than in the home of a Protestant. The title of the book has a special significance, for it is through the Eucharist on Ash Wednesday that one enters into a unique communion with God. But Bruno's supper is a secular affair. There is comment on the wine being passed round the table in the course of the meal so that the secular association with the religious is not missed. Bruno seems to imply that there is no need for a Church service in order to reach God, and that there is no need to argue about the meaning of the sacrament. All that is required is for men of good will, and especially leading figures, to get together to reach an accord, no matter what their original beliefs are. The implication is that a secular meeting, like the Ash Wednesday supper at Greville's house (or that of the French Ambassador) can result in attempts to reach important truths. At such a meeting one may attain a better knowledge of God.[9]

At a private residence, therefore, there was held a non-church form of the Eucharist, and in a sense Bruno preached a sermon. It is not surprising that the inquisitors in Rome were disturbed by this book, or that Bruno changed his mind about the venue. Working through the thought of Nicolas of Cusa, Bruno plays on the idea that opposites can always be reconciled through God. The individual must achieve unity with God. This can only be achieved by an individual act of mind. Each person is unique - possessing his own central identity - but there are inter-relations in nature, and ultimately all is combined in one whole in the Godhead. Thus, one can achieve unity even in apparent multiplicity. Bruno thought that there was a 'core identity', a 'oneness' in the universe, in spite of apparent differences. He thought that concepts formulated by human beings often suggested differences, and brought out the contraries in life, but that all these differences were ultimately reconcilable. Matter to Bruno had a dual nature. Individual phenomena existed, but were also working elements in 'the whole'. It could follow, therefore, that although there was an ultimate absolute, all values were relative.[10]   One might speculate on whether such opinions caught the imagination of the young Sidney whose mind, as his French tutor pointed out, was too readily open to new ideas. The dilemmas in the *Arcadia*, which will be referred to in the next chapter, raise questions on relative values.

Throughout Bruno's work, there runs the idea of the animation of matter. He thought, like many before him, that God breathes through all things. Here, he was doubtless influenced by Plato's *Timaeus*, and by the views of Ficino, Pico della Mirandola and others. He absorbs these ideas, but they do not flow evenly through the dialogues. He advances an argument and then turns back to previous statements in an attempt to link ideas, but this sometimes causes confusion. The influences are many - Aristotle, Plato, Lucretius, Paracelsus, Cusa, and the Hermetic writers. He may have been familiar with the work of Avicenna and of Averroes, for the notion of an eternity of worlds and of a unity of intellect was borrowed from early scholars. The wide reading of Bruno and men like Dee was not uncommon. Sidney and Raleigh were both avid readers, and the variety and complexity of thought which could not easily be reconciled in a world of shifting values, would have disturbed them as well as stimulated. One can but wonder what Sidney made of the two books which were dedicated to him.

The Expulsion of the Triumphant Beast, or *Spaccio*, is written in the form of dialogue like *The Ash Wednesday Supper*, but in

134

a different style. It is a rough and ready allegory in which Jove, repenting of his vices, decides to purge the heavens. The vices, or beasts of Jove, are represented by constellations. They have to be changed and made into virtues. The replacement of the beasts causes a discussion of values, and arguments are presented in a light-hearted way by the presence of Momus, the god of ridicule. If the book is something of a *jeu d'esprit*, it has an underlying seriousness - a blend of attitudes which might have appealed to Sidney, whose humour was sometimes evident in his serious moments. Bruno praises Sidney before depicting his mythology of the heavens.

In this book, Bruno shows that morality may sometimes seem to be relative. He refers to the contraries which life presents, and indicates that where contraries exist, there is bound to be both action and reaction. This adds to the quality of life; to its diversity. Christianity is valued, but Bruno suggests that there are some virtues in Paganism and that Pagan societies were aware that God existed in nature. One perspective is, that morality takes into account the needs of society. It is not a matter of concern that there are different faiths in the world as long as they can be interpreted on more or less neo-Platonic lines and fulfill the needs of society. Bruno does, however, criticize defects in the Protestant and Catholic religions. He dismisses the literal interpretation of the Bible.

In this colourful and somewhat satirical work, there is a serious commitment, according to Yates,[11] to a belief in a natural, magical religion - the sort of religion favoured by some Hermetic thinkers and supposedly based on the sun and astral magic of ancient, Egyptian worship. Such strange, mystical ideas were often derived from the *Asclepius*. In a supplement, he praises satirically the notion of 'holy foolishness' - no doubt with Cusa's *Learned Ignorance* and Cornelius Agrippa's *On the Vanity of Knowledge* in mind, for he did not believe that simplicity was a prerequisite for true religious knowledge.

If this work is a fantasy, touching on the relativity of human values in a world of complicated perspectives and changing identites, *The Heroic Furies (De Gli Eroici Furori)* is an ode, in poetry and in prose, to intellectual beauty with Plato in mind. He states that the religion of a people is part of its culture and it should be adhered to in the way that one adheres to national laws. At the same time, he favours intelligent and judicious criticism of national religions. He then moves towards the concept that true religion is not achieved by the teaching and pressure of external authority, but by the individual soul which is moved by inner light.[12] Like Dee, and other Hermetic thinkers, he stresses the role of the individual and the cultivation of a special identity. Heroic efforts are needed to subdue the common passions which affect the flesh or trouble the mind. There are many *humours* which disturb the faculty of reason, and human love is one of them. Divine love is of a different order altogether and it is difficult to cultivate, although there is a divine spirit which pervades the universe with which one can identity oneself, if one strives in the right way. Bruno conceives a progression towards a better world, in which wars and disputes recede, and where the contraries, which appear so often in life, are eventually reconciled in universal harmony.

When we examine the work of Sidney, it will be noticed that he, too, was concerned with the destructive force of passionate *humours*, and particularly with the passion of love. In the *Arcadia* there are several passions which undermine personality and which obscure identity. Love causes one of Sidney's characters to disguise his sex; a device which we have seen used by Shakespeare and others and which had a significance beyond that of older theatrical tradition. In the sonnets to Stella, love is, of course, the main theme, but in the end Sidney turns away from his debilitating passion and makes an affirmation in favour of divine love. It is interesting that Bruno should have dedicated a book to Sidney, which implied the relative nature of human values, without a knowledge of God, and which brought up the question of life's paradoxes and contraries. Such questions are raised by events in the *Arcadia*. If Sidney were tempted to think along Bruno's lines, or indeed those of Dr. Dee, it would go some way to explaining some of the apparent contradictions in his own nature. He was a strong supporter of the Protestant cause against Spain, and he believed in the essential Protestant virtues, but he also interested himself in Catholics, like Campion, who no doubt expressed ideas which appealed to him. At one point Campion thought Sidney might be ripe for conversion!

The second part of Bruno's book deals with heroic inspiration. Bruno indicates that inspiration may produce mental strife, and while emotion may seek high ideals it needs the control of the intellect. Conflict exists, and human nature has its warring elements which can only be transcended by the knowledge of a higher love. Bruno points out that people should develop according to their own natures, each differently, but they can be united and harmony can be achieved in diversity. The third dialogue deals with what he refers to as the 'coincidence of contraries', and the fourth with the weakness of the human will. The fifth dialogue is interesting, in that it raises a point which Sidney raised in the *Arcadia* when he compared the virtues of Pamela and Philoclea. One recalls that Pamela reasons her way in argument with the evil Queen Cecropia, but that Philoclea asserts her view through her steadfast innocence, reaching her judgements intuitively. In his dialogue Bruno describes how two women apprehend higher truths through intuition, rather than through reason.

Bruno's other works are concerned with theories about the universe. A work entitled *On the Infinite Universe and Worlds* dismisses traditional ideas on the structure of the universe. The second dialogue between Barchio and Fracastra shows how perspectives had changed:

Barchio   Where is that beautiful order, that lively scale of nature rising from the denser and grosser body which is our earth, to the less denser . . . finally to the divine which is the celestial body? From the obscure to the less obscure, to the brighter and finally to the brightest? . . . to liberation from all change and corruption?

Fracastro   You would like to know where this order is? In the realms of dreams, fantasies, chimeras, delusions. For, as to motion, everything endowed with natural motion revolveth in a circle around either his own or some other centre . . . I deny this order, this disposition that earth is surrounded and contained by water, water by air, air by

137

fire, fire by heaven . . . The famous and received
order of elements and of heavenly bodies is a
dream and vainest fantasy, since it can neither
be verified by observation of nature nor proved
by reason and argued . . .

Having demolished the Ptolemaic universe, Bruno goes on to state
that stars may be other worlds which may be inhabited. He conceives of the universe as infinite, and makes an interesting point
about perspectives being relative and dependent on position.

There is in the universe neither centre nor circumference,
but if you will, the whole is central, and every point also
may be regarded as part of a circumference in respect to
some other central point.[13]

Two books, *De Immenso et Innumerabilibus* and *De Minimo
at de Immenso*, draw upon ancient Greek ideas but Bruno fashions
his universe in his own way, and it is a universe far removed from
that of Aristotle and Ptolemy. According to Bruno, the minima of
matter is in eternal motion; it increases and it also diminishes. This
flux produces change and continuous growth. All things, and all
creatures, are impelled by their essential natures - they have their
own identities - but they are also part of a universal whole which is
an expression of the divine spirit. God is neither a minimum or
maximum in the changing universe, for He combines all creation.
De Immenso is a rambling hymn of praise and wonder in the contemplation of a universe which is limitless. In it, Bruno imagines
undiscovered planets revolving round each other, and worlds in
outer space which die and renew themselves by entering into new
combinations.

There is some truth in Bacon's view.[14] when he listed Bruno
with Gilbert, that he was one of those who sought knowledge
through the exercise of imagination rather than through a scientific
observation of fact, but few had the scientific skills which Bacon
sought. Bruno had, nevertheless, some skill in mathematics and his
views, however derivative, were forcefully expressed. He carried on
a neo-Platonic, Hermetic tradition which was influential in his day,

if less strong than that of Humanism. Both streams of thought existed in Europe, but since the former was less noticeable in England, its course in this country has not been sufficiently examined. Both Sir Philip Sidney and Sir Walter Raleigh would have been aware of the views expressed by people like Dee and Bruno. They were part of the intellectual climate of the time. They contributed to the sense of new perspectives in a changing and uncertain world, which made it difficult for some to take up firm positions and to know what role to play in life. Both Sidney and Raleigh, as leading courtiers, had to act out roles, and both were at times unsure of their true identities.

In the next chapter, certain aspects of Sidney's life and thought will be examined, and it will be important to keep in mind, as intellectual background, the work of Dee and Bruno and of earlier neo-Platonists. The influence of Humanism is more apparent, but Elizabethan writers were many-sided.

VII   The Lance and the Quill

Sir Philip Sidney has an elusive identity. At times he wrote plainly and with engaging honesty, but he is difficult to know. His lyric poetry is not complicated, but it is not easy to determine when his mood is sincere or assumed. Like his contemporaries he wrote as a craftsman, and not as a romantic with a need to express personal feelings. He can be very literary. His stylishness is often evident in poetry and in prose, and he is frequently concerned with making a point rather than expressing a feeling. In his *Apology for Poetry* he claimed that poetry had an educative value and shadowed forth important truths. Nevertheless, genuine feeling seems sometimes to break through the mould, and mistress Stella of the sonnets then becomes more of a real person and less of a symbol.

The question of the relation of the writer to his work comes to mind when one reads the *Arcadia*. It is an intricate work, although the basic narrative plot is simple. It began as a romance in the manner of the age, a fanciful love story, but as he wrote Sidney became especially interested in the minds and hearts of his figures, and he expressed and analyzed them during the course of his work. He became interested, too, in the political and moral issues resulting from situations in which his characters were placed. His growing interest changed the ambiance of the romance and he had to revise it. His change in attitude may have been due to his activities as a courtier, for he became frustrated over his role and his career prospects.

As he reworked the *Arcadia* he became more thoughtful and more serious. Moral and political issues were touched upon, in comments on the adventures of characters, or through their arguments and discussions. New tales were added to the original version of the book. They were interwoven in the main narrative, but many of them illustrated problems of conduct - like 'exempla'. The revised version of the *Arcadia* is larger than the original and the overall tone more serious. However, whether it is due to the unfinished nature of the book (for it was not completed and the revision was only partial), or whether he found difficulty in clearing a way through the contradictory moods and opinions which his intellectual explorations revealed, there is a sense of inconclusiveness about some of the issues raised. There are many uncertainties in the *Arcadia*.

Obviously it would be mistaken to regard Sidney's writing as if it were partly biographical, but one should not go to the other extreme and dismiss the relevance of personal experience to his work. His experience as an avid reader, a student traveller abroad, a frustrated lover, and as a courtier whose career did not fulfil expectations, would have been likely to have influenced his thinking. There are occasions when one senses that the stylist of the *Arcadia*, like that of the craftsman of the sonnets, moves towards a closer relationship with the reader, and that he writes from painful and puzzling experience.

He played a role that accorded with the legend that grew up around him after his death, for he had been brought up to regard himself as a future leader and as a Christian gentleman. In his early youth, he had high ideals, and these set the pattern for subsequent actions; but as he grew older he became aware of the gulf between life as it is and what it should be. The fact that reality often falls short of an ideal, is reflected in the *Arcadia*. There are several layers to Sidney's personality. He saw himself as a man of action; a warrior gentleman whose skill with the lance in courtly combat was but a symbol of the real thing. He was, of course, to meet his death as a soldier in active service. At another level he was a writer, a craftsman of lyric verse and a stylist writer of light romance. He once referred to his *Arcadia* as a 'toyful book'. Later he sought, according to his biographer, Fulke Greville, to produce a work which would be educative, and (not unlike Spenser's *Faerie Queene*) teach moral and political virtues. His revisions of the *Arcadia* no doubt had this aim in mind. He saw himself as a staunch supporter of the Protestant cause, and indeed he wrote to Elizabeth advising against a Catholic marriage, but his wide-ranging mind, which worried his tutor Languet, brought him into contact with men like Campion, Bruno and others, whose views were unorthodox, and even dangerous, to a young courtier. The different roles of man of action, Christian leader, poet, teacher, romance writer, patron of the arts and intellectual, did not easily blend together.

Sidney seems often to present to us the mask of the courtier and educative writer, but his individuality comes through his writing, and his personal problems do not always seem to be a literary game. One is aware of him as a personality, in spite of his doctrinal view of literature, as evidenced in the *Apology for Poetry*. When he treats of the passion of love, in the form of literary exercises, his own emotion seems often present and his voice retains a personal note, even in a contrived stanza or in a decorative piece of prose. In his sonnets, the image of Stella as a star is not always held before us, and Astrophel becomes a real person, as we move through the sonnet sequence.

Sidney's life, like his writing, was incomplete. He did not achieve the potential which he and others thought he possessed. He was born in 1554 and he died in battle at the early age of thirty-two. In spite of his achievements - and he died in a blaze of adulation - there are notes of frustration in his letters and in his creative writing. His death produced elegies from Spenser, Raleigh, Drayton and others. The poet Daniel, in an address to Sidney's sister, saw him as the leader of an English Renaissance, and Gabriel Harvey wrote as if he possessed all the virtues. His friend, Greville, thought so highly of him that he wrote his own epitaph in the following words: "Servant to Queen Elizabeth, Counsellor to King James, Friend to Sir Philip Sidney". Once the *Arcadia* was published it was read with interest and approval all over Europe. Yet he had not completed what he had set out to do, and on his deathbed he asked that his book be burned. He may have died a hero, but his military exploits were not successful and he did not achieve high office as a courtier or diplomat. Even his knighthood was awarded by the Queen more for his social status than for his personal merit.

The bare facts of his life are well known, but it is useful to keep them in mind when examining his work. He was killed fighting against the Spaniards at Zutphen, more as a result of lack of care than of physical combat. According to Greville, he saw the Master of Camp going into battle without full armour, and either wishing to emulate his courage, or not wishing to gain an advant-

142

age by being more protected, he neglected to put on his thigh armour. He was tragically unfortunate, being shot in the thigh by a musket ball, and he had to leave the field in pain. Calling for water, he saw a wounded soldier close by and ordered his flask to be passed to him with the words: "Thy necessity is yet greater than mine".[1] It seemed a characteristic gesture.

He lay at Arnhem, several days before dying and his body was brought to London for a funeral on the grand scale, although he had not been a notable courtier and was not especially favoured by the Queen. His death caught the public imagination. The cortège was led by gentlemen from the Inns of Court and in the forefront were thirty-two ordinary men, whose number represented Sidney's short life. In attendance, were officers of the military, members of his household, his physician and surgeon, and twelve knights, including Sir Francis Drake and Sir Edward Waterhouse. Horses were ridden by pages and heralds. Sir Fulke Greville and Thomas Dudley held corners of the pall. Robert Sidney and members of his family followed the coffin. There were also present, representatives of the Low Countries, the Lord Mayor of London and other dignatories. The merchant class was also represented. The enthusiasm at court for wearing colourful dress was restrained after his death, for months afterwards.

Fulke Greville's *Life* does not provide many facts, and one has to turn to Sidney's letters, and to other sources, to piece together the main elements of his life. In some respects his upbringing gave him an uncertain identity. He was an aristocrat, a man proud of his family, and he was not altogether at ease in an age of thrusting new statesmen. The feudal status of noblemen was almost a thing of the past, and to get on in life they had to do well at court and rely on court patronage. Sidney's father did not receive much encouragement from Elizabeth as Lord Deputy of Ireland. He was kept short of funds in his difficult administration. He felt it necessary, from time to time, to remind his son of his mother's noble lineage, for she was a descendant of the Dudley family, a sister of the Earl of Leicester. Sidney may well have felt that he and his family were somehow on the periphery of major affairs, although he entertained hopes of important office, as a nephew of Leicester. His tuition in high ideas may have been occasionally tarnished by the knowledge that his father had to resort to Machiavellian tactics in his administration of Ireland, and by an awareness of the political manoeuvring of his later father-in-law, Walsingham. Sidney's birth did not automatically entitle him to position. The family was not particularly wealthy and he had to struggle to maintain a useful place at court.

If Sidney's upbringing taught him the old notions of *noblesse* and the importance of chivalry, his schooling taught him to think like a contemporary Renaissance man. As for many of his age, the intellectual options were so varied that it would not have been easy to reconcile them and to see a clear way ahead. He entered the university of Oxford at a very early age and his contacts would have introduced him to intelligent 'new' men. As he grew older, he came to surround himself with intellectual companions and acquaintances, some of whom entertained advanced and unorthodox ideas. Moffet mentions that he was tutored by John Dee, and Dee's Hermetic neo-Platonism would have been at odds with the strains of Humanism at Oxford and Cambridge.

He was committed politically to the Protestant cause, but there is some ambiguity in his religious commitment. The religious background of his family is not well defined. His grandfather, the notorious Duke of Northumberland, was associated with the Protestant cause, but recanted when faced with execution over the plot to favour Lady Jane Grey against Mary. His father served the Protestant King Edward VI, but also worked under Mary. Two of his father's sisters were Catholics in Queen Mary's service. It was said that when the Catholic Edmund Campion was under threat in Elizabeth's reign, Sidney's father warned him, before he fled abroad. Sidney had Catholic friends, and during one of his visits to Europe he went to see Campion. It seems odd that although he was to fight against the forces of Philip of Spain, the Spanish monarch was one of his godparents.

Of course, the fact that Sidney's family had Protestant and Catholic connections was not unusual. Religious attitudes were for some, confused and ill-defined, after the Church settlement. It would not be of note that Sidney had Catholic friends, unless it were to indicate a lack of strong commitment. The background to the stories in the *Arcadia* is Christian, but there is no religious fer-

144

vour or doctrinal argument. The moral viewpoint is often seen from a neo-Platonic angle.

As a schoolboy at Shrewsbury school, he was under a Calvanist teacher, and one ought to bear in mind that his friend Greville had strong leanings in that direction. One wonders what influences worked upon him at Oxford and in his brief time at Cambridge? He was just over thirteen when he went up to Christchurch, but even at that age he could hardly have been untouched by the intellectual ferment in university circles. Campion was at Oxford at this time, and when Sidney was older he may have met Gabriel Harvey at Cambridge. Moffet in his *Nobilis* wrote of Sidney that "although he respected ancient learning, his mind was not closed to new ideas."[2] The intellectual changes at Cambridge at that time, were described by Gabriel Harvey in a letter to Spenser. Perhaps Sidney came into contact with Ramist thinkers? Respectful as he was towards Aristotle, he was not prepared to accept him totally, and one notices that Banos - a leading Ramist who was critical of the Aristotelians - later dedicated a book to Sidney and referred to Ramus' affection for him. The so-called *Areopagus* circle drew together writers like Greville, Spenser and Dyer and would have discussed Ramist ideas. Harvey mentions this circle in his *Marginalia*.

In 1584, one notes that William Temple dedicated to Sidney his *P. Rami Dialecticae Libri Suo* and became his secretary, and that the Ramist Abraham Launce, who owed his time at Cambridge to Sidney, also dedicated a work to him. He had connections, too, with the Ramist thinker Timothy Bright. If Sidney were a Protestant with Catholic sympathies, an Aristotelian with Ramist leanings, a man of action with a love of poetry and the arts, then it would go some way to explaining the contradictions in his character, and the difficulty of formulating attitudes and playing roles. His travels abroad as a young man must also have opened his mind to different intellectual perspectives.

The Queen gave him permission to go abroad in 1572, and for a while he stayed with Walsingham, who was then Ambassador in Paris. He was to marry Walsingham's daughter in 1593. He would have met several writers and thinkers in Paris, and especially after the Massacre of St. Bartholomew which took place during his stay. This would have occasioned much debate on political and religious issues and on problems of confrontation and reconciliation. He left Paris for Germany, Austria, and Italy, making a short visit to Hungary on the way. In Vienna, he met the Protestant scholar Languet, who became his tutor and adviser for many years. Languet carried on a long correspondence with Sidney when they were not together. From Sidney's letters, there emerges the idea of an alliance of Protestant leaders in Europe against Spain.

Sidney worked hard while abroad, learning several languages, and whilst in Padua, he got down to a serious study of Latin and Greek. It is not therefore surprising that he relaxed on his return. He improved his skill in horsemanship and in tennis. Jousting appealed to him in particular, and he was skillful with the lance. Once back in England, he took his place at court and became friendly with the Earl of Essex, who had known him since childhood. Essex took him to Ireland where he no doubt shared his father's frustrations.

At this time of life he would have met Penelope Devereux, Essex's daughter, with whom he was to fall in love. She became the inspiration of his sonnets *Astrophel and Stella*, and she was as unobtainable, owing to her marriage, as was Petrarch's Laura. His life at court began to pall after a while and he would surely have wanted to play a more important role than that of Cup Bearer to the Queen. He might well have been encouraged in his career as a courtier when he was sent on a mission abroad. This was ostensibly to convey the Queen's condolences to the Elector Palatine and to the Protestant leader Casimir on their bereavements, but he might also have been asked to report on trends in political thinking in Europe. Unfortunately, his mission did not seem to lead to more favour in court circles. It was, however, on this occasion that he visited Campion in exile and won his good opinion. Campion wrote about the visit and mentioned that he might be ripe for conversion to the Catholic faith. He wrote of his "wavering soul". His tutor Languet, in a letter to Walsingham, dispelled the idea that Sidney had Catholic leanings, but in writing to Sidney he was concerned that his young companion might open his mind to dangerous ideas on his travels.

Sidney's connection with certain Catholics was known in England. His cousin Richard Shelley was a Catholic, and he seems

146

to have given some help to the recusant Lady Kytson, but both Languet and Greville stressed his Protestantism. In Chapter III of his *Life* Greville writes: "Above all, he made the religion he professed, the firm basis of his life, for this was his judgement - as he often told me - that our true-heartedness to the Reformed Religion in the beginning, brought peace and safety to us . . .". Campion may have misunderstood the nature of Sidney's enquiring mind; equally Greville may not have wished to mention that Sidney could be open-minded on certain issues. During his visit to Europe he also met William of Orange and his letters indicate his enthusiasm over the meeting.

In England Sidney became anxious for action. He interested himself in a Frobisher expedition and in accompanying Leicester to the continent in some military capacity. The Queen did not, however, approve of these ideas and Sidney lingered in court circles possibly in some degree of frustration over his inactivity. His father received little support at this time for his work in Ireland, so that all round it would have been a depressing period for the Sidney family. Moreover, the Queen seemed lukewarm about supporting the Protestant cause in Europe which Sidney favoured. When Prince Casimir arrived in England hoping for support he was well enough received, but he had to leave without any firm agreement to strengthen political relations. Walsingham was in favour of a definite move to help the Protestant cause, but Burghley was more cautious. The Queen's advisers were divided on policy, and when the idea was mooted that she should consider marrying the Catholic Duc d'Alencon, Sidney, Walsingham and Leicester opposed it while Sussex and Oxford approved. Sidney became so concerned that he wrote a forthright letter to the Queen setting out the disadvantages of such a marriage. It was a bold move on his part, for he was still young and inexperienced. Elizabeth apparently discussed the matter with him. One does not know whether she took offence, but he certainly irritated her over his quarrel with the Earl of Oxford on a tennis court.

The story is mentioned by Greville in his *Life*. It appeared that Oxford arrived on the court and required Sidney to give way. Sidney retorted sharply and this led Oxford to refer to him as a 'puppy'. There were further exchanges in the presence of some visiting French Commissioners and Sidney left the court in a manner which suggested that the matter would be taken up further elsewhere. The Queen intervened and reminded Sidney of the Earl's higher status. Sidney was said to have replied that "place was never intended for privilege to wrong" - a thought which could have come out of the trial scene in the *Arcadia*. His view was that if the Earl had precedence he was not Sidney's master. It was a curious incident and suggested that Sidney was not always the polite and tactful courtier.

Shortly afterwards, he left court circles to retire into the country. He may have been out of favour, but since court life was expensive he may have found himself in straightened circumstances. He later wrote, somewhat ambiguously, that "necessity did even banish me from the place". Whatever the reason for leaving he had not achieved an important position or gained the ear of the Queen. He went to live with his sister, the Countess of Pembroke at Wilton House where he began to write his *Arcadia* and to hold discussions with his many friends. The Countess was interested in artistic matters, and Wilton House became something of a literary 'salon'. There were frequent gatherings of friends and acquaintances to discuss topics of the day. Here his friends Greville and Dyer, and possibly Spenser, came to see him. An important subject for literary men at the time was the theories stemming from the *Pleiade* in France and how they might usefully influence English poetry. The *Arcadia* contains many experiments in verse forms - hexameters, elegiacs, sapphics, asclepiads, anacreontics and so on. Wider questions would also have been discussed at Wilton, and it is reasonable to suppose that some of them found their way into Sidney's prose work. Harvey refers to the circle round Sidney as the *Areopagus*. The *Arcadia* probably owed much to it.

In 1581 Sidney returned to the court. The life of writing and of contemplation appealed to one side of his temperament; on the other hand, he needed the life of action. The value of poetry he maintained in his *Apology* was that it stimulated men to virtuous action. It was a view shared by Spenser and others and had its origin in Aristotle. Sidney quotes Aristotle in the *Apology* . . . "For, as Aristotle sayth, it is not Gnosis but Praxis must be the fruit". However, the return to court did not produce the life of action he sought. His father had left Ireland, but it was thought that he might return assisted by his son in some special office. However, this was not to be. Sidney became Parliamentary member for Kent, and was on several committees which dealt with laws against Catholics and with those who had committed seditious practices, but he did not play an active part in Parliamentary affairs as did his contemporary Raleigh. His main activity was jousting, and he turned from the use of the quill to that of the lance.

In 1582 he was knighted, but this was not due to any special or outstanding service. The Prince of Orange was to be given the honour of the Garter and in his absence he named Sidney as his proxy. Since protocol demanded that his stand-in should be at least a knight, Sidney was dubbed by the Queen. He did not rise much in her favour, however, for when in the following year he married Walsingham's daughter he did not seek her permission in advance. Nevertheless, he was at last given a definite income when he was appointed together with Warwick as joint master of Ordnance. The office provided various perquisites.

Sidney's frustrations continued as he contemplated the problem of the Protestant cause and Spanish dominance in the Netherlands. He changed his view on tactics, and at one point envisaged a scheme whereby the English, in collaboration with allies, might burn Spanish ships and make an attack on Seville. He then played with the idea that Spain could be weakened by attacks on her overseas possessions. Like Raleigh, he was interested in the New World, and when his suggestions for confronting Spain went unheeded he turned his attention to the Americas, deciding to sail with Drake on an expedition. He was set to go, when Drake - who may have been uneasy about Sidney's presence on his expedition - informed the Queen of their plans. Elizabeth promptly ordered Sidney back to court where he had to effect a reconciliation. He may well have succeeded in mollifying the Queen, for he was later sent as Governor to Flushing, and instructed to prepare for the arrival of Leicester as head of an expeditionary force.

At Flushing, Sidney rapidly set about organizing the garrison administration, for there was disorder and ill-discipline. This was his first real task as a leader and he performed it well enough. He also gave useful, preliminary advice to Leicester, counselling patience and caution in planning, so that he would not impetuously take on more than the Queen expected. He was perhaps beginning to mature politically, but it was on this service abroad that he was cut down in his prime in the battle of Zutphen. He had previously been involved in the abortive attempt to take Gravelines. He had not really made his mark as a soldier when he died, although the manner of his death at an early age made him a posthumous hero.

One wonders whether something of the frustrations of court life were expressed in the *Arcadia*, for the two princes in that book suffer setbacks which are due, not only to their inexperience, but to ill luck and the errors of rulers. It may not be going too far to see in the inadequacies of King Basilius a touch of Sidney's impatience with the Queen's lack of commitment for the causes he favoured. The ideal knights of old (Spenser's conception) were hardly recognizable in the new corridors of power. Courtly service under a changeable but strong-willed Queen must have sometimes seemed like ignoble servility. This would have been irksome to Sidney. Passages in the *Arcadia* reflect Sidney's concern for good government, loyalty in personal relationships, individual freedom and good justice. But the book also reflects an awareness that these ideals were not only difficult to achieve, but could even conflict with each other. The paradoxes and contraries mentioned by Bruno appear in the *Arcadia*.

If Sidney did not achieve total satisfaction in the world of military and political action, neither did he achieve it in the world of love. He married Francis Walsingham, but was apparently infatuated with Penelope Devereux who had married Lord Rich. As time went on, he became increasingly aware that his infatuation was getting him nowhere, for although she may have wished to reciprocate, she held him at a distance. He felt helpless to remedy the situation. His set of sonnets called *Astrophel and Stella* (i.e. Sidney and Penelope) expresses his frustration and his attempts to come to terms with his feelings and the reality of the situation. Some of the poems are exercises in the Petrarchan manner, and Stella is something of a Laura figure. One is therefore tempted to ask if his feelings were genuine, or whether he was playing the role of the rejected poetic lover according to literary convention. But some of the sonnets have the ring of genuine experience.

150

It has often been pointed out that it is not easy to determine when Sidney was being serious, or when he was suggesting a mock seriousness. The convention, especially in Italy, of idealizing a loved one in poetry was common enough. The loved one could be used as a symbol to express neo-Platonic views on humility, duty, self-abnegation and so on. If one detects a note of mockery in Astrophel's protestations this, too, was a convention. The use of 'ironia' was an accepted literary device. It was mentioned in treatises of rhetoric and Greville describes it as a style . . . "wherein men commonly (to keep above their works) seem to make toys of the utmost they can do".[3] Sidney's tendency to give an ironic twist to a serious theme is, nevertheless unsettling, in what is otherwise serious love poetry.

It is a feature of Renaissance poetry to make dialectical points with the aid of chosen imagery, already encrusted with traditional meaning. Mythological figures such as Cupid, were brought into love poetry for obvious effect. Sidney follows this practice. In sonnet 29, Stella comes to Cupid's aid in his amorous wars. Her eyes "serve him with shot". Equally artificial are the comparisons in sonnet 9 of Stella's face with a building:

> Queen Virtue's Court, which some call Stella's face
> Prepared by Nature's choicest furniture,
> Hath his front built of alabaster pure;
> Gold is the covering of that stately place.

The poem goes on to describe the porches as cheeks, the windows as eyes, and ends on a note of extravagant punning. Such poems are performances; they are contrived, and the pleasure they provide is in the skill and ingenuity, as well as in the humour, of the craftsmanship. However, in contrast to this, sonnet 14 speaks out more plainly - "Alas, have I not pain enough, my friend . . ." and Sidney complains about his mistress' "rhubarb words". In sonnet 24, there is some bitter, personal punning on the word 'rich'. Once again this is a literary device, but the tone is personal. He attacks Penelope's husband, Lord Rich, who does not know the value of the treasure he possesses. The poem is worth quoting in full:

> Rich fools there be whose base and filthy heart
> Lies hatching still the goods wherein they flow,

And damning their own selves to Tantal's smart,
Wealth breeding want, more rich, more wretched grow:
Yet to these fools Heav'n doth such wit impart,
As what their hands do hold, their heads do know,
And knowing love, and loving lay apart
As sacred things, far from all danger's show.
But that rich fool, who by blind fortune's lot
The richest gem of love and life enjoys,
And can with foul abuse such beauties blot;
Let him, deprived of sweet and unfelt joys,
Exil'd for aye from those high treasures which
He knows not, grow in only folly Rich!

Sonnet 28 addresses a real person beginning with "You that with Allegory's curious frame . . ." and continues:

> When I say Stella, I do mean the same
> Princess of beauty, for whose only sake
> The reins of love I love . . .

Sidney then dismisses "hid ways" and ends:

> But know that I in pure simplicity
> Breathe out the flames which burn within my heart,
> Love only reading unto me this art.

This echoes the final line of the first sonnet "Fool, said my Muse to me, look in thy heart, and write". The fact that 'know thyself', and 'look into thyself' were catchphrases of the age does not mean that Sidney was insincere, but it indicates the difficulty one has in getting behind the poetic mask of the accomplished stylist that he was. If one turns to the eighth song, Stella seems real enough, for the lovers meet, and there is a reference to her unsuitable marriage - "her fair neck a foul yoke bare". The language is straightforward, but then one comes across an element of the ridiculous at the picture of the poet on his knees at a temporary loss for words:

> Grant - O me! what am I saying?

and there is artifice in such lines as "Restless rest, and living dying".

Sidney himself is not always concealed behind the mask of Astrophel. In sonnet 30 he refers to the political problem of the Turks, the Dutch, the French and other nations. He also refers to "my father" and to the Ulster administration. One finds that he often shifts his position in the sonnets, which were written over a number of years. He changes his mood and his attitude, and in this he resembles the contemporaries already mentioned in other chapters. He hides behind the poetic identity of Astrophel, and then emerges as himself for a moment, only to retreat again. In general, the early poems are more literary and less personal than those which follow sonnet 33. From then onwards, one senses his genuine frustration. The development is not, however, an even one, and literary elegance occurs for its own sake in some of the later poems.

Sidney was aware that old conventions could inhibit. As early as sonnet 15, he mentions the drawback in imitating Petrarch:

> You that poor Petrarch's long deceased woes
> With new-born sighs and denizen'd wit do sing:
> You take wrong ways; those far-set helps be such
> As do bewray a want of inward touch . . .

He did not always follow his own advice, but even his literary experiments have an individual ring to them. He has a habit of standing back and seeing himself somewhat critically and even with amusement. He is yet another example of a writer who changes posture, identity and viewpoint in the course of writing; but he is an individualist even when he follows the fashion. In the final sonnet, he takes leave of earthly love in favour of spiritual love. This is a commonplace neo-Platonic sentiment, but the phrasing of the sonnet is moving and one senses its personal quality:

> Leave me, O love, which reachest but to dust;
> And thou, my mind, aspire to higher things;
> Grow rich in that which never taketh rust;
> Whatever fades, but fading pleasure brings.

So far the statement is not out of the ordinary, but then he goes on to use phrases in a more personal way:

> Draw in thy beams, and humble all thy might
> To that sweet yoke, where lasting freedoms be;
> Which breaks the clouds, and opens forth the light
> That both doth shine, and give us sight to see.
> O take fast hold; let that light be thy guide
> In this small course which birth draws out to death,
> And think how evil becometh him to slide,
> Who seeketh heav'n, and comes of heav'nly breath.
> Then farewell, world; thy uttermost I see:
> Eternal Love, maintain the Life in me.

It is interesting to turn for a moment to the poems of his friend Greville, who is a very different writer, but one who displays once again the Elizabethan tendency to alter posture. Greville wrote a sequence called *Gaelica*, expressing variations on a theme. The early poems have Petrarch in mind, but later a plainer style emerges and he tries to think through his verse. The style may sometimes be plain, but it is rarely simple. It can be tortuous, for Greville did not find it easy to express intellectual concepts in poetic form. He was not as skilled as Sidney in conceptualizing images, but when he is at his best he breaks through the conventional mould, like Sidney, and expresses a personal sense of urgency. Once he abandons models, his style has a terse individual quality with a flavour of its own.

Sidney's elusive identity hovers in the background when one reads the *Arcadia*. But even in the *Apology for Poetry*, a serious critical work which made Sidney one of the foremost, literary theorists of his time in England, he is not entirely himself. Sincerity and artifice are again intertwined in this work. He defends poetry, praising its educative quality; and as this is undoubtedly his belief he expresses his own view, even if he bases it on Classical authority. But he also plays a role. His essay is a response to a challenge; a form of literary jousting by which he hopes to unseat his opponent. His opponent was Stephen Gosson, whose *School of Abuse* supported Puritan attacks on poetry and drama. Occasionally the tone, and the formation of the arguments, recall old disputations in which the author presented his brief like a barrister at the bar. Few of Sidney's ideas are original. The notion of preserving dramatic unities can be found in Scalinger, and the concept of the poet as creator is expressed in Horace. The form of essay, known as the *Apology*, was used by Lodge and Puttenham. In his *Apology* Sidney puts forward arguments that already had currency.

The Elizabethans were adept plunderers of approved sources and Sidney was no exception. His essay owes much to Aristotle and to others. Yet when this has been said, the arrangement of ideas and their presentation are strikingly individual. If the seeds were borrowed the result was his own creation, and the *Apology* stands as a unique contribution to the literature of the age. As in the sonnets, sometimes genuine feeling comes through. At one point he almost gets carried away when he likens the poet to a divine creator:

> Only the Poet . . . lifted up with the vigour of his own invention, doth grow in effect another nature, in making things either better than Nature bringeth forth, or, quite anew, forms such as never were in Nature . . .

He draws back a little when he denies the perfection of the poet because of Man's fall from Grace.

> . . . our erected wit maketh us know what perfection is, and yet our infected will keepeth us from reaching unto it.

Nevertheless, the 'purifying wit' may

> . . . draw us to as high a perfection as our degenerate souls, made worse by their clayey lodgings, can be capable of . . .[4]

The aim of the *Apology* is clear, however, and the direction of Sidney's thought evident. This cannot be said of the *Arcadia*. In this work, Sidney changes his aim and his position as he continues revision, and his moods vary. As with other authors already mentioned in previous chapters, the opening of new perspectives, together with the claims of old traditions and early influences, may have caused uncertainty of vision and contradictions in thought. There were several influences at work in him. His immediate debt is to Armadis de Gaule by de Lobeira, from whom he took the bare bones of his romance story, and from Heliodorus' *Aethiopica*. Heliodorus also provided a love story and the structure of his work may have influenced Sidney. He expressed multiple points of view in his epic to deepen the interest of the reader, even when they blurred the consistency of the story. Sidney followed this tendency, and one knows from speculative thinkers like Bruno that awareness of multiple perspectives, and of life's rich contradictions, was in the air. In the *Aethiopica* there is a middle section, containing involved sequences and several hold-ups in the narrative to create suspense, which reminds one of the somewhat 'out of place' sections in the *Arcadia*. At the end of the Greek romance, the ravelled plot is untied by the device of a dramatic incident. This type of device is used in the *Arcadia*.

There were also examples of romance tales from Spain and Italy to follow. The Spanish writer Montemayor, who wrote sequences of pastoral love stories, interspersed with songs called *Diana*, is one obvious influence. Lyrics are, of course, scattered throughout Sidney's book. The title, and general form of the work, was taken from Sanazzaro's *Arcadia*. Ariosto's *Orlando Furioso*, with its strange stories of love and adventure - and which also had multiple and inter-connected plots - would also have appealed to Sidney. Ariosto makes frequent use of disguise, and of the device of mistaken identity. His wry humour would surely have amused Sidney.

Ariosto, in his romance, addresses himself openly to the reader as the narrator. From time to time, he speaks out with comments on the characters or the story. He adds a new dimension when he points out the ridiculous side to a situation. His identity as author is clear. He is in control of his fanciful material. There are some interesting insights into human behaviour and psychology, but the serious elements are not overstressed. Modern romance and old-fashioned chivalry blend well together. Sidney may have had Ariosto in mind when he began to write his romance, for he, too, tries to blend romance and chivalry. He, too, sometimes looks with amusement on his characters, and in the first version of the *Arcadia* he comments as a narrator in the guise of Philisides, a melancholy knight who disguises himself as a shepherd. Like Ariosto, Sidney uses disguise to complicate the story, create suspense and to indicate a problem in defining human identity. However, in depicting changes in personality, and in probing the workings of the mind, he goes deeper than Ariosto. On the other hand, he is not so much in control of his material.

There were many other influences on Sidney, and altogether they may have overwhelmed him. He is an example of the Elizabethan tendency to absorb avidly diverse, and sometimes contradictory influences and at the same time to strive to create an individual piece of work and to speak with one's own voice. The influences are too many to mention, but among the classical models was Vergil, whose Aeneas was tested, like Sidney's Princes, through various vicissitudes. Sidney regarded the *Aeneid*, as did his contemporaries, as an allegory of the development of a leader. In his *Apology* he wrote:

> Only let Aeneas be worn in the tablet of your memory, how he governeth himself in the ruin of his country, in the preserving of his old father, and carrying away his religious ceremonies, in obeying God's commandment to leave Dido . . .[5]

Some romances written in Europe give one a sense of travelling in a surrealist world of fantasy in which heroes experience purification through adventure. They may lose their identity temporarily in the new world of discovery (Orlando lost his wits in Ariosto's tale), but they recover on returning to the real world. The theme of the quest, so important in Malory's and Spenser's works, may not be obvious in the *Arcadia*, but in the revised version one does get the impression that Sidney's Princes are striving to attain ideals, and that the difficulties they experience will educate them to play a better part in life when they return to their own country. A sense of character maturation is present in Sidney's work.

157

The numerous influences on Sidney may well have contributed to the changes of mood and posture which occur in his work. Stories of chivalry alternate with stories of love. Stories in the manner of 'exempla' intrude; the tone changes from the light-hearted to the serious and one is not always certain of the main theme. Some have therefore seen the *Arcadia* as a romance with heroic elements, and others as a series of heroic tales set in a pastoral setting. The fact that Sidney did not complete his revision contributes to the difficulty in choosing a critical perspective.

It would seem that the *Arcadia* was first planned as a prose romance in five acts with pastoral eclogues to provide welcome breaks in the narrative. Some of the poems scattered throughout the work were literary experiments, and nowadays one may feel that they clog the narrative rather than provide relief. As time went on, Sidney became dissatisfied with what he had described in a letter as a 'toyful book' - a trifle written to please his sister and a few friends, a book to while away the time. He then began to recast it along more serious lines. He broke up the original version, added several martial or heroic episodes, gave up the idea of strict chronology by introducing 'flashbacks' and reminders, and made intricate connections between the new stories and the basic narrative. The complex world as seen by Bruno, with its multiple choices, paradoxes, contraries, and subtle inter-relationships - but without its transcendentalism - is reflected in the *Arcadia*.

The revision was never completed and Greville reports that on Sidney's death he requested the book to be burned. However, soon after his death there was a rumour of a possible publication and in order to forestall this, Greville allowed an editor to publish the revised papers he had in his possession. This was in three books. The edition contained textual errors and was not regarded as satisfactory by Sidney's sister, the Countess of Pembroke, who permitted another edition to be published. The work was expanded into five books.

The plot in the additional books was taken from the original and unrevised version, so that the new edition was something of an amalgam. The *Arcadia* proved popular in England and abroad and had considerable influence. Shakespeare took the sub-plot of Gloucester and his sons in *King Lear* from one of the tales, and

John Hoskyns and others regarded Sidney's style as a model of rhetorical usage. Greville, in his *Life*, states that Sidney's aims were serious and far-reaching, and he was obviously speaking of the partially revised work. He points out that the *Arcadia* does not do its author justice as it was his "unpolished embrio" . . .

> . . . yet that they were scribbled rather as pamphlets, for the entertainment of time and friends, than any accompt of himself to the world . . .

He adds that "his end was not writing", but moulding himself for a virtuous life. One recalls Spenser's educative aims and Sidney's view in the *Apology* that art is educative. However, in making his original romance into a serious work he jeopardized the clarity of his intention and the unity of the work.

The main plot of the *Arcadia* is simple, if extravagant. Two noble young men, Pyrocles and Musidorus, survive a shipwreck and find themselves in the land of Arcadia. The country is ruled by a King called Basilius, who is troubled by an oracular warning that his daughters and his kingdom are in danger. He is told that one daughter will "embrace an uncouth love", the other will be stolen from him, and that he will commit adultery with his own wife.[6] Furthermore his kingdom will be invaded. His counsellor, Philanax, advises him to face up to these dangers and not to abandon his responsibilities, but he decides to retreat into the country where he guards his family as if in prison. Philanax is left in charge of the nation in his absence. The abdication of responsibility was a theme which interested the Elizabethans. It occurs in *Gorboduc*, *King Lear* and in other dramas. Basilius plainly deserts his post.

Arriving in Arcadia Pyrocles falls in love with the picture of one of the King's daughters, Philoclea. This is a tribute to the power of art. Pyrocles gradually sinks into apathy, craving solitude. He becomes the epitome of the sick lover. His friend Musidorus finds him in this condition and criticizes his effeminate behaviour. An interesting debate ensues. Pyrocles puts the case for freedom of the spirit and for the whole enterprise of love, but Musidorus claims that love has eroded personality and destroyed the individual spirit. Sidney seems to be serious when regarding love as a

159

disease which undermines identity. At a later stage Musidorus also falls in love, and although he is less unbalanced than his friend by the experience, he resorts, like Pyrocles, to dubious tricks to achieve his ends. Both Princes make the mistake of stooping to deceit and to the doubtful use of disguise. If at first they achieve success, their acts rebound upon them and repercussions follow which are nearly disastrous. Musidorus falls in love with Basilius' other daughter, Pamela. Love, in both cases, motivates behaviour which is morally questionable.

In order to gain access to the King's country fortress the Princes disguise themselves; Musidorus as a simple shepherd, and Pyrocles as a woman so that he can attend Philoclea as a maidservant. This comic reversal of the convention by which women appear as boys or men (although boy actors took the part of women on the stage) is sometimes treated with humorous playfulness by Sidney; for example, when the sexual desire of Pyrocles is awakened as Philoclea is bathing and when the absurdity of Pyrocles' position as an imitation female is evident when he is pursued by King Basilius who thinks he is a woman. This humour may recall Ariosto's wry asides, but since Sidney treats the disguise theme seriously when considering the effects on the psychology of Pyrocles himself - his personal relationships and the reactions of others - the playful touches of humour seem a little odd. There is no problem of adjustment with Ariosto as there is with Sidney.

As in some of Shakespeare's plays, disguise begins as a simple deceit, but it creates situations which cause grave problems. Deception leads to further deception and eventually to a tangled web of distrust. When Pyrocles pretends to be an Amazon, Musidorus is concerned that his integrity will be undermined and that he will lose his essential manliness. Pyrocles asserts the claims of emotion against the cold claims of reason. If reason seems to win out in argument, one must recall the almost inhuman nature of reasonable men in other parts of the *Arcadia*. Pyrocles' father, Evarchus, who appears at the end of the work as the model of a just and honest ruler in contrast to Basilius, does not escape lack of sympathy for his rigorous attitude to the law when he supports the appalling sentence which the local law demands from his own son. Legality and justice seem at odds when the former is not tempered

160

by mercy (reason tempered by emotion); a point which emerges in *The Merchant of Venice.*

The tribulations which beset the Princes are not only due to the deceptions they employ, but to errors of judgement on their part. Other characters, too, are subject to criticism for trying to evade the consequences of their actions. Sidney's work, which began as a 'toyful book' develops as it goes along, and is revised, into studies of human conduct in the face of difficult responsibilities. People who pursue their own desires regardless of consequences are defeated in their aims by the turn of events and by the reactions of others. Pyrocles and Musidorus experience the paradoxes of life and cannot always reconcile the contradictions which arise in their minds. Perhaps this was true of Sidney.

Philoclea and Pamela are also confused in complicated situations when the taking of a decision could cause a conflict of loyalties. Philoclea is presented as pure and innocent, but cannot prevent the strength of her feelings for her so-called maid-servant. She has "whole squadrons of longings" which puzzle her. When the Princes gain access to Basilius' fortress the story makes some strange twists. Basilius is attracted to the disguised Pyrocles and uses his daughter as a go-between. This distresses her, but she feels obliged to obey her father. She is also concerned by the puzzling fact that her mother seems to be attracted to Pyrocles; for she is unaware that her mother, Gynaecia, has discovered the man beneath the disguise. Such relationship situations would normally be the basis of comedy - or the basis of a light romance, or 'toyful book' - and Sidney casts an amused glance at them from time to time, but the general handling is serious, and he indicates the play of conscious and unconscious motive with subtlety. Moral implications are of concern, although there is no preaching to the reader.

Pursued by both Basilius and Gynaecia, Pyrocles tries to escape by further deceit. He promises both his pursuers a secret midnight meeting at the same time. Basilius consequently meets his wife in the dark, thinking she is Pyrocles. His wife, too, thinks she is confronted with Pyrocles. Basilius seduces his hidden 'mistress' and therefore one of the oracle's prophecies is fulfilled. When they discover their mistake the King and Queen are filled with remorse. Gynaecia, in spite of her uncontrolled lust, is a person with a conscience. She recognizes her weakness and is distressed by her actions. She does not seem able to help herself, but like a tragic figure in drama she eventually shows strength and courage by openly confessing her faults and welcoming the punishment of death. She is portrayed with skill and is one of Sidney's more interesting conceptions. In her, passion is a disruptive force. Her remorse is increased when her husband drinks by mistake a drugged potion prepared by her, and appears to drop down dead.

Musidorus insinuates himself into Pamela's good graces as a shepherd in attendance. She shows no special interest in him at first, but as he flirts with her attendant, Mopsa, her interest quickens and she discovers a "second meaning" in his statements. When she discovers his identity she reciprocates his love. He then plans to escape with her. The idea is to beseige the fortress and also to help Pyrocles who eventually finds himself arrested. The oracle's prophecy is taking shape: one daughter to be stolen and the other engaged in an unseemly relationship, an 'uncouth love'. In the background to these strange events is a growing rebellion in the kingdom, for in the absence of Basilius from the seat of government the country has become unstable. The irresponsibility and excess of passion in the minds and hearts of leading figures is parallelled by similar disorders among the King's subjects.

There are many parallels and analogies in the *Arcadia*. The lusts which affect the King and Queen are parallelled by the surges of desire which affect Pyrocles and Musidorus, and which also affect the rebels who are greedy for gain. At one stage in the story Pyrocles sees Philoclea lying almost naked on a bed and is in danger of "quite forgetting himself". In the first unrevised draft Pyrocles and Philoclea make love before trying to leave the kingdom. In the revised version this is not permitted, and Philoclea argues with her lover about his intentions to "inveigle my simplicity". He does not therefore sleep with her but only near her; nevertheless he is discovered in what appears to be a compromising situation by a servant. This leads to his arrest. Once again desire is frustrated, and deceit brings punishment. Musidorus, too, has his setbacks. He escapes with Pamela into the country. They sleep in the open and Musidorus barely resists what would have amounted to rape if he had been successful in obtaining his desire.[7] A group of local dis-

sidents find them in their resting place, and after a fight Musidorus
is captured. Sidney describes Musidorus' desire to make love to
Pamela as follows:

> At what time she was in a shrewd likelihood, to have
> had a great part of her trust in Musidorus deceived, and
> found herself robbed of that which she laid in store, as
> her dearest Jewel, so did her own beauties enforce a
> force against herself.

Once again the narrator emerges as an identity with this comment.

In the land of Arcadia matters come to a head when the
King's men discover that Basilius is found dead, poisoned by his
wife, Pamela has been abducted, and Philoclea has a tender relationship with a very much altered 'Amazon'. Pyrocles' passionate
nature throws him into despair and he even contemplates suicide
in the hope that this might relieve Philoclea of any disgrace. Philoclea persuades him to give up the idea. Several pages follow on the
subject of suicide. The arguments are well sustained on either side,
although they hardly fit the mouths of the characters. The virtue
of courage in dying by one's own hand is set against the virtue of
self-control. It is argued that we have control over our own bodies,
but Philoclea feels that the rights of God prevail; in any case she
points out that suicide would not give her peace of mind for she
would continue to feel responsible for her lover's death. At the
end of this debate Philanax enters. He is at first torn between respect for Pyrocles, who had previously faced an angry mob and
addressed them in firm tones, calming their anger against authority.
On the other hand, he cannot get over the fact that Pyrocles seduced the King's daughter and contributed to his death. He impris-
ons Pyrocles who has to await trial.

Debates on serious matters like suicide, free will, and the
place of reason, may seem artificial and contrived when they issue
from the lips of characters like Philoclea, but they do arise out of
the situations which develop. The type of argument, as distinct
from the style of utterance, is not out of character, for Sidney had
a sense of individual differences. He was not a dramatist, and his
characters rarely speak like real people, but he was interested in

probing minds and motives. He indicates that people are not to be taken at face value and characters are contrasted with each other. Pyrocles is contrasted with the less complicated Musidorus, and Philoclea's temperament with that of the tougher Pamela. Basilius is contrasted with Evarchus, who later takes over his kingdom temporarily. Situations are parallelled and contrasted to throw light on their implications and they are seen from different viewpoints.

The additional stories in the revision, add to the contrasts and parallels and deepen our knowledge of some of the characters. The epic role of the heroes is more noticeable and they display more courage. There are examples of prowess in horsemanship and episodes which feature maidens in distress. The noble education of the heroes is outlined in a series of flash-backs, and the need emerges for them to learn and develop intellectual and moral virtue through an active and stressful life. Just as Aeneas learns from his travels and adventures, so must the heroes of the *Arcadia*. New episodes place them in ambiguous roles as knight errants. It is found that the exercise of some virtues may be opposed to others: the story of the Queen of Erona illustrates this.

This Queen is enamoured of an unworthy man, Antiphilus. She is loved by another, a leader called Tiridates, who invades her territory to take her. This invasion makes the heroes decide to come to her assistance. They kill her enemy and restore Antiphilus to her. Unfortunately his influence is not good for the realm, and thus it happens that for the best of motives the knight errants have supported a dubious cause. This kind of paradox came to interest Sidney, and the story of Plangus offers another example of conflicting values. Prince Plangus falls in love with the wife of one of his subjects, Andromana. The King, his father, therefore sends him away to do battle. Andromana then loses her husband and as a widow decides to win the favours of the King himself. The King proves weak and pliant and she dominates him. However, when Plangus returns from battle Andromana tries to renew her former love affair with him. Plangus, out of loyalty to his father, resists her. Having been spurned, she plots revenge and poisons the King's mind against his son. Plangus is finally sentenced to death, but escapes. He becomes involved in Erona's affairs and finally seeks the advice of Evarchus.

164

Authority is shown in a bad light in some of these stories, for it acts harshly and unwisely. But youth is also shown to be foolish, and turns in the end to a father figure. Sidney's attitude to authority is ambivalent. He upholds it on the one hand, while on the other he shows how it can be mistaken and tyrannical. He is not without sympathy for the rebels in Arcadia, although the need for their suppression is obvious. As Philanax is unable to cope with the forces of dissidence he calls on the assistance of a neighbouring ruler, Evarchus, to take over. In other words, he invites the invasion of another power. Evarchus quells the rebellion, but realizes he is in a difficult position as a foreigner when asked to sit in judgement on those brought before him. The local laws are harsh, but he decides he must abide by them. At this stage he does not know that the two people who are accused of betraying King Basilius and of contributing to his death are, in fact, his own son and noble friend, in disguise. When he learns the truth, he struggles with his grief, but decides that a sentence of death must stand. The trial scene in the *Arcadia* is the climax of the work.

Sidney's thoughts on rebellion are open to interpretation. He seems to believe in political stability based on good law and a strong magistracy, but he does not condemn rebellion outright. Like many of his age, he portrays the mob as crude and distasteful, but he has some sympathy for rebel causes. One wonders whether he would have been more sympathetic if rebellion against tyranny or weak rule had been carried out by noble leaders? He did at one time play with the idea of promoting a league of Protestant leaders to set Europe on the right course, and there was a theory circulated amongst some Huguenots that rebellion could, in extreme cases, be justifiable. Sidney does not commit himself to any political theory, although the issues he brings before us, raise certain questions in our minds. Evarchus may be right in dealing out his harsh sentences, but the audience at the trial show feelings of compassion for the victims and in the end some means has to be found to prevent legality suppressing justice.

It is interesting that a new character called Amphialus is introduced in the revised version, and his name suggests ambiguity. He seeks to justify rebellion on the grounds that loyalty to a country may be of higher value than personal loyalty to a ruler. Amphialus also implies that good government depends on a group of leaders rather than upon a single individual. These arguments are not pursued as the narrative develops, and no conclusion is reached. The thoughts are simply placed before us. Amphialus' real role is that of a feudal type of knight, urged into action by the passion of love. He is active, but manages to fall into a series of errors. He is not a character whose judgement we would trust.

Sidney's work provides many different perspectives and problems of identity. On quite a different plane, personal loyalty is given a high value. The two Princes confirm their loyalty to each other while awaiting trial. They blame themselves, deny involvement in the murder of the King, and defend their lovers from criticism. Gynaecia discovers a loyalty to her dead husband, and her true identity. She cuts short the angry, almost railing, prosecution of Philanax by accusing herself in open court and creating some compassion in the audience. Philanax is, of course, loyal to the dead King, but in his case it is arguable that his loyalty is overdone, since it clouds his mind and is based on passion only. Evarchus, refusing to let sentiment overwhelm him, finds Gynaecia guilty and condemns her to be buried alive with her husband - a sentence which she accepts and almost welcomes.

The case against the Princes raises some interesting points. It is claimed that they are not subject to local laws as foreigners, and as Princes they could request diplomatic privilege (an idea incidently that was expressed long before the Geneva Convention!). The claim is promptly denied. It is said that foreigners must learn and then obey the laws and customs of the land they visit, and that Princes, in the situation that Pyrocles and Musidorus find themselves, should be regarded as "private men" who offend against the "laws of nations". The idea that there is a natural law to which all people, including the monarch, are subject, had been debated in England and in Europe. There is an analogy with the concept of "natural justice" which exists in our own day. Sidney would have been interested in the different views expressed in his time.[8] Evarchus deals with this point by stating that the Princes, through the use of disguise and by their actions, have deprived themselves of any respect due to their rank. Philanax goes further, stating that disguise is deceit and their assumption of a false identity is an immoral act. He points out that Pyrocles forced his way into the bedroom of Philoclea so that he and his companion might take over the State - to seize "into their treacherous hands the regiment of this mighty province". He accused Pyrocles of "killing of the father, dishonouring the mother and ravishing the child".[9]

The trial scene in Book V is dramatic, the arguments strongly presented, and the reader is often held in suspense. A letter from Pamela is read out in court, the gist of which is to state that Musidorus has noble status and is worthy to be her husband. She claims that he has done no wrong other than consorting with her. Philanax contests this angrily. Musidorus produces a spirited defence, describing Philanax as a false accuser and praising Pamela for her virtue. He also points out that he and his friend have done the State some service in fighting the rebels. Both Princes deny complicity in murder, the blame for which is accepted by Gynaecia.

Evarchus accepts their guilt after weighing the arguments. He decides that local laws must be upheld, even if the punishment is death. He holds to this view even when he later learns that Pyrocles is his son in disguise.

> No, no, Pyrocles and Musidorus, I prefer you much before my own life, but I prefer Justice as far before you: When you did like yourselves my body should willingly have been your shield, but I cannot keep you from the effects of your own doing. Nay I cannot in this case acknowledge you for mine, for never had I shepherd to my nephew, nor never had woman to my son, your vices have degraded you from being princes and have disannulled your birthright".

He adds that they have caused a father "to rob himself of his children".

Musidorus criticizes the hard-heartedness of the judgement and pleads for the life of Pyrocles before his own. In turn Pyrocles pleads for his friend. Even Philanax is moved at this point, but Evarchus "that felt his own misery more than they, yet loved goodness more than himself" insists that the law be carried out.

The developments in the trial scene are important because they show clearly how Sidney brings an element of high seriousness into the light-hearted romance he had originally set himself to write. The trial occurs in the original version, before revision, and this suggests that by the end of his work, Sidney had already changed his views as an author and felt it necessary to go back to the beginning to revise. The arguments and issues in the trial of the Princes raise questions which particularly interested the Elizabethans. Indeed, they remind us of trials which actually took place or were under discussion - such as that of Mary Stuart. The responsibilities of rulers, of subjects, of judges, and the place of mercy in the giving of judgements, were themes which are expressed elsewhere. One also recalls Sidney's comment on privilege when reminded of Oxford's superior status in the tennis court quarrel.

Obviously the *Arcadia* could not end with the death of the Princes and of Gynaecia. There is therefore a contrived ending. No sooner has Evarchus delivered judgement than the supposedly dead Basilius revives from his coma. He revives in front of the court, accepts his share of the blame for all that has happened, forgives his wife and the Princes, and finally consents to the marriage of his daughters. And so all ends happily. But does it?

It is of course common for romances to have contrived endings. Heliodorus was one of several models, and later Shakespeare was to use the coming to life device in the *Winter's Tale*. Yet Sidney's ending is notably unsatisfactory. During the trial scene, we have grown accustomed to distancing ourselves from the frivolous world of romance, and feel too suddenly dismissed from the new world of serious thoughts and actions - a world in which questions raised are not always resolved. And it is not only in the trial scene that themes emerge which give rise to problems which are not resolved. There is a curious episode in the revised version which describes the capture of the Princesses by the evil Queen Cecropia, who tries to corrupt them. She tempts with ideas and persuasive arguments, and puts the Princesses through a form of mental torture. The Princesses, however, exhibit in different ways the qualities of constancy and courage; Philoclea through her steadfast innocence and purity and Pamela through her staunch counter arguments. The episode is long and the debates sometimes tedious. They express a gloomy outlook and the Queen is rather a contrived figure of evil.

At one point, Cecropia stages a mock execution of Philoclea, and this is seen from afar by Pyrocles and taken for the real thing. This causes one of his attempts at suicide - an attempt which he bungles. Cecropia's son is the Amphialus, already mentioned, and he falls in love with Philoclea, which complicates matters. He knows that he should try to set free the two Princesses, for unlike his mother, he has good instincts, but he is worried about losing Philoclea if she is not confined. He therefore wavers and does nothing. He is a character who knows what is right, but is unable to create opportunities for himself to act correctly. He waits until he is forced to act by circumstances which then conspire against him and corner him. He proves to be a courageous fighter when he eventually acts, but he suffers from a deficient Will. He is therefore prone to accident, and becomes the unwilling cause of several disasters, including the death of his own mother. She leaps to her death under the mistaken assumption that her son is arriving to punish her.

In the wavering Amphialus, Sidney shows once again his psychological skill in depicting character, and in showing how temperament may create social, moral, and political problems. Nevertheless, this skill does not prevent one from feeling that the captivity episode is somewhat tangential to the development of the narrative, at the point where it is introduced. It is possible that Sidney wished to draw more attention to the characters of the Princesses, since the emphasis is elsewhere on Pyrocles and his companion, or that he wished to re-examine moral problems, touched upon in other parts of the book from new angles. Whatever the reason, the captivity episode does not dovetail easily into the existing structure. Tone and attitude change noticeably; comic and ironic elements are abandoned in favour of a gloomy episode with long moral arguments, and when there is a return to the story of the Princes, there is a feeling of an emotional jolt.

The tendency to review themes from different angles is evident throughout the *Arcadia*. Love, in its various aspects, is a basic theme. Its general effect is to unbalance character and to weaken the Will, although there are examples, too, of the improving qualities of virtuous love. There is a strong implication that when passion has sway over reason, dangerous repercussions follow. The distress caused by love, features more than its pleasures. The Eclogues, which provide a commentary on love, almost portray a world which is sick with emotion; or else love is seen as "an old false knave". The stories of Erona and Plangus do not show love in an attractive light. In Book III, the ravages due to love are taken further and it is seen that there is an effect upon the public. The lusts of Basilius and Gynaecia cause them to abandon their duties. Love also causes disloyalty and disobedience, and it reduces the Princes to deceitful practices. In the fourth Eclogue which follows Book IV, marriage is recommended as a solution to the problems inflicted by love on mankind:

> Marry therefore, for marriage will destroy,
> Those passions which to youthful head do climb;
> Mothers and nurses of all vain annoy.[10]

There is another perspective, however, and that is the example of courtly love, as inherited through literary tradition. Love is then a form of service rather than a sexual relationship. The loved one, although capable of showing tenderness, is not portrayed as having sexual passions. This tradition influences some of the writing in Sidney's *Arcadia*, although he does not avoid mention of the physical side of ordinary love. Reference to the physical side of love also had its traditions in literature. It could be bawdy as in Boccaccio or Chaucer, or it could be referred to in a humorous vein, and then fine ladies sometimes came in for comment. Sidney tackles his love themes from many angles. Such variations of approach, and changes in tone and viewpoint, are not untypical of Elizabethan writers as we have seen from previous chapters.

The revision of the *Arcadia* obviously complicated the perspectives. Flashbacks to the early lives of the Princes, and the additional stories inserted at a later stage, were presumably intended to provide deeper insights and further examples which could throw light on issues raised elsewhere; and there was the example of Heliodorus to follow. Multiple plots provide contrasts and paradoxes, and they induce one to ponder on relative values. It is a cause for concern when certain qualities which are good in themselves lose some of their value when set against higher values. In some contexts, values contradict each other and choice becomes difficult. Thus, the admirable quality of loyalty becomes tarnished if it results in action which is immoral when seen from another point of view. Disobedience may gain credit if it is used in support of distress or to fight tyranny. Reason is a desirable quality in most circumstances, but it can become inhuman. Passion, which leads to so much turmoil, may sometimes be a spur to virtuous action.

In a literary world of ideas, in which there were many cross-currents of medieval and renaissance thought, it was not easy to create a workable hierarchy of values. There were too many yard-sticks: the changing views of the Church, the divergent ideas of new thinkers, and the teachings of one's own experience. It may have seemed at times, in such a world, that the solution of one set of problems resulted in the growth of other problems of a differ-ent nature. Inconsistencies and paradoxes were bound to occur and human relationships were seen to be more complicated than before. It is possible that Sidney was influenced by some of the ideas put forward by Giordano Bruno, who was himself influenced by ideas discussed in the academies of Europe. John Dee was briefly Sidney's tutor and may have made an impression on him. One detects little of the transcendentalism of the Hermetists in Sidney's work, but problems related to personal identity and to the establishment of absolutes are raised. The discovery of new perspectives, as Bruno knew, created problems of choice and of taking a position on life. The world of politics had also become complicated. Some of Jean Bodin's[11] views may have reached Sidney; such as his notion of a limited form of monarchy and of the way in which intelligent people, even of diverse faiths, may live together and practice tolerance. Bodin did not approve of reb-ellion, although he accepted that a Prince might interfere on behalf of the oppressed subjects of another State, just as Evarchus did.

Sidney saw conflict in abstract terms even though he told the story in the form of human action. He was not a masterly creator of characters as were some of the dramatists. He was, however, interested in the human heart and mind, and his people in the *Arcadia* are more than mere types drawn in outline to represent ideas. Amphialus is drawn with skill, and his other characters are interestingly contrasted. Temperaments are more carefully delin-

171

eated in the revised version in which it is pointed out that there is "more sweetness in Philoclea, but more majesty in Pamela".[12] Pamela is shown to be rational and strong, but not without heart. She is the true Amazon while Pyrocles is the false. Pyrocles displays, however, a sensitivity and an impulsiveness often associated with the female temperament, and his type of beauty almost suggests a female quality. The subtlety with which Sidney delineates his characters shows that he was not constrained by theories of the 'humours' any more than were the writers of drama. If Sidney's characters do not resemble real people then, and if they sometimes speak the language of rhetoric, they are more than embodiments of ideas.

The polythematic structure of the revised version of the *Arcadia* presents many contrasting and parallel issues which are not always resolved. Inconsistencies emerge, paradoxes are indicated and several perspectives are opened up. Some of the contrasts and parallels can be illustrated in note form:

Passion and Reason: Contrasts are shown in the hearts and minds of individuals and also in the conduct of affairs of State - e.g. in the trial scene. Passion is a major force in human affairs, and is often, although not always, a destructive force.

Love and Desire: A distinction is frequently made. The effects of lust are indicated in various episodes e.g. the infidelities of Basilius and Gynaecia. On the other hand, Ourania and Parthenia represent a kind of spiritual love, and Argalus loves Parthenia even when she is disfigured.

Knowledge and Activity: Knowledge and wisdom are shown as important, but excessive study and introversion may lead to melancholy. The melancholy person, like Pyrocles when he faces the first onslaught of love, is often at odds with society. Greville maintained that the *Arcadia* was meant to teach, through the knowledge of example, the way to a virtuous life. Knowledge did not necessarily of itself lead to virtuous action. Gynaecia and Cecropia are knowledgeable. Philoclea is hardly knowledgeable, but her virtue is based on innocence and instinct. Is it possible, however,

172

to rely upon instinct when human instincts have been corrupted since the Fall? Is there an innate goodness? Some of the characters in the book illustrate the view that 'self knowledge' is an important aim. Are the pursuits of knowledge and of the active life opposed to each other in some contexts? Does one choose the Quill or the Lance?

Nature and Art: Art may be seen as something contrived. It may give pleasure, but it may also be regarded with suspicion. Nature suggests purity and simplicity. Simplicity, however, can be contrived. Parthenia's beauty is natural and unadorned . . . "so far from all art that it was full of carelessness", but Sidney adds ". . . unless that carelessness itself (in spite of itself) grew artificial".[13] And simplicity is not always enough. Sidney had a high view of the function of art, as one knows from the *Apology*, but he had some reservations about its use. How far was the *Arcadia* meant to teach, as Greville expected it to do, and how far did the original intention remain of distracting and pleasing the reader?

Pleasure and Virtue: The reconciliation of pleasure and virtue was a Renaissance concern, especially when dealing with love.

Authority and Rebellion: This might also read *authority and liberty*. Sidney had some sympathy with aspirations for freedom and action, and was himself constrained under Elizabeth. He refused to subject himself to Oxford. In one of his letters he wrote: ". . . I see a picture of the age in which we live, an age that resembles a bow long bent, it must be unstrung or it will break". Authority is often shown in a poor light in the *Arcadia*, and the political story is one of weak government, avoidance of responsibility, selfish desire, and the effects of the resultant rebellion. In the revised version, there is a greater emphasis on the need for authority and for self-control; but the need is for good authority and sound justice. Tyranny is not supported, but neither is mob action. Rebellion is not condemned outright.

Justice and Mercy: Problems concerning justice are bound up with the question of authority. Some readers have felt uneasy at the operation of justice in the trial scene. Some have seen the contrived

173

ending, when Basilius recovers and forgives, as an example of the working of Divine Providence. Sidney refers to Divine Providence when Pyrocles is captured and when it is stated "that by the unlikliest means greatest matters may come to conclusion; that human reason may be the more humbled, and more wittingly give place to divine providence". But there is no clear thesis on Providence running through the work, and such a view is not dominant in the trial scene. Loyalty is a theme which may run counter to the operation of justice.

Male and Female Qualities: Ideals of manhood are contrasted with ideals of womanhood, but some women have so-called manly qualities, while some men have female qualities. Transvestism was a common device, but Sidney uses disguise to bring out personality traits and to raise questions about traditional sexual roles. Jonson and Shakespeare also use disguise to probe psychology, and to raise questions.

Constancy and Change: Constancy of purpose and loyalty are prime virtues in the *Arcadia*, but as the world is subject to change, adaptability may sometimes be as important as steadfastness. The Elizabethans were concerned about the effects of change, or mutability, and yearned for permanence in a decaying world. Spenser, Shakespeare and Raleigh reflect this concern too. It was important to hold onto absolutes, if possible, and constancy was a virtue. However, one is led in the *Arcadia* towards the idea that values which are sound in certain contexts, may be less sound in others. Some values seem relative.

Chivalry and Politics: The ideals of chivalry were not dead. His descriptions of knightly battles are detailed and enthusiastic, but he was likely to be aware that one could not fight real battles in the old ways, and that private affairs of honour might have to be subordinated to larger considerations. Sidney's quarrel with the Earl of Oxford and the manner of his death after Zutphen, suggest something of the old world of chivalry, but when Argalus is drawn into bloody battle with the resultant sacrifice of Parthagenia, because of "tyranny of honour," one is led to question the need.

Political considerations of the age made some former attitudes outdated. Falstaff questioned 'honour', and although we are not meant to agree with him, he was expressing a possible point of view, albeit in an amusing way.

The above themes are among many which raise in our minds ideas of contrasts and parallels, and sometimes irreconcilable viewpoints. Philosophical categories overlap or shade into each other. We may detect a bias in Sidney's thinking, but there is no definite thesis apart from that of the troubles caused by love. Intellectual arguments arise from time to time, but are set in contexts of ambiguity, and as an author, he frequently glances to one side or looks backwards when presenting a story. It is difficult to discover patterns of clear meaning, and the style in which the *Arcadia* is written does not help. It can be straightforward, but more often it is complicated and ornate.

Sidney's fascination with contrasts and paradoxes is reflected in his manner of writing prose. Sentences are constructed in sets of balanced clauses, or in the form of antitheses. The influence of older schools of rhetoric is evident, and the way in which arguments are put before us reminds us of the dialectic of schoolmen. Phrases are arranged for their elegance or wit rather than to convey clear meaning. Given Sidney's tendency to portray contrasting or parallel situations, he would have been easily tempted into stylistic niceties. Aristotle gave support to balancing contrary points of view in argument, but the *Arcadia* does not present a thesis like the *Apology*, and Sidney's balanced phrases are elegant rather than argumentative in many cases. When the shepherds discover Musidorus washed up on the shore after being shipwrecked, it is observed that the waves are lapping over him and may be a source of danger to him. Sidney comments:

> . . . that being in appearance dead, had yet saved his life, and now coming to his life, should be a cause to procure his death.

To the modern reader, this reduces the sincerity, or seriousness of the piece. Sometimes the tone of the writing or the angle of approach changes rapidly and disconcertingly. Pyrocles has a ser-

175

ious debate with *Philoclea* on the question of suicide and Sidney comments:

> Pyrocles was not so much persuaded as delighted by her well conceived and sweetly pronounced speeches.[14]

Maybe, but the tone makes one wonder whether the debate was really only an occasion for flirting.

The *Arcadia* presents many bewildering perspectives and the mixing of literary genres sometimes adds to confusion. Tradition permitted a mixture of genres in romance writing, but unless the blend were satisfactory, as in Tasso's work, the author might seem to lack overall control. Sidney was aware of the habit of mixing literary genres, and comments in his *Apology* under the heading of *The Various Species of Poetry*, that the mixing of prose and verse, or the heroic and pastoral could produce an effective result: "... for, if severed they be good, the conjunction cannot be hurtful ...". He was, however, concerned about some concoctions and did not favour the writing of *Tragi-Comedies*. He felt that the tone of high tragedy could not be harmonized with that of scurrilous comedy. It was a matter of moral and literary taste. In the *Arcadia*, elements of high seriousness are long and complicated, and do not go easily with fantasy and light-hearted stories of love and chivalry. Sidney changes his narrative form, and also his style and tone. If this sometimes brings relief, it sometimes confuses the reader. Issues are raised for us to ponder, but there is no move towards a resolution when there are resultant contradictions or paradoxes.

Under revision, the *Arcadia* possibly became too wide-reaching to bring under complete control. According to Greville, the first aim was "to please others", but he goes on to say that the work was an "unpolished embrio" and "both in form and matter ... much inferior to that unbounded spirit of his" ..."... if this excellent image-maker had lived to finish and to bring to perfection this extraordinary frame of his own Common-wealth ..." his higher aims might have been realized. The higher aims were certainly comprehensive:

> ... in all these creatures of his making, his intent and scope was, to turn the barren philosophy precepts into

pregnant images of life; and in them, first on the monarch's part, lively to represent the growth, state and declination of princes, change of government and laws: vicissitudes of sedition, faction, succession, confederacies, plantations, with all other errors or alterations in public affairs.

As if this were not enough Greville adds:

> In which traverses - I know - his purpose was to limn out such exact pictures, of every posture in the mind, that any man being forced in the strains of this life, to pass through any straights or latitudes of good or ill fortune, might - as in a glass - see how to set a good countenance upon all the discountenances of adversity and a stay upon the exorbitant smilings of Chance.[15]

Greville does not refer to the love themes which are basic, or to the light-hearted aspects of romance. He seemed to regard the *Arcadia* as a kind of political and social allegory. Did Sidney lose his way, the deeper he penetrated into his Arcadia? One is reminded of the unfulfilled aims of his friend Spenser, and of Raleigh's inability to complete his *Ocean* poem.

One critic of the revised version, Davis,[16] takes the view that Sidney was indeed moving towards certain conclusions. Davis sees the first book as depicting the changes which love brings to individuals and to society. The shepherds descant on different aspects of love. According to Davis the situation is further explored in Book II, in which incidents mirror the self-division of the heroes in struggles of passion against reason. Book III, then introduces the tragedy which results from self-division, and illustrates how reason, if allied to Christian patience, ultimately triumphs. "The rest of the *Arcadia*, therefore represents a reintegration of the divided mind". Books IV and V bring in political illustrations and culminate in the trial scene. Davis considers that they broaden the previous analogies and give them a universal implication. Through their vicissitudes the two Princes attain a knowledge of true virtue. They learn to know themselves, especially in captivity, and they recognize the importance of self-control.[17]

This seems to read more into the *Arcadia* than is evident or implied by the text. One can, however, accept this view if one looks at Sidney's work from a distance, and it does not go against the grain of his known thinking. As with Spenser, it is a matter of focus. The closer one focusses the less sure one is about the organization and harmony of the *Arcadia*. Sidney himself was, one has to recall, dissatisfied with it. The cross-patterns, contrasts, paradoxes, analogous repetitions may have related to the real world as Sidney began to see it, but the solution to these complexities may not have been clear in his mind. Greville does not suggest that Sidney had a philosophy to outline - only that he wished to 'limn out' pictures so that readers could take adversity as it came. Was he searching, with difficulty, for a hierarchy of values?

Another perspective is visualized by Maurice Evans in his introduction to the Penguin edition of the *Arcadia*. "The most important theme of the Arcadia is the mysterious but benevolent working of providence and the oracle itself is the central fact and symbol of this process". He adds that "the whole disordered pattern of action is presented in terms of a complete and orderly literary hierarchy. The level of style, throughout, is controlled with an impeccable decorum, every character speaking a language appropriate to his standing, each description in terms nicely graded to its social level and moral seriousness . . . Sidney insists on the permanence of hierarchy even when all order and decorum seem to have been lost". But the structure of accepted hierarchies is undermined if there is a growing sense of the relativity of values. And Providence, or the overall working of a benign will in the affairs of Man, is not made clear from the narrative. It is of course possible, that if Sidney had completed his revision, he might have amplified the scene of Basilius' revival and made it less hurried. The significance of Divine Providence might have been made more explicit. This is speculation, but there are so many lucky incidents in the work that Sidney might have used to indicate a divine purpose. He might, too, have wished to indicate that contradictions in values can only be resolved by a spiritual union with God, which takes us beyond the 'infected will', as taught by Dee, Bruno and other Hermetists. One will never know what a true and completed revision would have indicated. As it stands, however, the tone of the *Arcadia* is not markedly optimistic. Did Sidney become somewhat disillusioned with mental exploration as with the development of his own life?

It is doubtful whether Sidney had formulated a set of firm views by the time he died at thirty-two years of age. He was still at an exploratory stage and may have wanted a large canvas on which to trace his literary explorations. Like some of his contemporaries, who were skilled in the use of small poetic forms, he may have had problems in keeping his bearings in a larger structure. Spenser and Raleigh attempted large works and did not complete them, and with both these writers, one senses a play of contradictory moods and changes of attitude as their work continues.

Some of the questions which interested Sidney have a modern appeal. There is, for example, the question of the right of foreign invasion, even when this is requested by the ruling authority of the nation concerned. Evarchus has to act carefully when he enters Arcadia, and he feels that he must adhere to the local laws even if they do not please him. When giving judgement he has to bear in mind that he is judging local issues, as a foreigner. In dealing with such matters, Sidney may have had in mind Bodin's proposition that interference by a Prince in the affairs of a neighbour State could, in certain circumstances, be justified. The importance of national identity was, however, of growing interest; and especially in England under Elizabeth. Sidney was strongly opposed to a foreign Catholic marriage for the Queen, which might have compromised the country's newly found identity and its patriotic feeling. Another question with a modern appeal is that of special privilege for high ranking foreigners abroad.

The *Arcadia* means different things to different people. Harvey thought the work worthy for its "amorous courting", its "sage counselling", its "valorous fighting", while Hoskyns[18] thought it a model of good style. Greville thought of it in moral and political terms and was careful to point out that it had not been fully revised. Many would have agreed with Hoskyns, for Sidney's work was regarded as an example of style for many years. Here again, however, Sidney is indebted to predecessors, to earlier rhetoricians and to the notions expressed by contemporary grammarians. Like Spenser, he made deliberate use of archaisms such as 'spake', 'damosel', and 'gat' to give his story an old-world, romantic flavour. The use of balanced antithesis and elegant periphrasis,

179

which was particularly pleasing to Hoskyns, was also used by others. But Sidney was skillful in his own way, and he handled high-flown phrases with virtuosity without running into the excesses of Lyly's prose. He used stylistic conventions with artistry, providing judges, like Evarchus, with logical and forceful utterances, and shepherdesses like Mopsa with rambling, plain speech. However, the qualities admired by Hoskyns, were not those which were admired in a later age. Hazlitt was scathing. He attacked Sidney's poetic work as "an artificial excrescence transferred from logic and rhetoric to poetry", and his *Arcadia* as "one of the greatest monuments of the abuse of intellectual power upon record".[19] Today one may become impatient with stylistic virtuosity, but beneath the fine plumage of rhetorical device the real Sidney, as well as the literary Sidney, comes and goes.

Some, who preferred the romantic and heroic qualities in the *Arcadia*, have argued one way or the other, in favour. In the sixteenth century, too, there was debate on the best form to cast a heroic work. The example of Homer and Vergil, suggested that action should centre round a great hero, but Ariosto and others indicated that multiple plot sequences, with interwoven incidents, were more appropriate for contemporary readers, who demanded suspense and excitement. Sidney was pulled in several directions. He emulated the romance writers of his day, but he was also influenced by classical example; notably when he turned his mind to a more serious and didactic mode of exploration. Heroic qualities were introduced into the pattern of romantic fantasy.

Sidney is yet another example of those who opened their minds to new and exciting influences without altogether abandoning older traditions of thought which were frequently opposed to them; of those who were interested in finding new perspectives, but compromised their intellectual identities, which were strongly individual, by a tendency to face several ways and to imitate diverse models. They were uncertain of firm intellectual commitment in a complex and bewildering world of changing values. They often changed position, or re-worked what they had written as they continued to write. Spenser, Sidney and Raleigh had such problems. The *Arcadia* was, and still is, many things to different readers. If this is a measure of its rich interest, it is also a measure of its lack of cohesion.

VIII   "To Seek New Worlds . . . . . "

The theme of disorientation, due to the changing background of the life and thought of the late sixteenth century, can also be seen in the life and work of Sir Walter Raleigh. Like his contemporary Sidney, he was an individualist, and he, too, was concerned to establish his identity in an uncertain world. He cast himself in more than one role, but was ultimately frustrated in his endeavours. He, too, was an active man as well as a writer and thinker, and he was pulled in different ways by pressures and influences. He seemed to accept the Ptolemaic concept of the universe, but was suspected of having unorthodox views on religion.

Raleigh and Sidney were markedly different, but they had some traits in common. They were born within a few years of each other, were youthful apprentices at Court, and were often frustrated in their efforts to serve the Queen. Disillusionment with Court life may have been reflected in the *Arcadia*, and it is also reflected in some of Raleigh's poetry. Both men were at Universtiy at a time of intellectual ferment and were acquainted with thinkers who held unorthodox views. Raleigh was accused of atheism, and although Sidney faced no such accusations, his tutor Languet was concerned about some of the books he was reading and about the range of his views. Both poets knew leading figures in the literary world and would have been aware of new trends in theological thinking. They mixed with leading statesmen, concerned themselves with Irish and Spanish questions, and were interested in explorations in the New World. They opposed Spanish influence and sought an active as well as a literary life. As role players, they saw themselves in heroic parts.

Raleigh was known to be sharp-tongued and sometimes reckless in behaviour. He was involved in fights and escapades as a young man. Sidney was a quieter student, but he could speak his mind and the manner of his wounding at Zutphen indicated his impulsive side. The literary style of the poets was different, but both had a tendency to change from the writing of carefully constructed, and somewhat mannered, prose and poetry to simple and direct expression. Raleigh took himself more seriously in a central role within his poetry. In his long poem *The Ocean to Cynthia* he played the role of a forlorn and rejected courtier with earnest intensity. He did not stand back as Sidney sometimes did, to regard himself with wry amusement. But Raleigh was not without playful humour. Although he wrote his long poem in the allegorical manner, and made earnest protestations of love, he was able to mock affected writing in his reply to Marlowe's *Passionate Shepherd*, indicating the more likely results of a real life relationship with Marlowe's poetic shepherd.

Both Raleigh and Sidney wrote on the theme of love, and both often give the impression that they were writing from the heart as well as taking pleasure in craftsmanship. Behind Raleigh's fulsome compliments to the Queen, and his use of rhetorical devices in the poem *The Ocean to Cynthia*, there is a repeated note of genuine feeling. Love, in whatever form or disguise it assumed, became a passion which tended to unsettle and to wound both writers.

Raleigh had a long life, and at times his role seemed to be that of a grand hero in a dramatic tragedy. He appears almost larger than life, and is often in danger of over-reaching himself. Sidney's life was shorter and less turbulent, although he had his reverses, but he had a strong inner drive like Raleigh. Both were men, whose traditional ways of thinking conflicted with new trends in Renaissance thought, although paradoxically they seemed to accept new trends without troubling about contradictions. Raleigh's work, like that of Sidney, sometimes embraces opposing viewpoints. For example, he regarded God as a kind of puppet-master controlling human beings who were forced to dance to command, and his general outlook was fatalistic. In the *Preface* to *The History of the World* he wrote: "God is the author of all our tragedies". Yet, at other times, he believed in Free Will and in the power of individuals to create their own destiny. He wrote: "Men are the causes of their own miseries, as I was of mine". For someone to hold such contradictory views was not uncommon in the late Elizabethan age and as we have seen this was frequently due to the changing perspectives indicated in the first chapter. Heady enthusiasms alternated with uncertainty and even despair. Raleigh displayed these symptoms. He aimed, as he put it in *The Ocean to Cynthia*, "to seek new worlds", and was stimulated by exploratory ventures, by curiosity and by ambition. However, in his attempts to fulfill himself he found worlds which were unexpected and which produced disappointment and unhappiness.

The Elizabethan adage 'know thyself' was often contradicted by the wish to cast oneself in a role, to disguise and to act out a part on the stage of life. In some cases, this was due to vanity and to a desire for personal ambition. But it could also be due to an uncertainty about personal identity, an immature desire to fantasize and to allot oneself a dramatic role. And there was another perspective to consider. There were good practical reasons for assuming roles in the political context of Elizabeth's age, and there were writers who advised the donning of masks. Castiglione, whose book *Il Cortegiano* was influential reading in Raleigh's day, regarded the ideal courtier as having an artifical identity. The good courtier was rather like an actor who had to put a face on things. He might have to conceal his thoughts in the interests of good diplomacy. A different standpoint was taken by Machiavelli, but he, too, mentioned the need for pretence in the actions of an efficient politician. In such situations, an individual might feel that identity had to be 'fashioned' and could only be achieved by selecting a role and playing it well.

Sidney fashioned a part for himself as a noble leader, and a sense of duty led him to try to live up to his ideal. Raleigh was not brought up in the same way. He was more of an opportunist than Sidney, and he took on whatever roles circumstances required. He was a fighting soldier, a poet, a thinker, a penitent, and a martyr. This is not to say he was insincere in the roles he played - although untrustworthiness was a view of him which was held by some in his own day - but he did seem to have many selves. As with Sidney it is not easy to determine when he is acting or being sincere, and even when he assumes exaggerated postures, as in his long poem to the Queen, there is an element of sincerity. He may have gone behind the Queen's back in the Throckmorton affair, but one can hardly cite this as an example of general untrustworthiness. One suspects that Raleigh actually believed in the parts he undertook to play and that they were a true expression of his mood and personality. If he acted in different parts throughout his life, and indulged in fantasies, these were activities which allowed him to develop and to adapt in a world of deceptive appearances.

Raleigh was born in Devon in about 1552 of a respectable family that was down on its luck. His family had good connections but little money, and as Walter was a younger son by his father's third wife his prospects were poor. Aubrey reported that he was in financial difficulties at Oxford. He was an impetuous young man and eager for adventure. He set off early to join the Huguenots in the French wars and saw active service in the field. Perhaps he may have learned about advanced Huguenot thinking in his youth. In 1575, he was studying at the Inns of Court and was said to be an avid reader. He took part in various escapades in London and was, at one time, briefly imprisoned. A desire for adventure, coupled with a keen pursuit of knowledge, were traits that lasted throughout his life. When later he voyaged to distant lands he took care to stock his cabin with books, and at his trial, in James's reign, he referred to his early love of reading.

In 1578, he achieved command of one of his relative's ships, for Sir Humphrey Gilbert was his half-brother. He sailed as far as the Cape Verde islands, but the expedition got into difficulties on its return and the fleet took a battering in a sea skirmish. The Privy Council were critical of this exploit and were opposed to Sir Humphrey making similar attempts. Whether Raleigh made contact with the Court at this time, one does not know. He may have been noticed, but he did not make any obvious impression until he returned from active service in Ireland.

After his time in prison, he joined the army in Ulster to help suppress rebellion. There were accounts of his bravery in the field and also of his ruthlessness towards rebellious peasantry. He fought in the midst of danger and at one point had his horse shot from under him. It is told that he had a peasant hanged for insolence and he took part in the general slaughter which occurred when Smerwick castle was taken. This cruel side to his behaviour shows one side of his temperament and contrasts with his humane attitude towards the native population of Guiana, at a later stage in his life, when he set out to discover gold there. It can of course be argued that in Ireland he had the task of suppressing rebellion against the Queen. War is war, and the values of a Elizabethan fighting soldier were different from those of a peacetime civilian. In Guiana, on the other hand, Raleigh had, as a matter of policy, to win over the local population in order to encourage them to oppose Spanish influence. In this, he claimed later to have succeeded, citing their acceptance of the Queen's authority and their wish for Raleigh to return. Yet there would seem to be two sides to Raleigh. He could be indifferent to people. He showed little sympathy for the predicament of his companion Keymis (who committed suicide when he thought he had let down his leader), but he expressed a tender love for his wife, and was considerate towards the lot of the poor in his speeches in Parliament; although here again he could have been playing a role. Perhaps his outlook varied according to the part he was playing and to the situation in which he was placed.

He began to write poetry early, for in 1576 he wrote a verse in honour of Gascoigne's *The Steel Glass*. His youthful verse has been lost and there is still doubt about the authorship of some of the later verses attributed to him. It is not surprising that we have little of Raleigh's poetic output, for the verse of courtiers was circulated privately and not meant for public distribution. Such verse was often fragmentary and written for an occasion. Raleigh was not a professional poet and probably thought more highly of the active than of the contemplative life. He did, however, express an interest in intellectual matters, mixing with poets and scholars. He would have met the Fellows of the newly formed Society of Antiquaries including Camden and Lancelot Andrews. He knew of Sidney's work and wrote a tribute to him, as he did to Spenser. In the field of mathematics and science, he was a patron of Hariot the mathematician who was thought to be an atheist, and of Keymis, a former Fellow of Balliol College, Oxford. Side by side with his military and naval education, Raleigh was also educating himself in scientific and literary matters.

It was after his term in Ireland that he took a place in Court. He had been critical and outspoken about aspects of the military leadership in Ireland and wrote about these matters to Burghley and Walsingham. It is not known whether his views were sought at Court or how he gained entry, and it is strange that he was suddenly transformed from a Captain in the Irish wars to a dashing, finely dressed courtier in London. Once at Court, it is understandable that he drew the Queen's attention and that he cast himself in another role. To keep in the Queen's favour, flattery, diplomacy and sophistication were called for and Raleigh responded; although he still retained his rough edge and his Devonshire accent.

He seems to have regarded Elizabeth with genuine awe and admiration. His later confessed love for her was expressed in a poetic idiom and savours of an up-dated version of medieval courtly love; it may not have been sexual. He had a role to play as the Queen's loyal admirer, but in the broadest sense his love was probably heartfelt. Since he played his role well his rise was swift, so swift that it excited the envy of many at Court. In 1587, Sir Anthony Bagot referred to Raleigh as "the best hated man in the country". Unlike Sidney, he thrived in Court circles.

He also played the part of commercial speculator, involving himself in enterprises and growing rich. He was given lucrative monopolies, such as the export of broadcloth and the wine trade. He bought estates in Ireland and England, and as he built up a forfortune he spent lavishly on clothes and jewellry. The portrait in the National Gallery shows him as a handsome, richly-dressed young man of proud bearing. It is reported that his shoes were studded with jewels and his clothes were noted for their finery.

When he became interested in setting up a colony of settlers in America, the Queen was reluctant to let him go, and he decided to send out a fleet on his behalf to explore the coast of Virginia. Reports came back of a 'paradise' in North Carolina and with commendable initiative, Raleigh began to encourage investment in a colonial scheme. The idea was to send out a group of adventurers who would settle in America and work the land for trade. The proposed settlement was named Virginia in honour of the Queen. Sir Richard Grenville led the expedition.

At this time, Raleigh was in a position of considerable influence. He held the post of Captain of Guard and his duties kept him in frequent attendance upon the Queen. He was not formally an adviser, but he probably had her ear on several occasions. So much so that Essex blamed Raleigh at a later date for turning her favour away from him. Raleigh was knighted, made Warden of the

Stanneries, Lord Lieutenant of Cornwall, and a Vice-Admiral for Devon and Cornwall. Honours fell upon him, and as he was skillful in administration, he grew rich and increased his estates.

His colonial venture was not, however, a success and several settlers decided to return. A new scheme was considered. It was proposed that settlers should themselves own the land on which they worked. About one hundred and fifty set out under the leadership of John White in 1587. White later returned to England to pick up additional supplies and when he arrived back in Virginia in 1591, it was to find that the original settlers had disappeared without trace! Although Raleigh gave up the idea of further settlement at this point, a colony was eventually established.

There were, of course, marked dangers in being a favourite of the Queen. It was easy to fall from favour, and if one lacked friends, a fall could be disastrous. When the Queen learned that Raleigh had seduced one of her ladies-in-waiting, Elizabeth Throckmorton, she was incensed. She did not approve of courtiers forming serious liaisons without her knowledge and consent, and the fact that Raleigh married Bess Throckmorton did not make the matter less grave. The unapproved marriages of Sidney, Essex, and Leicester had caused offence. Both Raleigh and his mistress were packed off to the Tower of London, and for a time he was under sentence of execution. There was a sense of betrayal on the Queen's side, and possibly she wondered how far he could be trusted in his role as friend and loyal courtier. There may, too, have been an element of sexual jealousy in the Queen's anger. It was while he was in the Tower that Raleigh began his long unrevised poem *The Ocean to Cynthia* as an attempt to redeem himself and as a plea to the Queen to restore him to favour. She probably never saw it. It may have been part of an even longer sequence, and it is incomplete and in draft. The fragment is concerned with his banishment.

On reading the poem, one once again has a sense of Raleigh playing a part, taking on the identity of a shepherd in an allegorical role who is the lover of an idealized Cynthia. The Queen's playful Court name for Raleigh was 'Water'; a play upon his name and a reference to his love of the sea. His wife, too, wrote of him in her simple phonetic spelling as 'Sir Water' and perhaps many pronounced his name in this way. The fashion for using code names was encouraged by the Queen as it amused her and produced an atmosphere of playful intrigue in Court circles. The title *The Ocean to Cynthia* was therefore another way of saying 'Walter to the Queen'. The poem was a lament on Raleigh's fall from favour and on his melancholy banishment. The allegorical and pastoral game which Raleigh later mocked when answering Marlowe was now played seriously.

Like Sidney in the *Arcadia*, Raleigh had a problem of poetic stance. He wrote under the guise of a shepherd in the conventional pastoral mode. But at times, this did not suit his need for a passionate outburst, and he then abandoned the role in favour of a more personal statement. If many images are rhetorical, elegant, and exaggerated in the conventional way, there are also examples of original and striking imagery which give the poem a unique, personal flavour. The writing is even terse on occasions. His mood can change from a mournful tone to an intense and passionate lyricism. Emotion seems to come in a series of inspirational rushes, and the smooth flow is interrupted by a staccato lilt which suggests a personal anguish. On the other hand, one finds imagery which is contrived for the purposes of persuasion and of appeal.

In spite of its length, its repetitions and its 'longeurs' this long, rambling, and unfinished poem often holds the reader. It was only partially revised. Some stanzas are unfinished or roughly drafted. They seem to have been written in a hurry. Ideas run into each other, become confused, expand and repeat themselves. At some points there are breaks in the middle of sentences. Lines are added here and there and rhymes do not always conform to the overall pattern. The poem was probably conceived in stanzas of four lines, but as it was in draft, the form is obscured. Often the meaning is uncertain and there are personal allusions. It is a poem of extremes in which the author is playing a special part. Later we shall examine the poem in more detail.

During his captivity Raleigh was allowed freedom within the Tower precincts and was permitted visitors. Again he was seen dressed in fine clothes, wearing a "velvet cap and a rich gown". When not in a mood of depression, he was his arrogant self. The Earl of Northumberland once said of him that "he desired to seem able to sway all men's fancies, all men's courses". He quickly responded to a call for leadership when some of his ships arrived in Dartmouth with plundered treasure and looting broke out on board. He was temporarily released to restore order amongst the crew and to deal with the administration of the spoils. If he had grown unpopular at Court, he seemed popular enough with the Dartmouth sailors, for Sir Robert Cecil reported that they quickly responded to his authority, and there is evidence that he was highly regarded in Devon and Cornwall. After two months, Raleigh was released, but he and his wife were banished from Court. He went to live at Sherborne, the lease of which the Queen had previously given him, and he busied himself in the administration of his various estates in Ireland.

It was at this time, that rumours grew about his possible atheism. In 1592, the Jesuit Robert Parsons drew attention to Raleigh's heterodoxy, and it might have been during his exile from the Court that he wrote the sceptical reply to Marlowe's poem under the title of *The Nymph's Reply to the Shepherd* and the bitter comment on Court morals called *The Lie*. There is doubt about Raleigh's authorship of *The Lie*. It has been said that some of Essex's followers spread it about that the poem was by Raleigh and that it was dissident and atheistical in tone. But although the poem expresses contempt for worldly things and for established institutions, there is no internal evidence of atheism and it ends by referring to the Soul. Another view is that it is too crudely written for Raleigh and is Puritan in outlook; but Raleigh was known to dislike Puritans. It may have been written by a Dr. Latworth of St. John's College, Oxford.[1] The poem has, however, long been attributed to Raleigh, and even if he did not write it, the opinions expressed were not untypical of Raleigh in his darker moods. The style may lack grace and elegance, but the rough staccato quality of the verse was in the fashion of the time when writing satire,[2] and Raleigh had an occasional tendency to use short, staccato lines and epigrammatic statement when writing verse as we shall see later when the poem is quoted. The charge of atheism, however, does not depend on his poetry but upon Parson's specific accusation. Parsons refers to "Sir Walter Rawley's School of Atheism" and he goes on to make out that Raleigh and his friends mocked Biblical figures and spelt the name of God backwards.

Parsons was not the only accuser. The playwright Kyd mentioned Raleigh in connection with Hariot, Warner, Roydon and others who were known to hold irreligious views. Rumours came to a head when the Reverend Ironside reported a dinner conversation at which he had been present. He said that Raleigh had doubted the notion of the Soul. The dinner was at the house of a Sir George Trenchard where apparently an argument broke out on theological matters. Raleigh had then called for a definition of the Soul since "what the reasonable soul of man is . . . has not been resolved". He added that Aristotle's views on the subject were "obscure and intricate" and he did not accept his authority. When Ironside retorted that the Soul was breathed into Man by God, Raleigh demanded proof.

On the face of it, there is not much evidence of atheism in Ironside's report, and Raleigh was probably in a taunting mood at the dinner party, but Parson's accusation was definite and rumours continued about Raleigh's opinions. These rumours, the association with Hariot and others, and the tendency for intellectuals to form private discussion groups (Sidney's circle, known as the Areopagus, is a case in point) led to speculation among recent critics that Raleigh was a member of a dark school of thought, known as the School of Night; but this is doubtful. His work would suggest that he was given to periods of free thinking; but if there is an element of scepticism in some of Raleigh's writing, there is also frequent reference to God's intervention in the affairs of Man. This is noticeable in *The History of the World*. Nevertheless, the tag of atheist stuck to Raleigh in later life and Coke brought this up at his trial without producing any evidence for his views on Raleigh's thinking.

It is probable that the term 'atheist' was one of general abuse to describe Raleigh's unorthodoxies, for there was suspicion, too, about his political opinions. He antagonized the Howard family and they, too, accused Raleigh of irreligion and of holding secret meetings on political matters with Lord Cobham and the notorious Duke of Northumberland. He was also said to be intriguing against King James towards the end of Elizabeth's reign. Such criticisms of Raleigh may have been true, but they may also have been due to a desire, on the part of Raleigh's enemies, to poison James' mind against him when Elizabeth eventually restored him to favour.

Raleigh's writings indicate again and again a strong Christian bias. This is to be seen in the *History* and in his other prose writings. He wrote an essay called *A Treatise of the Soul* which is not in any way unorthodox. Elsewhere he presents many of the traditional metaphysical arguments which were current at the time. He argues that the Soul is a spirit and that it exists apart from the body. He considers that its functions are concerned with instincts and emotions, although there is an aspect of the Soul which may be called the reasonable Soul and which is concerned with Understanding and Will. This is not an original argument as we have seen in the first Chapter. He argues that the Soul is not located in one place, but is present everywhere. Another essay is called *The Sceptic*. This indicates conventional doubts, but is not anti-religious in argument. It is an example of an alert mind following intellectual currents and expressing them well. He argues that sense data vary with regard to objects according to circumstances, and that there is no fixed relationship between sense and object. One recalls Bruno's thesis that relationships depend upon perspectives, and that these change with the position of the observer. Bruno suggested that values were relative, that contradictions abounded in the world around us, and that true harmony only existed in union with God.

In his *History* Raleigh tends to play down the importance of Reason, since it cannot provide all the answers one needs in a universe which, to use his own words, "triumpheth in dissimilitude". This view runs counter to the Ptolemaic concept that there is an underlying coherence in Nature. Raleigh accepts in general the Ptolemaic universe, but sees Nature as a wild forest of contradiction in which it is difficult to follow a way leading to the truth. He finds it hard to establish absolutes in a world of relative values and in which Nature is subject to change. But these were thoughts which worried many late Renaissance thinkers - Spenser, Sidney and Hermetic thinkers like Dee and Bruno were also concerned, and Bruno tried to solve the problem of dissimilitude and coherence in his concept of 'the one'. There is no hint of transcendent-alism in Raleigh's work, any more than in the work of Sidney, but the basic Christian ethic seems to have been sincerely accepted even if the intellectual baggage accompanying it from former times is sometimes jettisoned. In Raleigh's work one finds, as in other works of the same period, the old and the new inextricably inter-twined and presenting a pattern of some confusion.

Raleigh's thoughts are in no way outrageous in an age which produced Sidney and Bacon and which was exploring new con-cepts. He was not alone in appearing to move towards the neo-Platonic idea that God exists above and outside Nature, and that in the world of the senses there is little that can be clearly defined - although it is beneficial to cultivate the sciences to find out what one can. Scientific knowledge based on careful observation and on calculation gave one some control over Nature's manifestations. But there is nothing in such views to suggest an anti-Christian stance. A belief in God and in a Christian morality is a ground theme in much of his writing. So too is the fear of change and decay; a fear which obsessed many writers - Spenser and Shakes-peare among them. Many of Raleigh's ideas are borrowed and aired, and sometimes there are contradictions and the perspectives alter. His intellectual identity is elusive. He seems to take on the parts of certain thinkers as he takes on roles in his active life.

As with Sidney, there were many influences at work on Ral-eigh. Aristotle continued to influence him, although he strongly denied his authority on some matters. Heraclitus was another influence and lay behind his thoughts in *The Sceptic*. Fashionable interpretations of the Stoic philosophy affected his thoughts and his moods, so that one is not quite sure how far genuine despair is coloured and aggrandized by the consciousness of Stoic models. Raleigh was aware, too, of writers on the continent from Montaigne to Bodin, and could well have sympathized with those who point-ed out contradictions in the Scriptures and who thought that mira-cles might have natural explanations. Like Bacon, he was interest-ed in practical approaches. Like Dee, who had to defend his belief in Christianity, he supported the idea of investigative magic. In his *History*, he wrote of science as a "lawful magic" which allows one to discover some of the secrets of Nature without recourse to the black arts.

192

The effect of varied and contradictory influences on a well-read mind would have pulled him in many directions, and the rapid changes in his fortunes would also have contributed to his disorientation. So many Elizabethans, psychologically anchored in inherited traditions, and whose ways of thought reflected former philosophical concepts, also floated some distance from their moorings on the moving currents of intellectual change. Spenser, Chapman, Sidney, Dee, Raleigh, and Jonson to some extent, exhibited symptoms of contradiction and uncertainty caused by a surfeit of received ideas. Unorthodoxies could become a fascination.

Before Raleigh's trial Sir John Harrington wrote an interesting comment on him: "I wist not that he hath evil design in point of faith or religion. As he hath oft discoursed to me with much learning, wisdom and freedom, and I know he doth somewhat differ in opinion from some others; but I think his heart is so well fixed in everything, as far as I can look into him". This suggests that Raleigh was basically Christian, but may have been disposed to argue and to question points of Church doctrine.

The Queen gave no sign of favour while Raleigh stayed at Sherborne, and eventually the idea of an expedition to seek gold in Guiana began to fire his imagination. This would result in action and adventure and perhaps renew the Queen's interest in him. His optimism, which alternated with feelings of despair, was rekindled. He had sold some property in 1594 and sent off a reconnaissance fleet to Guiana. Reports came back of the location of a rich gold mine. His friend Keymis claimed to have seen it. He therefore made up his mind to lead a fully equipped expedition himself, in spite of his wife's objection that he was heading "toward the sunset". In 1599, he led four ships piled up with men and provisions.

On arrival in Guiana, his policy was to gain the friendship of the local population and to enlist their help in finding the mine. It took the expedition fifteen days to reach the Orinoco, and by that time food was scarce and the men were tired. They set off, nevertheless, into the interior and claimed later to have reached areas of splendid scenery where "every stone that we stooped to take up promised either gold or silver by his complexion".[3] They also claimed to have prized some gold from rocky ground and took it back to England as evidence. Unfortunately the rainy season came upon them and they were forced to return to their boats.

Back in England, the voyage was greeted with some scepticism. It was said that the gold had been taken from somewhere less distant, and represented a fraudulent claim. In order to vindicate his venture, and to persuade the Queen and others that a further expedition was a sound proposition, Raleigh wrote his tract *The Discovery of Guiana*. It was well written, colourful and persuasive; a piece of Raleigh's direct, narrative prose at its best. But it failed to convince the Queen and the merchants. As time went on, Spain began to increase her hold over the territory and this meant that future English expeditions were bound to be hazardous. There would be political as well as practical dangers. Raleigh had to abandon his attempts until he revived the idea of discovering gold when he was later imprisoned by James. The Guiana idea not only represented a challenge to Raleigh, it gave him a grand role to play on the world's stage.

The tract on Guiana is a propaganda tract, but it is a fine piece of prose. The writing is direct, colourful and moves at a good pace. The descriptions of the country are appealing as this well-known extract illustrates:

> On both sides of this river, we passed the most beautiful country that ever mine eyes beheld: and whereas all that we had seen before was nothing but woods, prickles, bushes, and thorns, here we beheld plains of twenty miles in length, the grasses short and green, and in divers parts groves of trees by themselves, as if they had been by all the art and labour in the world so made of purpose: and still as we rowed, the deer came down feeding by the water's side, as if they had been used to a keeper's call. Upon this river there were a great store of fowl, and of many sorts: we saw in it divers sorts of strange fishes, and of marvellous bigness . . .

Some of the other essays are dry and unimpassioned, and parts of the *History* are ponderous and rhetorical, but Raleigh is also able to write a straightforward, muscular prose which sets him apart from many of his contemporaries. When he attempts the grand style, he also often brings it off. In literature, as in life, he was a good performer. His prose style, sometimes like his dress, was fashioned for the occasion, and his heart and mind were often in the performance.

With Spain, Raleigh took the view that attack was the best form of defence. He was eager to serve under Howard and Essex in an attack on Cadiz and was given command of twenty-two ships. He persuaded Essex to enter the harbour with his fleet instead of standing off-shore and loading soldiers into boats to land as a fighting force. It was sound advice, for Essex's manoeuvres would have been difficult to achieve in rolling seas. Raleigh's own ships attacked the Spanish fleet directly and he inflicted much damage on his enemy. This was one of his more successful exploits and it was on the heroic scale. It was said that it left him with a leg wound which made him slightly lame. He was therefore unable to take part in the actual taking of the town. He wrote a description of the battle in a note which is both vivid and exciting:

> . . . they all let slip, and ran aground, tumbling into the sea heaps of soldiers, so thick, as if coals had been poured out of a sack, in many ports at once, some drowned, and some sticking in the mud. The *Philip* and the *St. Thomas* burnt themselves: the *St. Mathew*, and the *St. Andrew* were recovered by our boats, ere they could get out to fire them. The spectacle was very lamentable on their side; for many drowned themselves; many half burnt leapt into the water; very many hanging by the ropes' ends by the ship's sides under the water even to the lips; many swimming with grievous wounds, stricken under water, and put out of their pain; and withall so huge a fire, and such tearing of the ordnance in the great *Philip*, and the rest, when the fire came to them, as if any man had a desire to see Hell itself, it was there most lively figured.[4]

The battle of Cadiz pleased the Queen, who eventually restored Raleigh to partial favour. In the battle "Sir Walter Raleigh's service", according to Carew, "was so much praiseworthy as those who were formerly his enemies do now hold him in great estimation; for that which he did in the sea service could not be bettered". However, he had had his disagreements with Essex, and if these receded they were again to flare up on a later voyage when they both aimed to attack Spanish treasure ships in the Azores. Raleigh again came under Essex's command, but since Essex's ships arrived late on the scene and Raleigh saw an early opportunity for successful action slipping away, he decided to lead an attack himself. His action was successful, but Essex was incensed by Raleigh's premature and unauthorized involvement. The enmity between them continued to smoulder and later Essex was said to have influenced the future King James against Raleigh, and Raleigh was accused of influencing the Queen against her former favourite.

Raleigh was, of course, all that King James disliked. He was a former friend of the Queen; he was proud, outspoken, virile and had a reputation for holding unorthodox views on religious and political matters. In addition, he was a smoker of tobacco and helped to make smoking a habit at Court. When Howard and Essex suggested that Raleigh was intriguing against him, James was naturally suspicious. He would not have liked some of the views Raleigh was expressing in Parliament, and may have heard rumours that toward the end of Elizabeth's reign Raleigh favoured some kind of republic. Cecil, who had been a friend to Raleigh on occasions, also warned James to be careful.

Raleigh's partial restoration to the Queen's favour coincided with Essex's decline and his later execution. He was reinstated as Captain of the Guard and made Governor of Jersey. In 1601, he gave evidence at Essex's trial which led to the Earl's execution, but by then he had increased the number of his enemies. Soon after the Queen's death Raleigh was deprived of his Captaincy and arrested. Charges of treason were soon brought against him and he found himself back in the Tower. Gradually his possessions were peeled away from him, including his beloved Sherborne which James wanted for his favourite, Carr. He was accused of intrigue and even of planning to abduct the King. His former friend Cobham had by then been implicated in secret dealings with Spain and Raleigh was suspected of being involved, in spite of the fact that he had maintained a strong anti-Spanish policy throughout his life. Under cross-examination, Cobham said that Raleigh had incited him, and although he was later to retract this statement the affair left a lingering suspicion that Raleigh was somehow involved in secret dealings. There was no concrete evidence against Raleigh that could stand up to examination, and it is difficult to avoid the impression that he was falsely accused. He was also suspected of intriguing with the French at a later date when he led his final expedition to Guiana. He strongly denied this, as we shall see, but he was unundoubtedly testing the ground for a French deal. It is not difficult to understand why Raleigh was regarded by many as someone not to be trusted or believed.

Faced with the possibility of conviction for treason, Raleigh attempted suicide, but failed in the attempt. If one reads Cecil's account there is a hint that the act was more theatrical than sincere. Cecil wrote to the English ambassador in Paris saying that Raleigh had given himself "a cut rather than a stab", but his suicide note is passionate and anguished. It seems sincere enough, although if Raleigh was again acting a role he would have been capable of contriving such a note. Greenblatt in his book on Raleigh considers that Raleigh conceived his identity "as a dramatic role",[5] and it is possible that the attempt at suicide was dramatic play-acting.

Raleigh was placed on trial in 1603 and made a good impression by his bearing and defence. The record of the trial reads like a drama, and Raleigh was something of a hero, presenting a calm and dignified performance which won him much support. He seemed a different person from the angry, passionate, and impetuous suppliant of previous years. There was no definite evidence to bring against Raleigh and the judges were no doubt partisan. It is interesting to note that after the trial four judges received pensions from the Spanish ambassador.[6] While in the Tower Raleigh wrote to his wife:

> My love I send you, that you may keep it when I am dead; and my counsel, that you may remember it when I am no more. I would not, with my last will, present you with sorrows, dear Bess. Let them go to the grave with me, and be buried in the dust . . . Remember your

poor child for his father's sake, that comforted you and loved you in his happiest times . . . and know it (dear wife) that your son is the child of a true man . . .

It was a tender, affectionate note, and there is no reason to doubt its sincerity. But did not Raleigh still have an eye on his image, just as he did later when he asked his wife to recall his pleading letters before his final performance on the scaffold?

At the last moment, James decided to grant a reprieve. But Raleigh had to linger in the Tower for many years afterwards and his health began to deteriorate. Even so he had privileges and was allowed visitors. He saw his family and friends; he entertained Hariot and other scholars, and he was able to write and to study. He won the sympathy of the Queen and prescribed various medecines for her. His 'elixir' became known to many. He also gained the interest of Prince Henry, who commented: "Who but my father would keep such a bird in a cage". Raleigh was supported by the Prince in his writing of *The History of the World* and he wished to dedicate the work to him. Henry's death in 1612 at eighteen years of age was a blow to Raleigh, and may have been one reason why he abandoned his work, ending it on a note of resignation and despair. The *History* might have impressed the Prince, but it did not impress the King. Raleigh then revived the idea of yet another expedition to Guiana to obtain gold. He petitioned the Queen and the Lords, but did not get strong support. Cecil, who had given marginal assistance in his attempt to keep his Sherborne estate, had warned the King against Raleigh and did not commit himself in Raleigh's favour.

It is surprising how little Raleigh tried to gain the King's favour by his writing. He wrote pleading letters, which he regretted and attempted to recall, but there was no parallel work on the lines of *The Ocean to Cynthia*. Much of his writing would have irritated James. Tracts on Parliament, on shipbuilding and on the navy would not have appealed, and nor would his views on marriage proposals for the Prince. In his writing he advised rulers to accommodate themselves to Parliament. He also made the point that virility and skill in the martial arts were desirable qualities in Princes; qualities which James lacked. The King disapproved of parts of the

History since it criticized the actions of rulers, and when the un-finished book came out in 1614, James commented that Raleigh was "too saucy in censuring Princes". He tried unsuccessfully to suppress the book, which proved popular.

Raleigh's writing in prison often deals, as one would expect, with themes of fortune and destiny, but there is always a personal element in his prose and poetry. His study of history is based on many sources and his views are often borrowed, but the personal accent is there. He produces his own biassed selection of events and examples which enable him to comment on human action. For Raleigh, history was also an experience with relevance for the present and the future. The basic philosophy is Christian, as I have indicated, but there is a strong vein of scepticism. "We are all in effect become comedians in religion", he wrote at one point. There was a religious role to be played on the world's stage, but he probably would not have gone as far as his acquaintance Marlowe who made Machiavelli say:

> I count religion but a childish toy
> And hold there is no sin but ignorance.[7]

Raleigh is traditional in the sense that he sees the universe as an interconnected whole, geocentric, with the earth surrounded by heavenly spheres, but he also sees Nature as an expression of 'dis-similitude'. This may not be a contradiction, but it appears so and there is no attempt to reconcile apparent differences. On the one hand, he believes that God shapes the destiny of Man, but he also believes in Man's power to shape his own fortunes. His general view of the universe depends on Aristotle and Ptolemy, but he rejects Aristotles's overall authority.In the Preface he comments that all learning was not shut up "within the lanthorn of Aristotle's brains". The *History* was like another voyage of discovery for Raleigh, and like Sidney's *Arcadia* it was an incomplete expedition into the world of new ideas and strange perspectives. In the end it led to a gloomy view of the world and of human achievement.

When the King's favourite, Carr, began to lose favour Raleigh pressed again to be allowed to take an expedition to Guiana. The death of Cecil, and of Howard in 1614, diminished opposition to the idea and the new favourite, Villiers, was inclined to befriend Raleigh. In 1616, the King, lured by the idea of obtaining gold, released Raleigh conditionally, stressing that there should be no attacks on Spaniards. He saw Raleigh's venture only as a means of bringing back gold and that this should be done, somehow, without coming into conflict with Spain. He even took the precaution of informing the Spanish Ambassador without Raleigh's knowledge of the general plans of the expedition. Raleigh, on the other hand, thought of the Spaniards as intruders in Guiana, and that on his earlier expedition he had taken possession of the land, with the consent of the local population, on behalf of the Queen. Since the views of Raleigh and the King were apart at the outset it was highly likely that the venture in Guiana would end in failure.

The expedition left England with fourteen ships and about one thousand men in the year 1617. Raleigh's friend Keymis and his son Walter were among the leading officers. The fleet was dogged with ill fortune. There were bad winds, desertions and disease, and the voyage took too long. By the time the fleet reached its destination the crew were tired and unfit. Raleigh himself was laid low with fever and unable to walk. Sickness also took its toll on his nephew George and other officers. Since Raleigh could not go ashore, he sent Keymis, unsuited to the role of expedition leader, to seek out the mine of gold which he had previously claimed to have seen. It would appear that after moving along the river a little way a skirmish took place with a group from a Spanish settlement. Keymis may have been uncertain of their position up river and unable to appreciate the proximity of Spanish forces. It has been argued that a former settlement had moved position. Near to San Thome, Keymis' men were fired upon and they retaliated. There was some confusion and Raleigh's son Walter was allowed to lead a charge. He was killed in action and Keymis did not seem able to control the situation. Three Spaniards were killed before the expedition continued further up river to find the mine. After three weeks of searching, Keymis returned to report lack of success, the death of Raleigh's son, the story of a battle and of a burned Spanish settlement.

Raleigh blamed Keymis for his handling of the expedition. He grieved deeply over his son's death and was angry over the attack on the settlement. It was a disastrous failure and the end of a major dream. In writing home he felt that his "credit was lost for ever", his honour tarnished, and humiliation would be the result. Keymis, who had served Raleigh for many years, also felt the disgrace keenly and after Raleigh had berated him, retired to his cabin and committed suicide. Raleigh's reaction was in no way sympathetic, and he regarded the suicide as a confession of guilt. The total failure of his expedition, his grim future and the tragic death of his own son, overwhelmed him to the extent that Keymis' suicide was diminished in its effect. He wrote tenderly to his wife, and to Secretary Winwood he wrote: "What shall become of me now I know not". On the voyage home the crew became disaffected and difficult to handle. There was a suggestion that they should turn to piracy - a proposal which Raleigh rejected. There was even an attempt at mutiny and men had to be landed in Ireland before the docking in Plymouth. On shore, Raleigh tried to explain the failure of his expedition, claiming that the taking of a Spanish town was an unfortunate necessity in a territory which was not Spanish.

The King was not prepared to accept such explanations. He was then currently involved with negotiations over Prince Charles' marriage proposal to the Spanish Infanta and Raleigh's exploit was a political embarrassment. Moreover, James considered that Raleigh had disobeyed instructions, and when the Spanish Ambassador, Gondoma, demanded Raleigh's death it was agreed that he should be placed on trial. Raleigh hesitated over the possibility of escape to France, decided to brave it out, feigned illness in order to gain time to write his *Apology*, decided to escape after all, took a boat down the Thames, but was eventually captured. The *Apology* sets out his failure to bring back the promised gold, and he blames Keymis for not obeying his instructions.

As before, the case against him was treason, but he was now also accused of inventing the story of the Guiana mine to obtain his release. He was accused of intending to prey on the Spanish fleet, of attacking a Spanish settlement, and of generally disobeying the King's instructions. In addition he was suspected of intriguing with the French before setting out on his voyage. In spite of the Queen's pleas, Raleigh was found guilty by a tribunal and exe-

cuted at Westminster, in 1618, before a large crowd. There are
only imperfect reports of his last speech, but he apparently spoke
for about three quarters of an hour and impressed the crowd with
his bearing. He defended himself against disloyalty, rejected the
accusation that he had invented the story of a gold mine and
denied any complicity in the death of Essex - for this too had been
held against him. He explicitly denied having a secret treaty with
the French.

Raleigh died in the grand manner with appropriate remarks
to the executioner which were notable and quotable. The death
scene on the scaffold was his last dramatic role, and he played it
well. He gave his rich cap to an old man in the crowd, he asked to
see the axe - "Dost thou think that I am afraid of it?" He refused
to be blindfolded and did not seem to care which way his body
was laid. "So the heart be right, it is no matter which way the
head lies". He then gave the command to the executioner, who did
not immediately act on his signal, "Strike man"! It was an impres-
sive performance.

Even on the scaffold, Raleigh was careful to arrange matters
with dramatic skill. He dressed for the occasion, but without over-
doing it. He spoke to the old man in the crowd, and he made sure
the attendant Lords were able to hear his speech. He refuted all
the charges against him, implied the total injustice of the trial, and
he called upon God to punish him if he lied. His denial of intriguing
with the French is interesting:

> I do therefore call the Lord to witness, as I hope to be
> saved, and as I hope to see Him in his Kingdom, which I
> hope will be within this quarter of this Hour; I never
> had any Commission from the King of France, nor any
> treaty with the French Agent, nor with any from the
> French King;"

This was an earnest denial and God was called upon to witness it.
Yet it is known that Raleigh was in touch with French agents
before he set sail for Guiana since he knew the French King was
also interested in the possibility of discovering gold. It is known
because a letter was eventually discovered in Raleigh's handwriting

202

to De Buisseaux, a member of the Council of State. In this letter, he asked for a commission to be arranged. The letter was not delivered to the King, but one of the agents confessed his dealings with Raleigh to a Jesuit. Strictly speaking Raleigh's statement on the scaffold was true in that he had not entered into any agreement with the French, because his letter was ineffective and was lost. Nevertheless, the impression which Raleigh gave on the scaffold was totally misleading. He selected and manipulated the facts to convince his audience. It was almost as if he were determined to arrange his final exit as a dramatic work of art.

Raleigh was something of a puzzle to his contemporaries as well as to later historians. He had a chamelion identity, changing as he sought to play his part in Court life and to find a suitable intellectual stance. His enthusiasm for borrowing ideas, for trying out new notions like new clothes, could obscure his essential identity; although the way in which such notions were refashioned was strongly individual. It is arguable that a man like Raleigh could only realize and express his identity by acting out an imagined role. This, as we have seen, was an Elizabethan trait.

It is not surprising that Raleigh can be viewed from different angles. He was a man of many parts: a martial man, an intrepid sailor, a bold adventurer, a landowner and man of affairs. He was also a studious person, a philosopher in a general sense, and a writer with imagination. He seemed to some almost larger than life, a man to follow and to praise. Yet he could be small-minded, arrogant, and moody. He was both respected and distrusted, hated and admired. He suffered from fits of melancholy and depression, and he could be passionate and impetuous. Yet once he realized that the end was really near he ceased to plead and to give way to fits of emotion. Perhaps he saw himself in the role of martyr, and it was then necessary to be calm and dignified.

With Raleigh's life in mind as a background, one might turn to examine examples of his work in greater detail. His poetry was unpublished except for the anonymously published *The Phoenix Nest* which contained some of his verses.[8] Much of it has an ephemeral quality, and a suggestion that it is part of a pattern of the fashioning of an image. But if Raleigh's art was to some extent contrived to support a life-style, his personality is expressed in his art. The terse and often direct elements in his personality are to be seen in some of his lyrical verse. His style often takes the form of sets of assertions and he is fond of staccato lines. Examples of this style of writing may be seen in *The Nymph's Reply to the Shepherd* and in the poem *To Prove Affection is not Love*:

> A honey tongue, a heart of gall,
> Is fancies spring, but sorrowes fall.
>
> Thy gowns, thy shoes, thy beds of roses,
> Thy cap, thy kirtle, and thy posies,
> Soon break, soon wither, soon forgotten:
> In folly ripe, in season rotten.

Raleigh indicates that light-hearted love is only a transitory emotion, and in the second poem he again stresses the ephemeral nature of superficial love. Once more the style is assertive and the lines are short:

> Conceipt begotten by the eyes,
> Is quickly born, and quickly dies.

or

> Affection follows Fortune's wheels;
> And soon is shaken from her heels;

and similarly

> Desire attained is not desire,
> But as the cinders of the fire.

The ballad *As You Came From The Holy Land* . . . has the same theme which contrasts light-hearted love with a more permanent and deeper emotion. It is reworked from a known ballad and is only original in the manner of its expression. The customary short phrases are in evidence:

> But love is a durable fire
> In the mind ever burning:
> Never sick never old never dead
> From itself never turning.

It is, of course, a convention to dwell upon the adverse effects of time and upon the unsatisfactory nature of human love. The convention was handled by Sidney and by Shakespeare and by numerous other writers. We therefore have a problem in trying to assess sincerity of emotion. Raleigh was possibly reworking the old ballad to suit his role as a lover who had rejected carnal love in favour of a higher form of love, but he is not implying a spiritual love in Sidney's sense. His love is an idealized love for an idealized Queen. He is using a convention and turning it to personal advantage with regard to his relationship to the Queen. But this is an assumption on our part. One is not sure; and whatever Raleigh may be contriving the individual tone of his verse leads one to think that he believes what he says.

The importance of attaining a higher form of love is also a theme in *The Ocean to Cynthia* as one would expect. Although the poem is somewhat rambling in style, one finds clusters of Raleigh's typically short, assertive phrases. The accent is usually four beats to a line, and the lines are often end-stopped. This mark of Raleigh's style is noticeable in the poem called *The Lie* and is one reason why it should not be rejected too easily as the sort of poem he could not have written (as Lefranc does.[9]) Here are some selected verses:

> Go soul the body's guest
>   upon a thankless arrant,
> Fear not to touch the best
>   the truth shall be thy warrant:
> Go since I needs must die,
>   and give the world the lie.
>
> Say to the Court it glows,
>   like rotten wood,
> Say to the Church it shows

whats good, and doth no good.
If Church and Court reply,
  then given them both the lie.

Tell Potentates they live
  acting by other's action,
Not loved unless they give,
  not strong but by affection.[10]
If Potentates reply,
  give Potentates the lie . . .

Tell Arts they have no soundness,
  but vary by esteeming,
Tell Schools they want profoundness
  and stand so much on seeming.
If Arts and Schools reply,
  give Arts and Schools the lie.

Tell Faith its fled the city,
  tell how the country erreth,
Tell Manhood shakes off Pity,
  tell Virtue least preferred.
And if they do reply,
  spare not to give the lie.

So when thou hast as I
  commanded thee, done blabbing,
Because to give the lie,
  deserves no less than stabbing,
Stab at thee he that will,
  no stab thy soul can kill.

The ill effects of time, the sadness at the heart of things, the prevalence of corruption, the unsatisfactory nature of lust, were all themes which appealed to Raleigh, as they appealed to his contemporaries. The poem recognizes the divergence between role playing and reality; and if trying to combine the two in his life were a fault in Raleigh, he again recognizes the divergence in his reply to Marlowe's shepherd.

206

The paraphernalia of allegorical poetry is noticeable in his work, and in this respect his writing is along traditional lines. *The Ocean to Cynthia* is cast in the conventional pastoral form and accustomed rhetorical devices and hyperbole are found in the tribute to Spenser and in the Epitaph on Sidney. In the sonnet on *The Faerie Queene* there is a reference to Homer, a conceit on weeping Petrarch, a personification of 'oblivion' which "laid him down on Laura's hearse", and the exaggerated praise is nothing new. Even so, one is left with the feeling that Raleigh is writing with conviction.

Raleigh's tendency to assert goes with a tendency to reiterate. Frequently he says the same thing in different ways. This is, of course, an Elizabethan characteristic. It is a feature of Sidney's *Arcadia* and it is evident in the work of Bruno and others. It is not simply a technique which is inherited, but a way of thinking. The search for universal parallels was necessary for those who still believed in the nature of the Ptolemaic universe, even when they were at times sceptical about its structure. The short poem *The Advice* relies upon a reiterative technique, and in *The Ocean to Cynthia* themes are repeated again and again. This can be wearing, but it sometimes has a cumulative effect on the reader which impresses. This is perhaps due to the personal tone of Raleigh's insistence. When Raleigh uses traditional modes of expression he is often able to invest them with a quality of his own. If he were given to playing roles in life, and yet somehow playing them with such conviction and feeling that he discovered a new personal identity in each role, the same ability may be seen in his writing. The literary cloak he chooses to wear, in prose or in poetry, is made to suit him.

Reference has been made to Raleigh's uncertain views on religious matters. This uncertainty is reflected in his writing as in his life. He yearns for something permanent in a world of change - "a durable fire"; but although he may feel the need for faith he is inclined to cynicism. God is mentioned again and again in his writing, but one is not sure about his specific religious beliefs. One is reminded of Marlowe who reflects a Christian atmosphere in his work, but who was said to be an atheist - or at times of Sidney, who was considered a true Christian, but who may have flirted with unorthodox opinion on religious matters. In the Pilgrimage poem, Raleigh refers to a staff of faith:

> Give me my scallop shell of quiet,
> My staff of faith to walk upon,
> My scrip of joy, Immortal diet,
> My bottle of salvation:
> My crown of glory, hopes true gage,
> And thus I'll take my pilgrimage.

Yet there is an air of detachment, even of mockery, a touch of amused make-believe about the joys of the after-life which he later describes:

> And by the happy blissful way
> More peaceful pilgrims I shall see,
> That have shook off their gowns of clay,
> And go apparelled fresh like me.
> I'll bring them first
> To slake their thirst,
> And then to taste those nectar suckets
> At the clear wells
> Where sweetness dwells,
> Drawn up by saints in crystal buckets,
> And when our bottles and all we,
> Are filled with immortality:
> Then the holy paths we'll travel
> Strewed with rubies thick as gravel,
> Ceilings of diamonds, saphire floors,
> High walls of coral and pearly bowers.

The poem continues with a vision of a heavenly court case, complete with jury and an "unblotted lawyer". Christ is cast in the role of an attorney

> Who pleads for all without degrees
> And he hath angels, but no fees.

The poem ends ironically with the thought of his death and a request for an "everlasting head".

The same quizzical attitude is found in that sad verse which is said to have been written as his epitaph and which was inscribed on the flyleaf of his bible and left at the gatehouse in Westminster. It is a rewrite of a previous verse from the poem beginning "Nature that washed her hands in milk". This time he borrowed from his own work and arranged the verse to suit another circumstance:

> Even such is time, which takes in trust
> Our youth, our joys, and all we have,
> And pays us but with age and dust,
> Who in the dark and silent grave,
> When we have wandered all our ways,
> Shuts up the story of our days:
> And from which earth, and grave, and dust,
> The Lord shall raise me up I trust.

This deft, dry humour, reminds one a little of Sidney. Both poets assume poetic postures, but occasionally reflect with amusement on their situation. Sometimes uncertain of himself, in an age in which disorientation occurred, Raleigh's moods vary from the calmly reflective to the mocking, or to the angry and turbulent. Such variations are noticeable in *The Ocean to Cynthia* in which rhetorical phrases alternate with a crisper, individual imagery. He is now of the old world and now of the new.

The reiterative tendency, already referred to - and which was to some extent inherited from 'trouvère' verse - is strong in *The Ocean to Cynthia*, but what is also striking is the circling movement of repetitive themes. This cyclical approach is at times untidy and wearisome, but it can also be effective when done well. The theme of obliterated joy is seen in so many aspects, and produces so many telling phrases, that its moving, personal nature outweighs the tedium of other passages. The rough, unfinished quality of much of the verse contrasts with oldfashioned flourishes; the sudden leaps of thought, the unconnected meanings, the twists in logic, convey the pain and tumult of the writer, as well as his confusion of mind. The syntax often becomes wrenched and uneven, the metre loses its beat, verbs drift and allusions are uncertain; these are symptoms not only of a lack of revision, but of a state of mind. There are reflective passages over which disturbing turbulences break like waves over a still shore.

As Raleigh circles round his subject he varies his attitude and the images change too. Meanings may flow into each other. Raleigh's predicament in prison was special, but the shifts in focus and in viewpoint in this long poem remind one of the reorientations and disorientations of other Elizabethan writers who attempted long works and whose attitudes changed as they continued to write. In prison, Raleigh was naturally driven to rethink about many things and about himself. He was "Alone, foresaken, friendless on the shore". He reflected on "broken monuments of my great desires". He felt a loss of identity. What was his role to be now? In his mood of dejection, the significance of the universe itself was called in question and one may at times be reminded of Hamlet's doubts about the universe, and even more of King Richard's loss of identity when he is deposed in Shakespeare's play.

If one looks at this long poem in more detail, its movements express contrasting emotions. It begins by depicting a waste land, and the images reflect desolation. There is a wan light, and the land is covered with dust and fallen blossom. There is a hearse, and fruitful trees are contrasted with withered leaves. The sad mood then changes to a feeling of adoration as the poet contemplates Cynthia, and the style is heightened. His ambition is described as "To seek new worlds, for gold, for praise, for glory". He daydreams about the past and soon becomes melancholy. He feels that his time as a faithful courtier has been wasted:

Twelve years I wasted in this war
Twelve years of my most happy younger days,
But I in them, and they now wasted are
Of all which past the sorrow only stays.

These lines are borrowed from a poem he wrote earlier and which was published in the *Phoenix Nest* in 1593 and called *Farewell to the Court*. He borrows from previous work and uses his words in a new context with effect, admitting "So wrote I once, and my mis-

210

hap fortold". He describes his feeling of banishment and from about line 221 there is writing of a melancholy cast, until a plunge into self pity disorders his thought. Line 341 renews his praise for Cynthia:

> Divine in words angelical in voice
> That spring of joys, that flower of love's own setting.

and he recalls the past. Soon this mood gives way to a sense of injustice and he contemplates his fate. The uncertainty of his position is caught in lines concerning Leander's failure to reach Hero: "She is gone, she is lost, she is found, she is ever fair". The long poem ends with the helpless conclusion: "Her love hath end, my woe must ever last". Then follows a short unfinished piece likening Cynthia to the sun, which may be life-giving by day, but can cause life to decline when it moves in orbit and allows night to take over.

Raleigh's prose work is also of uneven quality. As in his verse, he borrows frequently and he can be tedious; but often he is able to refashion the influences which work upon him to express his own moods and attitudes. When he is strongly moved, or when he writes descriptively, his prose catches fire and he is easy to read. His report on Grenville's action against Spain is an enthusiastic account of heroism in battle and of courage in the face of heavy odds. His account of the battle of Cadiz, and the opening passages of the essay on Guiana, which we have already quoted, are examples of Raleigh at his best. The prose moves easily and the interest of the reader is held. The later *Apology* does not stand up so well for he loses direction and sometimes resorts to bluster. Other essays, already mentioned, on the soul and on the senses, are not specially remarkable, but they are written in a direct way which is characteristic of Raleigh when not striving after rhetorical elegance. He wrote an interesting tract called *Discourse* on the subject of war, in which he pities the ordinary soldier who may die without appreciating the cause for which he is fighting. He touches on the imperfections of governments, but is concerned to prevent anarchy. These are themes which interested Elizabethans. Sidney raised similar issues, and Henry V, in Shakespeare's play of that name, has to explain his country's cause to the ordinary soldier who has doubts before battle. Raleigh was following others in dealing with themes which were debating points in Europe, in the French academies and in some writing.

The *History of the World* is Raleigh's longest and most ambitious prose work. It was to have been dedicated to the Prince, and perhaps Raleigh thought that it might help his cause, if it pleased Prince Henry; but he made no attempt to please King James, who was irritated by some of his comments. He had been planning a history for some time, although it was not until 1614, when he was advanced in age, that the folio edition appeared. The work was, in a sense, another voyage of discovery and of exploration. Once more he sought "new worlds" and found them lacking. Once more he borrowed ideas and tried to refashion them in his own way, but the task was difficult and he did not always find a straight intellectual track through the undergrowth of his sources.

The history was to begin with the Creation, advance to the era of the Roman civilization in the second century B.C. and possibly continue. The Old Testament gave Raleigh some trouble and he found difficulty in getting through it. He wanted, like many historical writers of his day, to show the lessons that history could produce, but the early Christian period was difficult to sort out. There were doubts in many minds about some of the Old Testament statements. Raleigh had to struggle with interpretations, and to reconcile factors which seemed irreconcilable. He took some trouble to produce evidence from contemporary scholars which supported the idea of the Flood, but in other matters he came close to the notion that some truths were allegorically expressed. This was a view he held about Greek legends, which he said "did maimedly and darkly express" ancient truths. When he reached the classical period he planned further volumes to bring his history closer to his own times.

The work was unfinished and revision probably caused changes in attitude and viewpoint - as it did with Sidney's *Arcadia*. There were so many influences working upon Raleigh that they could have overwhelmed him. Ben Jonson who wrote a piece for him, said that the "best wits in England were employed for the making of his history". Raleigh consulted Hebrew scholars for the

212

biblical parts and the first three chapters were based on a commentary by Benedict Pererius. He also used historical digests. The work was really a treatise on Man - on his nature, and on his relation to God and to the universe around him. Man's background and his early history are described and discussed. Raleigh's notion was that as history develops it sheds light on Man's nature and it reveals lessons for the future. His justification for reporting historical events is that they have a contemporary moral or political application. He says ". . . the end and scope of all history (is) to teach by examples of time past such wisdom as may guide our desires and actions.[11] The work soon became popular. Eleven editions came out before the end of the seventeenth century.

Raleigh draws practical and moral lessons from certain events by means of asides or commentaries. Like the historical poems in the *Mirror for Magistrates* there are stories of the fall of great men which illustrate truths about life. He indicates the way in which Providence works, and how human beings should attempt to frame their lives. He is pessimistic about the nature of the human race after the Fall, and he is critical of the record of monarchs.

Raleigh's view in the *History* would seem to imply that he was no atheist, but he obviously had doubts about religious doctrines. The working of God's will is shown to be a complicated matter. Patterns in history present him with contradictory strands of evidence. History reveals God's mercy and justice, and also God's severe retribution. God intervenes, but he also sometimes allows freedom of action. Raleigh's book may have become popular over the years because it taught, in general, that God punished the wicked in the biblical sections. But Raleigh did not find it easy to pick his way through the uncertainties, ambiguities and contradictions in human history, and this is more noticeable as the story of human endeavour moves into the classical period. At times he seems confused, and there are tensions and variations in the way he develops his themes.

He is Elizabethan in the way he changes perspective. At one point he dismisses Fortune, since it is clear that people are responsible for their own actions; but later Fortune is shown to be a force in the affairs of human beings.[12] He is not sure whether eclipses foretell disaster. He refers to the noble simplicity of primitive Man, but also to his unenlightened savagery. Influences from Montaigne and Pico della Mirandola produce contradictions which are not resolved. He is aware of the studies of Galileo, but his thoughts are shaped by the notion of the Aristotelian and Ptolemaic universe. He believes that God usually works through angelic agents - ". . . second causes . . . being but instruments, conduits, and pipes which may carry and disperse what they have received . ."[13] He is able to move from orthodoxy to a more radical way of thinking and on occasions he exhibits a religious cynicism. God moves in a Ptolemaic universe, but as the narrative develops God's presence is not so evident and there is a sense of the desolation and emptiness of life. Raleigh's *History* unfolds before us a poor record of nations warring and enslaving themselves and others. One is not aware of the possibility of redemption or of the working of a divine plan. At the end of the book it would seem that only death is able to liberate human beings and provide them with a final identity. The work ends on a grand, but despairing note, in spite of previous themes which had indicated Man's enormous potential.

If optimism and pessimism alternate, the latter mood is dominant towards the end. In the final analysis Raleigh has little to say on behalf of human achievement. Great leaders, like Alexander, are viewed as "troublers of the world" who achieve glory through bloody destruction. "Valour", says Raleigh, "is in no way praiseworthy but in daring good things", and there is not a preponderance of such actions. The attack on falseness and corruption, which was expressed in the poem called *The Lie*, is noticeable in the *History*, and he states the view that people are unfortunately honoured for qualities which are not worthy of praise - such as flattery - and that glory is, in any case, obliterated by time and by death. "Ambition, which begetteth every vice" is commented upon, as is the pride of Princes. In chapter V (2) there is a discourse on tyranny, and a comment on the rarity of true Christian monarchs in the history of the human race.

The *Preface* sets the tone and indicates the main theme. Raleigh considers that the attainment of material things is ultimately of no account if one wishes for peace of mind and to live in the hope of a blissful eternal life. Across a large span of time, minor incidents are selected from history to illustrate a point or to reinforce a prejudice. He frequently draws parallels and the conventional morality of the *Mirror for Magistrates* is behind his attitude to many of the lessons of history.

The style of this long work is heavier than his other prose writing. It is not as lively as his accounts of battles, although the stories of Alexander and other leaders are vividly told. There are, however, memorable phrases and in general the narrative of the history is clearly and straightforwardly expressed. Sometimes we get great surging sentences which live in the mind, like the famous invocation to Death which ends the work. Such passages may be theatrical, but they are moving.

> O eloquent, just and mighty death! whom none could advise thou hast persuaded; what none hath dared, thou hast done; and whom all the world hath flattered, thou only hast cast out of the world despised; thou hast drawn together all the far-fetched greatness, all the pride, cruelty, and ambition of man, and covered it all over with these two narrow words. *Hic Jacet*.

The changing moods and attitudes in the *History* remind one of the changing moods in his poetry. As in the *Ocean to Cynthia* sentences state a position and then drift away towards something else. Ideas change. God is a presence in the biblical history, for Raleigh is influenced by his sources, but later in the work, God is often invoked for rhetorical purposes only, and the motivations of Man (good or bad) are dealt with in more detail. The brooding, meditative style of the early history changes and a terser, more aphoristic style is used. The writer has assumed a different mantle - a more classical pose, perhaps. As Raleigh's sources change, he too changes. There is more preoccupation with the effects of Time, and as the critic Greenblatt points out: ". . . the perspective and meaning ceaselessly change".[14] If the background is still Ptolemaic, names such as Copernicus and Galileo and Machiavelli are referred to. At one point history teaches that good practical planning - for example, a modern fleet of manoeuvrable ships, good defences, tactical awareness - is essential. However, elsewhere Raleigh takes the view that practical plans are of little avail. If God was once present in Man's affairs, he later recedes; only death prevails. A wry pessimism is the underlying tone.

Even so, one is left with the notion that had the work continued, and had Raleigh's circumstances altered, optimism could have bubbled to the surface again if given a chance. Raleigh had a strong belief in the power of the individual to discover, to conquer, and to reconstruct. His aggressive policies towards Spain, his love of fine clothes, his wide-ranging intellectual curiosity - in chemistry, shipbuilding, navigation, military matters, occult sciences, philosophy, politics, geographical discovery, and so on - give evidence of the optimistic side of his nature.

Raleigh's works, like his life, reflect the variety of his skills and the variable nature of his temperament. He took on different roles in his life and in his writing. If much of his verse and prose was intended to support and to add lustre to his chosen life-style, his personal emotions and preoccupations give spirit to his work, although it is not easy to judge how far he is writing sincerely and in what identity. He possessed some chameleon qualities and it is understandable that he gained different reputations. It could perhaps be argued that he was so conditioned by the varied intellectual trends of his time that he had no original mind of his own; but he is no dull regurgitator of other men's opinions. He was, by temperament, an individualist and eager to go his own way. By trying out current ideas, and by playing roles in life, he was expressing his identity and fulfilling himself. To search for a role and then to play it well was an Elizabethan trait. Identity was elusive, as we have seen, in Miranda's 'brave new world', and there was a need to achieve an acceptable persona. This was not easy under the strong personality of the Queen, whose temperament was variable. In his book on Raleigh, Greenblatt concluded that "his life was his greatest work of art",[15] and at the end Raleigh may have decided, like Leander in his long poem to the Queen, to "Do then by dying what life cannot do".[16]

IX   Critical Perspectives

The feudal concept of an ordered, hierarchical, social life, existing within an ordered if mysterious universe, did not encourage self-realization as a supreme aim. Once, however, this concept was subject to modification there was an increasing interest in ego-centricity. It is noticeable in the literature of the later sixteenth century, especially in drama, in spite of an inherited stereotype portrayal of character. Individual characteristics were more subtly expressed, as time went on, and dramatic characters became more varied and unusual. The adage 'know thyself' was turned, in the hands of a playwright or romance writer like Sidney, into meeting the challenge of creating fictional individuals who sought to express themselves as individuals. If such characters represented historical personages, or were based on previous models, they were neverthe-less 'fleshed out' to resemble living people with thoughts and emotions of their own.

The identity problem was complicated. It was obvious that in real life there was a divergence between appearance and reality; that the world itself was something of a stage on which people played roles, masked their thought as well as their appearance, and that human psychology was more unpredictable than early theorists on the 'humours' contemplated. Observation of life as it seemed to be lived in Elizabethan England must sometimes have been difficult to reconcile with the conventions of drama as handed down by successful playwrights and by respected classical models. Every age produces its noteworthy individuals, but the Elizabethan age produced particularly colourful and varied examples compared with the previous century. Changes in the economic and political climates encouraged strong, thrusting personalities. For entrepreneurs who had sufficient funds to tide them over bad times there were exciting chances for the future. The rise of Puritanism, with its offshoots, was not always an influence for restraint. It was a spur to individualism and it emphasized the need for self-realization.

It was natural for an age which produced colourful characters, and emphasized personal heroism, to be preoccupied with unusual personalities on the stage. There were frequent debates about the influence of the stars, as we have seen, but there was a greater awareness than before of the unique self and of the ability to carve at least part of one's own future. If one believed in the dominant influence of outside forces there were those like Machiavelli who taught techniques to master the play of Fortune. In their different ways the Hermetists sought to control the future and to create a special human identity. The search for identity was difficult, and it is not surprising if playwrights, in presenting character on the stage, did not move too far away from previous models and sometimes manage to involve themselves in contradictions.

The chapters in this book have indicated the contradictions and unresolved paradoxes which resulted from the uncertain stance of some of the major writers of the Elizabethan age, and how their uncertainty was due to the opening up of new philosophical and scientific perspectives. Old theories about the universe were still held, but they were held in doubt. There was the possibility that the universe was infinite - and the parallel possibility that individual potential was also infinite - and that the movements and functions of the stars were uncertain. Theories on the nature of Man, and on the part played by the 'humours' in determining individual dispositions had become so complex that confusion was to be expected. People could be seen to be both puppets controlled by Fate and also responsible for their actions. Doubts about traditional philosophy created doubts about traditional authorities, including classical models. Plato was given several identities to support divergent trends of thought. New models appeared, and new fashions were taken up, but not necessarily with total commitment.

The many influences in Shakespeare's time were not satisfactorily integrated before they were absorbed, and the absorbtion was often fitful and incomplete. One may sympathize with Bacon in his attempt to bring order into people's minds and to stress the need to concentrate on physical evidence. Bacon was himself, however, positioned between the old and the new and could be contradictory in his arguments. He was not always forward-looking.

In his day, one sees the flickering influence of Ficino, Mirandola, and the Hermetic thinkers side by side with the steadier flame of Humanism. Men like Dee and Bruno were prone to contradictions, and they were a source of confusion as well as a stimulus. While they were putting their views forward the Ramist school of thought was also making itself felt.

Writers like Sidney and Raleigh were typical in that they interested themselves in ideas, but produced few ideas that were not derivative. Their originality was in manner of expression and in dramatic presentation. If some of their literary plumage were borrowed, they wore it with style. The discipline of small verse forms was valuable and many of the Elizabethan lyrics were carefully crafted. Yet it has to be said that even within the space of the fourteen line sonnet, some writers seem unsure of the poetic development. Some short verse forms seem to be part of a larger continuing sequence, but not necessarily as part of a fixed plan. One readily calls to mind Sidney, Greville, Raleigh and Shakespeare; and even Spenser who began his *Faerie Queene* with a poetic plan in mind, gives the impression at times of setting forth on a voyage of discovery, well supplied with borrowed baggage. Elizabethan writers were hungry for knowledge and for adventure, and plagiarism came easily to them. Playwrights, as we know, borrowed from each other and collaborated in theatrical ventures.

Literary influences were so numerous that it is hardly surprising that beside small lyrical forms, larger canvases were used to express a wealth of ideas and to enable the artist to work through to the final picture. There were long works such as *The Faerie Queene, The Arcadia, Hero and Leander, Venus and Adonis, Eugenia, The History of the World*, and long five act plays. Within these larger forms, there emerged inconsistencies and changes of approach. Ambiguities may sometimes have been expressions of imaginative apprehension; on the other hand, they were sometimes due to untidiness of mind or to uncertainty. There were, as we have seen, attempts at revision, and some works were incomplete.

There was naturally enough a large body of translation work, for there was a desire to absorb knowledge and to make it part of oneself. Jonson digested classical sources and borrowed useful quotations, Shakespeare borrowed plots. Most translations read well because the original work is rewritten as if it were the work of the translator. Chapman is so enamoured of Homer that one is not sure whether Homer has become Chapman or Chapman has become Homer. The translation is not exact, the style and manner of expression is far removed from any semblance to Greek, but the work is a work of art. Nevertheless, translation, or the reworking of sources into an original work, again poses problems of identity. A person may exist within borrowed clothes, but the outside picture is not always convincing.

Shifting attitudes, and an addiction to wholesale borrowing, were obstacles in the way of self-realization, but they were also symptoms of the struggle to achieve it. There is a sense in which Elizabethan writers were serving an apprenticeship, and many were beginning to outdo their masters and to establish their own identity. In the process of development, there were changes in posture and in perspective. Occasionally it is difficult for us today to determine when a writer is speaking for himself or performing a literary exercise. In a literary sense, both Sidney and Raleigh are hard to know. And role playing, which may be learning by experience, was not confined to the stage or to writing in general. Elizabethans took on roles in the drama of life, and wanted at the same time to get behind the mask of appearances.

The changes in perspectives and the modifications in posture create critical problems. The critic, too, has difficulty in deciding upon a viewpoint. Critical appreciation of Elizabethan literature from the seventeenth century onwards has moved from one extreme to another, and in our own day it has been notably vagarious. The study of influences outside the field of literature by literary scholars has been sporadic and small attention has been paid to foreign sources of interest outside the work of major writers. As England moved towards civil war, political confrontation caused people to take sides in the seventeenth century and to make up their minds on other issues. Individual perspectives varied, but the reasons for differences became clearer and the field of view less hazy. Identity became easier to define, and the dramatic focus on character narrowed. This in turn enabled critical appreciation to specialize with less uncertainty of approach.

Today one may find the late sixteenth and early seventeenth centuries both remote and close. The present day interest in questions of individual and national identity can lead one too readily to identify similar problems and concerns in the previous age. Our critical perspective needs to be carefully adjusted; but the evidence of these Elizabethan concerns gives the age an added interest for us in our time.

Notes

Chapter I

1. Ptolemy or Claudius Ptolemaeus lived in Alexandria 139-161 A.D. His compendium on astronomy was generally known by its Arabic name of *Almagest*. Improving on the work of his predecessors he expounded a system according to which the sun and other planetary bodies revolved round the earth. Surrounding the earth were eight spherical shells and to seven of these a divine spirit was attached. The eighth sphere was the area of the fixed stars. Irregularity of motion was explained by theories of epicycles. The system was based on ideas expressed by Plato and Aristotle, and his astronomical work was influenced by Hipparchus, who noted the eccentricity of the sun's path, estimated the distance of the sun and moon from the earth, and produced latitudes and longitudes to determine geographical position. Ptolemy's geographical treatise remained a textbook in the 16th century, although many of his comments were superseded by discoveries in the previous century. Ever since Copernicus, his work had been questioned in much of its detail, but it continued to exercise great influence in the sixteenth and seventeenth centuries.
2. Apart from the astronomers, it is interesting that Leonardo da Vinci (1452-1519) had written in his Notebooks "The sun does not move". It is not known how he came to state this so definitely, but Copernicus was not unique in his views on the motion of the earth. Copernicus formed his theories from astronomical calculation, however; other theorists were mainly speculative thinkers. Early Greek thinkers like the Pythagoreans did not make the earth central to their system, and Lucretius, who was read in the 16th century, touched on the idea of infinite space. There were divergent authoritative opinions, but generally the Ptolemaic view prevailed. Leonardo believed in a universe in which all elements were interrelated, but that perspective geometry changed visual concepts. He had difficulty in determining the perspective for the 'Last Supper' fresco as it was painted high on an end wall. See Chapter VI on Bruno's concern with religious perspectives.
3. Thomas Digges wrote several treatises and in 1576 revised and augmented a work by his father on climate and astrology called *A Prognostication* ... He was a pupil of John Dee (see Ch. V).
4. Bacon, *Advancement of Learning* and Book I of the *Novum Organum* frequently make the point that received doctrines need to be examined carefully.
5. See Spenser's *Hymn of Heavenly Beauty* and Milton's *Paradise Lost*.
6. Jean Bodin (1530-1596) *Les Six Livres de la République*.
7. *Troilus and Cressida* Act I, sc. iii.
8. *Coriolanus* Act 5, sc. iii

9.   Raleigh. *The History of the World* Bk. I, Ch. 2 (sec. 5) states that "...
a person's ... blood which disperseth itself by branches of veins through all
the body, may be resembled to those waters which are carried by brooks and
streams all over the earth". He likens the moisture of our bodies to the fertil-
ity of the earth, our hair to the grass, our eyes to the light of the sun or moon,
our youth to the flowers of Spring, and our thoughts to the motion of Angels.
Our Souls were said to have the stamp of God's image.
10.   Marlowe *Tamburlane the Great* Part I, Act 2, sc. vii.
11.   *Anthony and Cleopatra* Act V, sc. iii.
12.   George Chapman *Eugenia*.
13.   Ficino *De Vita Libri Tres* (Basel 1549).
14.   The origin of 'vital spirits', which animate the body, is not clear. They
were created in the heart according to one view; others thought they were
generated in the liver.
15.   This point was mentioned in John Davies' *Microcosmos* (1603) and in
Thos Newton's *The Touchstone of Complexions*.
16.   Chapman, *Byron's Tragedy* Act IV, sc. i.
17.   *A Midsummer Night's Dream* Act II, sc. i.
18.   *King Lear* Act I, sc. ii.
19.   *Othello* Act I, sc. iii.
20.   *The Tempest* Act I, sc. ii.
21.   Learned men like Dr. Dee, whose advice was sought by the Court, believed in the influence of the stars. Sidney refers to their influence in Sonnet
XXVI and scorns "dusty wits" who deny their power, but as often with
Sidney, there is a 'stand off' quality in his expression.
22.   Cornelius Agrippa *De Occulta Philosophia* (1531-33).
23.   *Mirror for Magistrates* (1559).
24.   Chapman *Eugenia* - Virgilia Secunda l. 120.
25.   See Chapter *To Seek New Worlds* ...
26.   Coeffeteau (1574-1623) *A Table of Human Passions* trans. by Grimes-
ton in London 1621.
27.   Chapman *The Revenge of Bussy d'Ambois* Act V, sc. i (Clermont).
28.   The notion that the poetic 'furor' was a divine possession was touched
upon in the writings of the French *Pleiade* and was reinforced by neo-Platonists. Chapman believed in this kind of inspiration, and of the high calling of
the poet, holding that withdrawal from society into dark seculsion encouraged
the imagination (see his *Shadow of Night* and *Eugenia*). Monastic seclusion is,
of course, an old tradition and many religious thinkers valued darkness as an
aid to contemplation and to the control of troublesome senses.
29.   Chapman *Byron's Tragedy* Act V, sc. i (Epernon).
30.   Bacon *Essays* - on Truth.

Chapter II

1.   Dr. Johnson *Lives of the Poets* - Cowley.
2.   Chapman *Ovid's Banquet of Sense* st. 69.
3.   John Donne *An Anatomy of the World* l. 215.

4.   Macrobius - a 5th century Latin grammarian. Commentary on Cicero's *Somnium Scipionis*.

5.   See *Boccaccio on Poetry* - ed. Osgood, p. 51 (Indianopolis 1956).

6.   Sidney *Apology for Poetry* - section on function of poetry.

7.   Gabriel Harvey *Letter to Edmund Spenser*.

8.   See Ch. VII 'The Lance and the Quill'.

9.   *The Faerie Queene* Book I (i) 38.

10. See chapter on hermetism 'Darkness and Light'.

11. *The Faerie Queene* Book VI (10) 24.

12. *The Faerie Queene* Book VII (59) 3.

13. I.G. Maccaffrey *Spenser's Allegory* (Princeton 1976), p. 431.

14. *The Faerie Queene* Book VII (7) 9.

15. *Hero and Leander* - end of poem.

16. *The Rape of Lucrece* ll. 810 and 1240.

17. *Arcadia* Book I, ch. 9.

18. *Hymn to Night* - Chapman Book II l 370.

19. Marston *The Scourge of Vilanie* Book III, satire 9.

20. Chapman *Bussy d'Ambois*, end of Act V - death speech.

21. Chapman *Byron's Conspiracy* end of Act III.

22. Chapman *Eugenia* ln. 1745.

23. J.F. Danby *Poets on Fortune's Hill* (Faber 1952), p. 148.

24. Dryden *Essays* (Oxford, ed. Kerr) p. 43.

25. Jonson *Discoveries* - Praecepta Elementa.

26. Jonson *Discoveries* - Ingeniorum Discrimina nota 10.

27. Jonson *Volpone* Act III.

28. Jonson *Epicene* Act IV, sc. ii.

Chapter III

1.   Reputed to have been written by Willoughby or Willobie on the theme of the courtship of Avisa. It contains several innuendoes and possibly refers to Shakespeare.

2.   Shakespeare *Comedy of Errors* Act II, sc. ii, 194.

3.   Shakespeare *Merchant of Venice* Act I, sc. ii, 26.

4.   Shakespeare *Merchant of Venice* Act III, sc. ii, 73.

5.   Shakespeare *Twelfth Night* Act I, sc. ii, 26.

6.   Shakespeare *Twelfth Night* Act I, sc. v, 125.

7.   Shakespeare *Twelfth Night* Act III, sc. i.

8.   Shakespeare *Henry VI* (part III), Act III, sc. ii, 182.

9.   Shakespeare *Richard II* Act III, sc. ii, 173.

10. Shakespeare *Richard II* Act V, sc. v, 31.

11. Shakespeare *All's Well* Act V, sc. iii, 304.

12. Shakespeare *Henry IV* (part I), Act I, sc. ii, 86.

13. Shakespeare *Henry IV* (part II), Act V, sc. v, 58.

14. J. Danby *Shakespeare's Doctrine of Nature*.

15. Shakespeare *King Lear*, Act IV, sc. vi, 125.

16. Shakespeare *King Lear*, Act I, sc. iv, 230.

17. Shakespeare *King Lear* Act I, sc. i, 225.
18. Shakespeare *The Winter's Tale*, Act III, sc. ii, 80.
19. Shakespeare *The Winter's Tale*, Act IV, sc. iii, 35.
20. Shakespeare *Cymbeline*, Act IV, sc. ii, 83.
21. Shakespeare *Cymbeline*, Act V, sc. i, 32.
22. Shakespeare *Henry IV* (part I), Act III, sc. ii, 318.
23. Jonson *Poetaster* Act IV, sc. iii, 35.
24. Jonson *Timber*, II, 1093.
25. Jonson's masques present self-distortion as well as disguise.
26. Jonson *New Inn* Act V, sc. i.
27. Jonson *Epicene* Act IV, sc. ii.

Chapter IV

1. T. Rhymer *Tragedies of the Last Age*.
2. Johnson *Preface to Shakespeare*.
3. M. Morgann *An Essay on the Romantic Character of Sir John Falstaff*.
4. M. Bradbrook *Elizabethan Stage Conditions*.
5. J. Wilders *The Lost Garden* (Macmillan 1978), p. 37.
6. J. Dillon *Shakespeare and the Solitary Man* (Macmillan).
7. Shakespeare *Troilus and Cressida* Act II, sc. ii, 169.
8. See chapter on Sidney, 'The Lance and the Quill'.
9. Shakespeare *Love's Labour's Lost* Act V, sc. ii, 406.
10. Shakespeare *Henry VI* (part III), Act III, sc. ii, l. 182.

Chapter V

1. F.A. Yates *French Academies of the 16th Century* (Warburg Inst. 1947).
2. Raleigh in the *History of the World* Book II, chapter 6 mentions that Hermes was older than Moses and ought to be venerated.
3. Raleigh was accused at one meeting of discussing atheism. See chapter 'To seek new Worlds'.
4. Lull (or Lully) - (c. 1232-1315) was born in Majorca. After a military life he devoted himself to a spiritual crusade to convert Mussulmans. He invented a method of manipulating fundamental propositions, based on Aristotle's categories, which he claimed could solve all problems. He was fascinated by systems and believed in the magical properties of numbers and of letters.
5. P.J. French *John Dee* (Routledge 1972).
6. P.J. French *John Dee*.
7. See Chapter VI. Bruno probably put forward Hermetic views which upset the Oxford Humanists.
8. P.J. French *John Dee* (Routledge 1972), pp. 110, 113.

Chapter VI

1. F.A. Yates *French Academies of the 16th century* (Warburg Inst. 1947).
2; F.A. Yates *ditto*. Yates makes the point that views on reconciling Cath-

olic and Protestant religious differences were common in Europe. The notion that there might develop a universal religion in which all intelligent people could believe, and the creation of a Christian Commonwealth under a leading monarch, was probably mooted at the Palace Academy.

3.   See chapter on Sidney 'The Lance and the Quill'.

4.   This was a view Bruno expressed in *Ash Wednesday Supper (Cena de la Ceneri* trans. Gosselin & Lerner, Archon 1977).

5.   Harvey praised Copernicus in his *Musarum Lacrimae* of 1578.

6.   Bruno *Cena de la Ceneri* - see above.

7.   F.A. Yates *Giordano Bruno and the Hermetic Tradition* (Routledge 1947), Ch. XIV.

8.   Bruno *Cena de la Ceneri* (trans. Gosselin & Lerner) - see above.

9.   One recalls Bodin's *Colloquium Hepta Plomeres* where there is discussion between men of different faiths who find that they can come together in charity.

10.   It was a Hermetic tendency to draw upon ideas from different faiths to form a theistic philosophy. Bruno was not original in thinking that an individual could find God without the aid of the Church. Similar views were held by Dee.

11.   F.A. Yates *Giordano Bruno and the Hermetic Tradition*.

12.   *ditto* Ch. XIV.

13.   D.W. Singer *Giordano Bruno* (Hen. Schuman N. York 1950), pp. 313 ff, 322, 365.

14.   Francis Bacon. Introduction to *Historia Naturalis*.

Chapter VII

1.   Fulke Greville *The Life of the Renowned Sir Philip Sidney* Ch. XII.

2.   Moffett - Physician and author. Patronised by Earl of Pembroke and Sidney's sister. May have lived at Wilton House, the Earl's home, towards the end of his life.

3.   Greville's *Life* Ch. XIX (Grosart ed. 1870) p. 154.

4.   Sidney *Apology for Poetry* - section on Functions of Poetry.

5.   *Ditto* - Section on Epic or Heroic Poetry.

6.   Sidney modified the oracular statement when he revised his book so that the Princes could only be tried for the murder of Basilius and not for dishonouring the mother.

7.   In the revised version, Sidney cools Musidorus' ardour and he is only accused of wishing to come closer to Pamela.

8.   Goodman, who was helped by Sidney to obtain a living in Cheshire, wrote a Puritan tract arguing that monarchs were only fit to rule if they obeyed the Will of God. Only then could they demand the obedience of their subjects.

9.   See note 6 above. The oracular statement was modified but Sidney did not revise the end of his first draft of the book.

10.   This recommendation in favour of marriage to reduce unbridled lust was also counselled by the Church.

11. Jean Bodin (1530-1596) - a French writer on history and political ideas.
12. Sidney *Arcadia* (ed. Feuillerat. OUP 1912) BookI, Ch. 3.
13. *Ditto* Book I, Ch. 16.
14. *Ditto* p. 278.
15. Fulke Greville *Works* (ed. Grosart) Vol. IV, pp. 19-22.
16. Davis & Lanham *Sidney's Arcadia* (Yale Univ.).
17. *Ditto* p. 77.
18. Hoskyns was a contemporary of Sidney and wrote *Directions for Speech and Style* in 1599.
19. Hazlitt *The Age of Elizabeth*.

Chapter VIII

1. Lefranc *Sir Walter Raleigh - Ecrivain* (Quebec) 1968.
2. Marston's satires sometimes take on a rough quality.
3. Sir W. Raleigh *The Discovery of the Large and Beautiful Empire of Guiana* . . . . first published in 1596.
4. Sir W. Raleigh *A Relation of Cadiz Action* . . . .
5. Greenblatt *Sir Walter Raleigh* (Yale 1973) p. 115.
6. E. Thompson *Sir Walter Raleigh* (1935) p. 201 ff. See also A.L. Rowse *Raleigh and the Throckmortons* (Macmillan 1962) on the accusation that Raleigh had intrigued in favour of Spain.
7. Marlowe *The Jew of Malta* - Prologue.
8. It is uncertain which poems were written by Raleigh, but he undoubtedly wrote some in *The Phoenix Nest*. He refers to one in *The Ocean to Cynthia* see p. 210.
9. Lefranc *Sir Walter Raleigh - Ecrivain* (Quebec) 1968.
10. A possible reference to the idea that monarchs needed the goodwill and consent of the people and were subject to "natural justice". The Huguenots and certain political thinkers like Bodin discussed notions like Divine Right. See Ch. VII pp. 166, 167.
11. Raleigh *The History of the World* Book II (21) 6.
12. *Ditto*. Preface. See also my reference to Preface on p. 182.
13. *Ditto*. Preface.
14. Greenblatt *Sir Walter Raleigh* (Yale 1975) p. 140.
15. *Ditto*. p. 170.
16. Raleigh *The Ocean to Cynthia* l. 496.

Bibliography

GENERAL

Agrippa, C.	*De Occulta Philosophia*
Alexander, P. (ed.)	*Studies in Shakespeare*
Aristotle	*Works*
Babb, L.	*The Elizabethan Malady* (Michigan)
Bacon, F.	*Works* (ed. Spedding)
Boccaccio	*Boccaccio on Poetry* (ed. Osgood, Indianopolis 1956)
Bolgar, R.R.	*The Classical Heritage*
Braden, G.	The *Classics and English Renaissance Poetry*
Bright, T.	*A Treatise on Melancholy* (Facs. Text Society)
Campbell, L.B. (ed.)	*The Mirror for Magistrates*
Castiglione, B.	*The Book of the Courtier*
Chambers, E.K. (ed.)	*The Oxford Book of 16th century Verse*
Coeffteau	*A Table of Human Passions* (trans. Grimeston)
Craig, H.	*The Enchanted Glass* (New York)
Danby, J.F.	*Elizabethan and Jacobean Poets*
Davies, J.	*Nosce Teipsum*
	Orchestra
Dryden, J.	*Essays* (see comments on Jonson)
Eliot, Sir T.	*The Castle of Health*
	The Governor
Empson, W.	*Seven Types of Ambiguity*
Ficino	*De Vita Libri Tres*
	Commentaries
Fletcher, A.	*Allegory : The Theory of a Symbolic Mode* (Ithaca)
Gordon, D.J.	*The Renaissance Imagination* (ed. Orgel)
Gregson, J.M.	*The Public and Private Man*
Guibbory, A.	*The Map of Time* (Illinois, 1986)
Harvey, G.	*Letters* (see letter to Edm. Spenser)
Hill, C.	*Society and Puritanism in Pre-Revolutionary England*
	The Intellectual Origins of the English Revolution
Hunter, G.K.	*Dramatic Identities*
Kermode, J.F.	*Shakespeare, Spenser, Donne*
Lewis, C.S.	*The Allegory of Love*
Lovejoy, A.O.	*The Great Chain of Being* (Cambridge, Mass.)
Moffet	*Nobilis* (trans. Heltzel & Hudson, California)
Newton, T.	*The Touchstone of Complexions*
Nicholson, M.	*The New Astronomy and the English Literary Imagination* (Studies in Philol xxxii, 1935)
Nicoll (ed.)	*Shakespeare Survey*

228

Ovid	*Metamorphoses*
Plato	*Works*
Rowse, A.L.	*The Elizabethan Renaissance*
	The England of Elizabeth : The Structure of Society
	The Expansion of Elizabethan England
Spingarn, J.E. (ed.)	*Seventeenth Century Critical Essays I*
Tillyard, E.M.W.	*The Elizabethan World Picture*
Trevor-Roper, H.R.	*History and Theory*
White, H.O.	*Plagiarism and Imitation during the English Renaissance*
Wiley, M.L.	*The Subtle Knot : Creative Scepticism in 17th century England*
Willey, B.	*The 17th century Background*
Wilson, T.	*The Art of Rhetoric* (ed. Mair)
Yates, F.A.	*Queen Elizabeth as Astraea* (Warb. Inst. X, 1947)

DRAMA

Bamborough, J.B.	Ben Jonson (Writers and Their Work 112)
Bradbrook, M.C.	*George Chapman*
	Elizabethan Stage Conditions
	The Living Monument
	Shakespeare
	Themes & Conventions of Elizabethan Tragedy
Chaudhuri, N.	*The Infirm Glory*
Danby, J.F.	*Shakespeare's Doctrine of Man*
Dillon, J.	*Shakespeare and the Solitary Man*
Lewin, H.	Ben Jonson (Cambridge, Mass.)
	The Overreachers (Cambridge, Mass.)
Maclure, M.	George Chapman. A Critical Study
Mahood, M.M.	*Shakespeare's Word Play*
Muir & Schoenbaum (ed.)	*A New Companion to Shakespeare Studies*
Rowse, A.L.	*Shakespeare*
Wells, R.H.	*Shakespeare and the Politics of the Stage*
	Shakespeare
Wilders, J.	*The Lost Garden*

BRUNO, G.

Boulting, W.	*Giordano Bruno*
Singer, D.W.	*Giordano Bruno* (New York)
Yates, F.A.	*The Religious Policy of Giordano Bruno* (Journ. of Warburg & Court Inst. iii 1939)
	The French Academies of the 16th century (Warburg Inst. 1947)
	Giordano Bruno & the Hermetic Tradition (Warburg Inst.)

229

DEE, Dr. J.

French, P.J.   *John Dee*

SIDNEY, Sir P.

Amos, A.K.   *Time, Space & Value - Narrative Structure of the New Arcadia* (Lewisburg P.A.)
Buxton, J.   *Sir Philip Sidney & the English Renaissance*
Davis & Lanham   *Sidney's Arcadia* (Yale)
Hamilton, A.C.   *Sir Philip Sidney : A Study of his Life & Works*
Lindheim, N.   *The Structures of Sidney's Arcadia* (Toronto)
McCoy, R.C.   *Sir Philip Sidney - Rebellion in Arcadia* (New Bruns., N.J.)

SPENSER, Ed.

Alpers, P.J.   See essay on the *Faerie Queene* in Penguin Critical Anthology 1969
Evans, M.   *Spenser's Anatomy of Heroism*
Hamilton, A.C.   *The Structure of Allegory in the Faerie Queene*
Kermode, F.   *Shakespeare, Spenser, Donne*
MacCaffrey, I.G.   *Spenser's Allegory : The Anatomy of the Imagination* (Princeton)

RALEIGH, Sir W.

Greenblatt, S.J.   *Sir Walter Ralegh : The Renaissance Man & his Roles* (Yale)
Irwin, M.   *The Great Lucifer*
Lefranc, P.   *Sir Walter Ralegh, Ecrivain* (Quebec)
Rowse, A.L.   *Ralegh & the Throckmortons*

Index